Staging Decadence

Methuen Drama Engage offers original reflections about key practitioners, movements and genres in the fields of modern theatre and performance. Each volume in the series seeks to challenge mainstream critical thought through original and interdisciplinary perspectives on the body of work under examination. By questioning existing critical paradigms, it is hoped that each volume will open up fresh approaches and suggest avenues for further exploration.

Series Editors
Mark Taylor-Batty
University of Leeds, UK
Enoch Brater
University of Michigan, USA

Titles
Contemporary Drag Practices and Performers: Drag in a Changing Scene Volume 1
Edited by Mark Edward and Stephen Farrier
ISBN 978-1-3500-8294-6

Performing the Unstageable: Success, Imagination, Failure
Karen Quigley
ISBN 978-1-3500-5545-2

Drama and Digital Arts Cultures
David Cameron, Michael Anderson and Rebecca Wotzko
ISBN 978-1-472-59219-4

Social and Political Theatre in 21st-Century Britain: Staging Crisis
Vicky Angelaki
ISBN 978-1-474-21316-5

Watching War on the Twenty-First-Century Stage: Spectacles of Conflict
Clare Finburgh
ISBN 978-1-472-59866-0

Fiery Temporalities in Theatre and Performance: The Initiation of History
Maurya Wickstrom
ISBN 978-1-4742-8169-0

*Ecologies of Precarity in Twenty-First Century Theatre: Politics,
Affect, Responsibility*
Marissia Fragkou
ISBN 978-1-4742-6714-4
Robert Lepage/Ex Machina: Revolutions in Theatrical Space
James Reynolds
ISBN 978-1-4742-7609-2
*Social Housing in Performance: The English Council Estate on and
off Stage*
Katie Beswick
ISBN 978-1-4742-8521-6
Postdramatic Theatre and Form
Edited by Michael Shane Boyle, Matt Cornish and Brandon Woolf
ISBN 978-1-3500-4316-9
*Theatre in the Dark: Shadow, Gloom and Blackout in Contemporary
Theatre*
Edited by Adam Alston and Martin Welton
ISBN 978-1-4742-5118-1

For a complete listing, please visit
https://www.bloomsbury.com/series/methuen-drama-engage/

Staging Decadence

*Theatre, Performance, and
the Ends of Capitalism*

Adam Alston

Series Editors
Mark Taylor-Batty and Enoch Brater

methuen | drama
LONDON • NEW YORK • OXFORD • NEW DELHI • SYDNEY

METHUEN DRAMA
Bloomsbury Publishing Plc, 50 Bedford Square, London, WC1B 3DP, UK
Bloomsbury Publishing Inc, 1385 Broadway, New York, NY 10018, USA
Bloomsbury Publishing Ireland, 29 Earlsfort Terrace, Dublin 2, D02 AY28, Ireland

BLOOMSBURY, METHUEN DRAMA and the Methuen Drama logo are trademarks of Bloomsbury Publishing Plc

First published in Great Britain 2023
This paperback edition published 2025

Copyright © Adam Alston, 2023

Adam Alston has asserted his right under the Copyright, Designs and Patents Act, 1988, to be identified as Author of this work.

For legal purposes the Acknowledgements on pp. xii–xiv constitute an extension of this copyright page.

Cover image © jaamil olawale kosoko, *Séancers*, American Realness Festival, 2017. Photo by Ian Douglas

All rights reserved. No part of this publication may be: i) reproduced or transmitted in any form, electronic or mechanical, including photocopying, recording or by means of any information storage or retrieval system without prior permission in writing from the publishers; or ii) used or reproduced in any way for the training, development or operation of artificial intelligence (AI) technologies, including generative AI technologies. The rights holders expressly reserve this publication from the text and data mining exception as per Article 4(3) of the Digital Single Market Directive (EU) 2019/790.

Bloomsbury Publishing Plc does not have any control over, or responsibility for, any third-party websites referred to or in this book. All internet addresses given in this book were correct at the time of going to press. The author and publisher regret any inconvenience caused if addresses have changed or sites have ceased to exist, but can accept no responsibility for any such changes.

A catalogue record for this book is available from the British Library.

ISBN: HB: 978-1-3502-3704-9
PB: 978-1-3502-3708-7
ePDF: 978-1-3502-3706-3
eBook: 978-1-3502-3705-6

Series: Methuen Drama Engage

Typeset by Deanta Global Publishing Services, Chennai, India

For product safety related questions contact productsafety@bloomsbury.com.

To find out more about our authors and books visit www.bloomsbury.com and sign up for our newsletters.

For those in search of putrid bounty
Alice Condé, Jane Desmarais, Jess Gossling, and Owen Parry

Contents

List of figures	xi
Acknowledgements	xii

Introduction		1
	Uselessness, wastefulness, outmodedness, and alternative productivities	4
	Decadence in context: From page to stage	11
	Slowdown and the pursuit of busyness	16
	What follows	19
1	Zombie time: Sickness, performance, and the living dead	25
	Interminable waiting	28
	Zombie time	35
	Conclusion	41
2	Para-sites and wired bodies: Decadence, scenography, and the performing body	43
	Parasitical space: Julia Bardsley	47
	Techno-productivism: Marcel·lí Antúnez Roca	56
	Conclusion	62
3	Alien nation: Afropessimism, Afrofuturism, and the decadent society	65
	'What beasts they are': jaamil olawale kosoko	69
	Alien Nation: The Uhuruverse	76
	Conclusion	87
4	Frenetic standstill: Decadence, capitalism, and excess on the Japanese stage	89
	Unstoppable motility: Toshiki Okada	91
	Theatre as explosion: Toco Nikaido	96
	Conclusion	109

5 'A dangerous form of decadence': Decadence, performance, and
　the culture wars　　　　　　　　　　　　　　　　　　　　111
　'We should not subsidize decadence': Ron Athey　　　　　115
　Art, outrage, and austerity: Paul McCarthy and Wunderbaum　122
　'A dangerous form of decadence': The war on woke　　　130
　Conclusion　　　　　　　　　　　　　　　　　　　　　138

Conclusion　　　　　　　　　　　　　　　　　　　　　　141

Notes　　　　　　　　　　　　　　　　　　　　　　　　155
Works cited　　　　　　　　　　　　　　　　　　　　　192
Index　　　　　　　　　　　　　　　　　　　　　　　　215

Figures

0.1	Nia O. Witherspoon, *Priestess of Twerk* (2021)	4
1.1	Martin O'Brien, *The Last Breath Society* (2021)	31
1.2	Martin O'Brien, *The Last Breath Society* (2021)	34
2.1	Julia Bardsley, *Aftermaths: A Tear in the Meat of Vision* (2009)	53
2.2	Julia Bardsley, *Aftermaths: A Tear in the Meat of Vision* (2009)	55
3.1	jaamil olawale kosoko, *Séancers* (2017)	71
3.2	jaamil olawale kosoko, *Séancers* (2017)	74
4.1	chelfitsch, *Super Premium Soft Double Vanilla Rich* (2014)	93
4.2	Toco Nikaido, *Miss Revolutionary Idol Berserker: Extreme Voices* (2016)	100
5.1	Wunderbaum, *Looking for Paul* (2010)	126
5.2	Krys Alex, original image used for CyberFirst campaign	133
6.1	Hasard Le Sin, *Fairy Boudoir* (2022)	142

Acknowledgements

Decadence has long been associated with atomization. However, my experience of writing this book tells a different story. Despite the scale of the political and economic challenges faced by Arts and Humanities departments in universities across the UK, and despite periods of lockdown during the Covid-19 pandemic, I have been struck by the willingness of colleagues and friends to give up their time and energy to discuss the ideas in its pages. Its completion would not have been possible without the generosity of others.

The development of this book benefitted from a reading group convened at Goldsmiths by a few of us with an interest in decadence and performance, and for that, I would like to thank Sarah Cefai, Elly Clark, Alice Condé, Jessica Gossling, Eleanor Keane, and Owen Parry. I am also tremendously grateful to colleagues who gave up their time to comment on draft chapters: Shane Boyle, Meredith Conti, Clare Finburgh Delijani, Jane Desmarais, Liam Jarvis, Eirini Kartsaki, Elyssa Livergant, Cody Poulton, Robert Stilling, Ben Walters, and David Weir. Clare and Jane also offered mentorship, both formally and informally, offering the kind of insight that comes from a happy but all too rare coupling: erudition and empathy. Kyoko Iwaki and Cody Poulton also offered invaluable guidance on the contexts underpinning the work of Toco Nikaido and Toshiki Okada. Amanda Waddell helped with both organizing and translating the discussion with Nikaido, including the translation of an interview (as with several other interviews informing this book, it can be found on the Staging Decadence blog: www.stagingdecadence.com). Marielle Pelissero also put me on the scent of work by jaamil olawale kosoko, and Eva Bru-Domínguez kindly shared insight into performances by Marcel·lí Antúnez Roca. I would like to thank Dan Jacques from the London International Festival of Theatre, Wednesday Sue Derrico from Experimental Bitch Productions, Nanami Endo from chelfitsch, Margreet Bergmeijer from Wunderbaum, and Richard Jordan Productions for sharing recordings of performances by the artists, and Marcel·lí Antúnez Roca, Julia Bardsley, jaamil olawale kosoko, Toco Nikaido, Martin O'Brien, Toshiki Okada, Normandy Sherwood, Hasard Le Sin, and Nia O. Witherspoon for sharing a wide range of materials linked to their work, including images. Indeed, visual illustration has greatly enriched this book. For that, I would also like to thank Krys Alex, Emma Jones, Holly Revell, Manuel Vason, and Amanda Waddell.

Staging Decadence: Theatre, Performance, and the Ends of Capitalism was made possible thanks to the support of an Arts and Humanities Research

Council ECR Leadership Fellowship: 'Staging decadence: Decadent theatre in the long twentieth century' (AH/T006994/1). There were several strands to the Fellowship, which had a formative impact on this book's development. I would like to thank HERE Arts Centre, Rich Mix, and Iklectik Arts Lab for hosting and supporting live events associated with the project, which are discussed in the Introduction and Conclusion, especially: Cole Bonenberger, Kristin Marting, Meredith Lynsey Schade, and Amanda Szeglowski from HERE; Dennis Cooke, Jack Edwards, Monty Hoffman, Josh McNorton and Martha Rumney from Rich Mix; and Atay Ilgun, Isa Ferri, and Eduard Solaz from Iklectik, as well as Anjali Prashar-Savoie, who co-produced the event at Iklectik. The wider project also benefitted from the expertise of Patricia Pulham and Duška Radosavljević, who sat on its advisory board alongside Jane Desmarais. A special note of thanks goes to Owen Parry, whose collaborative work on the project led to a fruitful exchange of ideas. I would like to thank heads of department who backed the Fellowship – Andy Lavender at the University of Surrey, and Ben Levitas and Pamela Karantonis at Goldsmiths – and I am particularly grateful to Goldsmiths for granting a sabbatical that enabled the completion of this book, as well as the institutional support offered by its Professional Services Team. I am also indebted to the Methuen Drama Engage series editors, Mark Taylor-Batty and Enoch Brater, for their invaluable feedback, and the editorial team at Bloomsbury for backing and supporting the project, especially Anna Brewer and Aanchal Vij.

Each of the chapters has benefitted from the sharing of work in progress at various conferences, symposia and seminars, including the British Association of Decadence Studies 'Jeudis' seminar series, the Cultural Studies Association, the Performance Research Forum at Goldsmiths, and the Utopian Studies Society. Several papers were also presented at the International Federation for Theatre Research (IFTR) and the Theatre and Performance Research Association (TaPRA). I would particularly like to thank colleagues in the Political Performances WG and the Scenography WG at IFTR, and the Performance, Identity and Community WG, the Bodies and Performance WG, and the Documenting Performance WG at TaPRA. I have also discussed the work of Martin O'Brien and Ron Athey in an earlier article, although my analysis of relevant examples has been substantially updated and revised. See Adam Alston, 'Survival of the Sickest: On Decadence, Disease, and the Performing Body', *Volupté: Interdisciplinary Journal of Decadence Studies*, 4 (2) (Winter 2021), pp. 130–56.

The writing of this book came at a strange and difficult time, and its completion would not have been possible were it not for the support of my family: Jim, Marion, John, Mel, and Evelyn. Their interest in – and healthy querying of – this project proved an invaluable touchstone from the very beginning. Pubs and dance floors also had a formative impact on my thinking. I often find that it is in such places that the real work of research is achieved: time for reflection and meandering discussion, and, in the context of this book, indulgence in ecstatic revelry. In this, I am eternally grateful to my fellow travellers, Will Philps and Dan O'Gorman, and Gareth White and Josephine Machon.

The prospect of dedicating time and energy to a book about theatre, performance, and decadence was welcome when mapping its shape, as was the prospect of working alongside colleagues in the Decadence Research Unit – now the Decadence Research Centre (DRC) – when I moved to Goldsmiths in 2020. It has proved less a 'centre' than a sanctuary, and my final note of thanks goes to my colleagues in the DRC, particularly Alice Condé, Jess Gossling, and Jane Desmarais. It may seem counterintuitive to think of decadence as a 'thriving' field, but their steadfast commitment to its study has played a significant role in making that the case – or if not 'thriving', then at least ensuring that this corner of the academy is rife with fabulous pestilence.

Introduction

It's September 2021 and I'm cocooned in the Temple of Isis, surrounded by billowing white gauze and pillows. The goddess Isis is flanked by two languorous disciples who recline at her feet, chins resting nonchalantly on their wrists like cherubs. Their fingernails are excessively long, pointed and encrusted with shimmering gold, haphazardly reaching into the air in search of half-formed notes as if to conduct the musicians who surround them: a cellist carving effervescent melodies, a guitarist warping harmonies through a synthesizer, a percussionist binding these sonorities to a gentle, pulsating metre. It is easy to forget the city's streets in here. Tonight, this place plays host to decadent bodies dressed in ornate costumes – feathered, glowing, flowing – that befit a paean to pleasure.

This temple was created by the African American performance maker Nia O. Witherspoon as part of a performance called *Priestess of Twerk* (2021). It was one of several performances and talks comprising a 'decadent salon' at HERE Arts Centre in New York City, which was produced as part of a wider project of which this book is a part.[1] There were talks on the fall of empires, and the reclamation of opulence and luxury. We heard about Nero, Rome's first actor-emperor, and the queer iconography of St. Sebastian in the work of the Italian author and playwright Gabriele d'Annunzio and the North American live artist Ron Athey. It was a promiscuous affair. The timing was also unusual, with theatres only recently reopening as the latest wave of the Covid-19 pandemic entered a sustained period of decline. Asking audiences to wear masks and provide proof of vaccination seemed anathema to the theme, but what struck me when the night got underway was the willingness of those involved to engage with decadence when its popular association with orgiastic excess had been all but extinguished. A longing for sensuousness and revelry, it seemed, was birthed by the devastating effects of pervasive sickness.

Another performance that was presented that night, this time from the North American performance maker Normandy Sherwood, took matters in a rather different direction. Sherwood's *Psychic Self Defense* (2021) takes its name from an obscure work of esoteric literature by the British occultist Dion Fortune (Violet Mary Firth). Fortune's book is essentially an instruction manual for protection against psychic attacks. In Sherwood's hands, these attacks come not from people but the injunctions of twenty-first-century capitalism that manifest as paranormal apparitions feeding off our psychic energy, each one draped in delightfully crafted garments: monsters with innumerable arms that claw at the chest of a magus cloaked in bejewelled fabrics, for instance, or a bloated creature made from layers of thick curtains, which open to reveal a dime-store skeleton costume.

For Sherwood, the decadence of design has nothing to do with meaning or function, and everything to do with filigree and ornamentation.[2] She draws inspiration from the legendary artist Jack Smith, who worked in New York City until his death in 1989. She reads Smith's obsessive interest in filigree and ornamentation as 'decadent', particularly in works that are 'constantly in process. To be inefficient or wasteful in that way is antithetical to how businesses work or even any artworld works. [. . .] The thing is never finished, and is always being torn up and put back into something else'.[3] The iteration of *Psychic Self Defense* presented at the salon was the latest version of a work that had already been through a lengthy process of development, endlessly searching for the aesthetic qualities of discarded but useful materials – curtains, prosthetic limbs – and their being used in useless but delightful ways.

Fascination with filigree and ornamentation unrelated to function aligns with how I think about aestheticism, which is related to decadence, but decadence bears a more complex relation to everyday life. Where aestheticism seeks to transcend the everyday, celebrating the autonomy and intrinsic value of art for art's sake, decadence transgresses. Decadence is an art of border crossing.[4] It courts borders in order to breach them – for instance, by revelling in the transgression of 'good' taste and social acceptability, or by breaching the binaries that order gendered types. Decadence also travels across different cultures and histories, each with their own prejudices and preoccupations. In one iteration, it evokes ancient Roman orgies, indulgence in oysters and champagne in gilded hotel bars, and the freshly powdered nose of a corporate fat cat. In another, it refers to the ivory tower of an academy out of touch with realpolitik and the demands of effective socialist praxis. A third describes the personal and political freedoms of the liberal West as a corruption of divine Law. The list goes on, but it is the etymological association of decadence with decline and decay that caught the attention of late nineteenth- and early-twentieth-century novelists, poets, and playwrights, such as Joris-Karl Huysmans, Rachilde (Marguerite Vallette-Eymery), Oscar Wilde, Edgar Saltus, and Jun'ichirō Tanizaki, who were interested in stylizing and refining these associations.

The word 'decadence' literally means 'a falling' (from the Latin *decadēre*), and it is related to the word 'decay'.[5] It is this sense of decadence as falling or flowing away from an established order or hierarchy – of transgressing their borders – that will become a frequent touchstone in this book's theorization of decadence. Things can fall apart or flow away without being decadent, but these processes can become decadent when that falling or flowing lends itself to a critique of modernity and (I venture to add) late-twentieth- and twenty-first-century capitalism, not least when utility, efficiency, and incessant calls to consume and produce more – and to consume and produce more intensely – are subverted or perverted.

Sherwood privileges filigree and ornamentation over use and functionality, but she also cultivates a taste for 'the perverse aspect of the circulation of trash in theatre' that resists categorization as a complete product.[6] The conjunction of aestheticism with this 'perverse' interest in refining theatrical detritus and practising deliberate inefficiency is what gives her designs a decadent flavour. However, to grapple with the political significances of decadence as a practice of border crossing, it is worth returning to Witherspoon's *Priestess of Twerk*: a work that was not grounded in the stylized refinement of theatrical detritus, but in her background as a composer, performer, and activist (Figure 0.1).

The Temple of Isis is one of three 'worlds' that Witherspoon stages in this performance. The music helps a great deal in creating this world – it is essentially an extended prelude without resolution or climax – as it does in each of the scenes that follow. As one world crumbles another is built, and next up is a club-like space where Witherspoon and her co-performers sing and dance to hip-hop. Their routines occupy the whole of the stage, revelling in the excesses of choreographic pops and locks. They delight in movement and the look and feel of one another's translucent garments. Their appearance is opulent, and their energy abundant. In all this, Witherspoon pays homage to the activist adrienne maree brown, whose work informed the piece. '[W]e all need and deserve pleasure', writes brown, and 'our social structures must reflect this. [. . . But in] this moment, we must prioritize the pleasure of those most impacted by oppression.'[7] In the scene that closes the performance, Witherspoon emerges adorned with innumerable blue feathers, peacock-like, with melodies that soar high into the air, and bodies set to take flight.

Witherspoon identifies decadence as one of the ways in which brown's ambition might be achieved.[8] However, like the mask-wearing and proof of vaccination, I initially understood 'pleasure activism' to be at odds with the pleasures that I had come to associate with decadence, such as a taste for abjection and delight in decay. I was also reminded of the antithetical relationship between decadence and progressive politics that served as a hallmark of the decadent imagination in the nineteenth century.[9] Nonetheless, Witherspoon's performance invites us to ask some fundamental questions about the appeal and relevance of decadence in the twenty-first century. Who is or might be empowered to define its conceptual parameters? How is decadence being staged today – as a practice, as an issue, as a pejorative, as a site of pleasure? Where might we find it, why might we look for it, and who is decadence for?

Figure 0.1 Nia O. Witherspoon, *Priestess of Twerk*, HERE Arts Centre, New York, 2021. Photo: Michelle Y. Thompson.

Uselessness, wastefulness, outmodedness, and alternative productivities

It is a truism in Performance Studies to suggest that live performance follows 'a trajectory of mortality', continually reanimating ephemeral offerings.[10] Many of the scholars best known for their work on the ephemerality of performance were associated with the Department of Performance Studies at

New York University (NYU) in the 1980s and 1990s, including Fred Moten, Diana Taylor, Barbara Browning, Barbara Kirshenblatt-Gimblett, André Lepecki, José Esteban Muñoz, Peggy Phelan, Richard Schechner, and (as a doctoral researcher) Rebecca Schneider. These scholars forwarded divergent theories of the ephemerality of performance, which have been adapted, contested, and reimagined ever since, and invite reflection on the practice of performance as an art that forever 'falls away' from the live event.

Phelan's book *Unmarked: The Politics of Performance* (1993) has proved particularly influential, as well as contentious. 'Performance's only life is in the present', she writes, and 'becomes itself through disappearance'.[11] Phelan positions performance as an art conditioned by entropy, suggesting that something at the heart of performance dies, or tends towards death, as its life in the present marches towards the final curtain. What remains of performance after the event – artefacts, documents, memories and feelings, its material traces and immaterial reverberations – is neither reducible to nor synonymous with a performance event, functioning only as distorting reflections of a transient experience, or so the argument goes.[12]

It is tempting to see the entropic nature of live performance as evincing a kind of decadence (recognizing the rather dated distinction between the radical in 'performance' and the commercial susceptibility of 'theatre'), but clearly not all theatre and performance is 'decadent' along the lines set out earlier. Rather, this book contends that theatre and live art lend themselves to a decadent sensibility when their outmoded resistance to utility and productivity (understood here in a strictly economic sense), and their wasteful dissipation of energy in the live act of creation, are foregrounded. This is especially the case when bodies and actions are staged in ways that fall or flow away from established social mores and aesthetic conventions.

Theatre and live art have the potential to do things with decadence that other art and literary forms cannot. They enable its embodiment and enactment, like film – although unlike film this embodiment and enactment takes place in a space shared with actual bodies that may be doing things with decadence very close to an audience. In a similar vein, where decadent literature lends itself to the mind's eye and the imaginative stimulation of sensation, theatre and performance lend themselves to the body and what a body and crafted objects can do on stage. The processual and affective qualities of the live arts open new avenues for exploring decadent practices as practices of falling, flowing and crossing, not least by staging their effects on bodies and objects in a space shared with others in a particular moment and context.

Decadence has gained its firmest scholarly footing in the study of nineteenth-century European literature, although the field has been expanding in recent years.¹³ It has also enjoyed a renaissance in the commentaries and speeches of conservative columnists and politicians in the late twentieth and twenty-first centuries. *Staging Decadence* is informed by these two discourses, especially, but it also reaches beyond them. The questions raised at the end of the previous section invite reappraisal of how decadence was codified in nineteenth-century literature and literary criticism, on the one hand – where decadence tends to be linked to the influence of writers like Charles Baudelaire, Théophile Gautier, Paul Bourget and Huysmans – and conservative discourse about societal decadence, on the other. These questions also challenge us to decentre the authority of the scholar and the writer in order to learn from perspectives emerging from other professions and backgrounds, which in the context of this book means turning to theatre makers and live artists who derive insight from different kinds of cultural experience.

Witherspoon's invitation for women and queers of colour to prefigure a radically opulent and abundant future is at odds with the pessimistic assessment of the state of North America forwarded by the *New York Times* columnist Ross Douthat. In his book *The Decadent Society: How We Became the Victims of Our Own Success* (2020), which was published during the pandemic, Douthat argues that the liberal West has reached an end-of-history state of 'sustainable decadence': a perpetual status quo in which economic growth and productivity is stagnating, fertility rates are declining (Douthat is a committed Catholic), cultural production is content with re-hashing the same tired forms and narratives, and humankind is languishing in a complacent stupor. Not since Apollo 11 has 'mankind' evinced any real transformative and invigorating ambition, he says, it being the last historical moment when the conquest of new frontiers seemed achievable. '[T]he speed with which we experience events has quickened', he writes, not least with the boom in telecommunications at the turn of the new millennium, but 'the speed of actual change has not. Or at least not when it comes to the sort of change that really counts: growth and innovation, reform and revolution, aesthetic reinvention and religious ferment.'¹⁴

The problem with Douthat's thesis has nothing to do with his observation that economies are stagnating, which in advanced capitalist economies is demonstrably the case, or that cultural production in these economies tends to centre on the commercially friendly reproduction of the tried and tested. Rather, Douthat takes for granted a very narrow understanding of what 'really counts' as meaningful change. The massive (although as yet inadequate) advances made by social and political movements like #BlackLivesMatter and #MeToo do not 'count' as meaningful change for Douthat to the same extent as religious fervour, faith in the myth of perpetual growth, and the promise of ever-more bountiful rewards deriving from commitment to an intensified work ethic and the pursuit of technological innovation. In fact, for many conservative critics similarly invested in 'declinism', socially progressive advances are not seen to be advances at all, but a retreat into a state of barbarism or 'decadence' (in a negative sense of that word), although in fairness Douthat's commentary is considerably more sober than the more vociferous outpourings that pepper the pages of puritanical, nationalist, and radically libertarian diatribes.[15] In contrast to the diagnoses of these critics, Witherspoon's performance takes the decline of an empire and the enslavement of Black people that enabled its growth as points of departure for prefiguring an alternative world in which abundant pleasure is unleashed, and opulence redistributed. She uncouples decadence from narratives that either condemn it as a symptom of liberalism 'gone mad', or that seek to legitimize infinite expansion, colonial appropriation, and the turbo-charging of business, science, and industry over and above people who have little stake in their rewards.

I have enjoyed reflecting on the opulence of this performance in the months since the salon, but what sticks in my mind most of all was Witherspoon's refusal to allow it to be contained within a set timeframe. The piece was commissioned as a thirty-minute performance, and in the dress rehearsal – the day of the performance – it emerged that it would be closer to double that length. And at some point between the dress rehearsal and the performance, another ten minutes was added. The performance luxuriated in time, and it made time for slowness: for rhythms and ethereal sonorities to breathe and stretch, and for obscure hymns to defer climactic fulfilment in the show-stopper, preferring instead to 'reclaim the present as a territory of pleasure', and as 'a prelude and an outpost of revolutionary thinking', to borrow from the performance scholar Giulia Palladini.[16] This was a work in progress destined for perpetual development, as with Sherwood's *Psychic Self Defense*, only in this case getting ever-grander and more luxurious in scope, ideally resulting 'in a live spa and performance installation in a temple, an actual temple', if Witherspoon's ambitions for the work are anything to go by.[17]

All of which leads me to one of the central contentions of this book. Although Douthat is right to identify economic stagnation as a concern of significant interest in advanced capitalist economies, his solution – to reignite faith in continual growth, the pursuit of perpetual technological innovation, and productivist enterprise – is not a solution at all, but the issue. Economic growth, innovation, and intensified productivity no longer simply serve as means to the end of wealth creation; they have become ends in themselves, which are 'the ends' referred to in this book's subtitle.

A stubborn adherence to productivism – understood here as the valorization of intensified productivity, and the introjection of productivity as a basis for self-realization[18] – is getting us nowhere fast. The issue is not with productivity per se. The problems come when productivity develops into productiv*ism*, where productivity is pursued and intensified for its own sake, regardless of effectiveness. This has given rise to a paradoxical phenomenon that several influential philosophers and sociologists have come to refer to as 'frenetic standstill'. This phrase has its roots in a neat translation of Paul Virilio's book *Polar Inertia* (*l'intertie polaire*, 2000).[19] Frenetic standstill refers to the experience of a situation governed by stagnation, on the one hand, and a directionless busyness, on the other. It is the consequence of the instrumentalization of everything, including our capacities to think more, do more, and act and interact more, even as the quality and desirability of each is eroded.

Where an economically incentivized focus on use and efficiency in the industrial period produced significant economic growth and productivity gains, productivism today is having no such impact. Instead, it is fuelling cultures of planned obsolescence, cluttering a global marketplace with redundant commodities, and plaguing workers with burnout and the gradual erasure of the line dividing working life from a time outside of work. However, for the cultural theorist Mark Fisher it is more appropriate to compare our current situation not with the industrial period, but with the advent of postindustrialism in the second half of the twentieth century that found advanced capitalist economies transitioning from the raw materials and manufacturing industries to the provision of human and information services. It was not long before this transition brought with it an unprecedented privileging of economic interests in place of a wider range of social and civic interests. A favourite slogan of Margaret Thatcher's in the 1980s is indicative: that 'There Is No Alternative' to the primacy of a free market unfettered by social conscience. However, where Thatcher's slogan was originally intended to persuade as many people as possible that this was, indeed, the case (i.e. that there was a choice to be made), for Fisher that claim now 'carries an *ontological* weight' – what he refers to as 'capitalist realism' – in which capitalism is positioned not merely as the best possible socio-economic system, but the only *viable* system.[20] As a phenomenon linked to these conditions, frenetic standstill, too, risks being taken for granted as a necessary evil.

The 'ontological weight' of the claim that There Is No Alternative to a form of capitalism that has become stagnant, despite its debilitating fixation on intensified productivity, is what draws me to the uselessness, wastefulness, outmodedness, and alternative productivities that are central to the kinds of theatre and performance considered in this book. Of course, these characteristics are not unique to theatre and performance. For a start, workplaces and marketplaces are awash with processes and things that are neither useful nor efficient. Obsolescence is built into the lifespan of commodities, especially technologies, and sustaining material affluence produces an extraordinary amount of waste. However, rather than hiding inefficiency and unproductivity behind the veneer of the latest upgrade, the performance makers in this book find inspiration in the retrieval of outmoded things, beliefs and practices, and pleasure in their lack of economic utility. They also revel in productivities that pervert the injunctions of productivism. Rather than fixating on perpetual growth, they seek sustenance in that which falls or flows away from demands to 'grow' and 'progress'. They also embrace wastefulness in ways that redefine what constitutes waste, finding value in that which is deemed obsolete and redundant, or enjoying expenditures of energy ill-suited to an economic logic. In short, rather than transcending the conditions of the capitalist everyday – which includes the conditions of producing and consuming theatre and performance – the artists in this book deliberately seek the transgression of productivism by experimenting with alternative productivities based on creative and cultural gain.

These introductory observations can be distilled into four core theses, which will be providing way markers in the cultivation of a decadent sensibility in the chapters that follow:

1. Theatre is useless. This uselessness has often been put to work in useful ways – for instance, when theatre is attached to categories like 'socially-engaged' or 'applied' – but its being treated as useful is usually linked to its capacity to inspire a change in oneself, another, or society. Theatre can also produce effects in people that are profoundly useless but deeply stimulating and fulfilling, like pleasure. In fact, pleasure is one of the most enriching aspects of theatrical experience for those watching and making theatre. Theatre is by no means the only producer of useless things – the contemporary marketplace is full of them – but it has the capacity to produce useless things in ways that refuse or pervert economic priorities: by corrupting them, perhaps.
2. Theatre is wasteful. It is resource-intensive, and it requires a lot of time and energy to create a work that is usually shared for a limited time. There are 'poor theatres' – which tend to be labour-intensive and time-consuming – and there are performances made on shoe-string budgets. However, the energy expended in the making of theatre is dissipated rather than stored, flowing out into societies that

are fickle in what they choose to remember as important, meaningful, or influential. Productivism breeds inefficiency and wastefulness as well, but it seeks constantly to expunge that inefficiency and wastefulness, often with dire consequences for those tasked with fixing the problem. In contrast, the act of creating live performance is inherently wasteful in its 'mortality'; it makes a spectacle of expended energy night after night, and has the capacity to turn that expenditure into stimulating critiques of what constitutes a 'proper' use of one's time, energy, attention, skill, resource, and intellect.

3. Theatre is outmoded. Because of its resource intensity, it can be expensive to attend. Subsidy is often required if theatre, particularly innovative or experimental theatre, is to reach the widest possible audience, which frequently draws the ire of those invested in the utility of things – and even then there are additional barriers that make theatre elitist in the eyes of many who refuse or are yet to benefit from its offerings, as well as those who have been knocking at the doors of cultural gatekeepers to no avail. But it has also persisted despite challenges deemed existential at the time of their emergence, including the economic and social turbulence wrought by the coronavirus pandemic. It has also persisted despite the massive roll-out of on-demand technologies and the global distribution of cultural products at odds with the antiquated act of congregating to watch a time-bound performance in a space shared with strangers.

4. For all these reasons, and despite the influence of many of its commercially minded stakeholders, theatre also has the capacity to resist forms of productivity based on economic imperatives. To clarify: theatre is *profoundly* productive in terms of generating ideas, images, and actions – which is to say, in a creative sense – but its uselessness, wastefulness and outmodedness make it resistant to metrics and policies that measure and prioritize economic gain over other benefits that are not so easily aligned with the imperative to seek a financial return on an investment. Theatre can most certainly reap economic rewards, as any number of lucrative megamusicals illustrate; it has persisted through countless economic and geopolitical crises; and it has also made highly significant contributions to creative economies.[21] However, it would be wrong to suggest that theatre is likely to be regarded as a major contributor to the strategic plan of a government, say, that pitches financial interests and productivity gains as priorities, although it might be positioned at the margins of such a plan. It is also worth questioning the limitations of orienting theatre around commercial gain – creative limitations being the most obvious, but

also demographic limitations in the making and watching of theatre once we acknowledge the faces, bodies and issues that tend to sell well with those empowered as cultural consumers in the commercial arena.

Rather than trying to spin what theatre has to offer to make it align more neatly with the ends of capitalism – be it with regard to economic growth, technological innovation, or the intensification of productivity, noting the elision between means and ends discussed earlier – *Staging Decadence* suggests that we should take theatre's uselessness, wastefulness, outmodeness, and alternative productivities as points of departure for thinking about how and why we value what we value. It also contends that the same themes are as relevant to other kinds of performance made by performance makers who resist the term 'theatre', *especially* its being 'outmoded': either in the sense of its being old hat or behind the times (Schechner once described theatre as 'the string quartet of the 21st century'),[22] or because it is seen to be antithetical to the progressive or radical politics of those making performance (in the sense of it being unduly susceptible to the whims of commerce). Live art and performance more broadly can be just as useless, wasteful, outmoded, and resistant to economically oriented forms of productivity as mainstream theatre. Even the assumption that live art is somehow more resistant to outmodeness is at odds with the antiquated act of gathering in a room to watch bodies talk or move in a space shared with an audience over the course a timespan that cannot be paused. But these very issues, I argue, are what make theatre and performance uniquely valuable. Once focused and refined, they are also what lend specific performances to the study of decadence in both aesthetic and political terms – a lending that we would do well to celebrate.

Decadence in context: From page to stage

In twenty-first-century theatre and live art – which this book addresses – decadence manifests as a reaction to the incursion of productivism and commerce in the creative lives, working practices, relationships, and creative offerings of artists who take issue with the valorization of intensified productivity in workplaces and commodity-saturated marketplaces that fracture and vie for our attention. Sometimes this finds expression in delightfully perverse forms of over-identification with the excesses of twenty-first-century capitalism (a concept related to José Esteban Muñoz's notion of 'disidentification', but that places additional emphasis on the exaggeration or augmentation of a normative cultural logic),[23] and sometimes it is expressed through a radical dissociation from these excesses. What unites these otherwise diverse forms of performance is a steadfast commitment to ways of thinking, being and doing that fall and flow away from the purely economic. Moreover, in the hands of the performance makers addressed in this book, decadence refers to a re-valuing of all of those things that have for so long been put at arm's length from how theatre and performance are valued in cultures geared towards the demonstration of financial sustainability and resilience, including their uselessness, wastefulness, outmodedness, and deviation from or perversion of productivism.

Many writers associated with decadence who were working around the time of the fin de siècle, or shortly after it, turned to the multiple and often contradictory resonances of decadence as a framework for exploring modernity and industrialization. I mentioned a few examples in the opening pages. Writers like Huysmans, Rachilde, Wilde, Saltus, and Tanizaki shifted the association of decadence with decay and decline into a critique of modernity, particularly urban modernity and the 'progress' that a newly modernized and industrialized cityscape had come to represent.[24] Also, while decadence is often meant as a pejorative intended to castigate behaviours, sexualities, and relationships, many decadent writers embraced it as a badge of honour, queering the prejudices of a society built on imperialism, industrialism, and heteronormativity. This has often been true not just of the characters depicted in decadent literature, but the author's own championing of the countercultural potential of decadence in social circles as well – for instance, in the way that they dressed, behaved, and spoke.[25]

This is an important context for understanding decadence, but it is not the only context. For instance, in the mid-fifteenth century, Philip the Good, Duke of Burgundy, held ostentatious and unorthodox feasts in which musicians and animals erupted from gigantic pies, including a 'live sheep dyed blue with gilded horns', and 'a man dressed as an eagle [. . .] releasing a flock of white doves which flew about and settled on the tables'.[26] Louis XIV upped the theatrical anti in the mid-seventeenth century with his *grands divertissements*: spectacular festivities that went on for days incorporating sumptuous banquets, performing animals, musicians, and extravagant spectacles devised by the leading impresarios of their day, including Molière.[27] The dances of 'vice, horror and ecstasy' performed by Anita Berber and Sebastian Droste (Willÿ Knobloch) were also seen to be part and parcel of the 'decadence' of the Weimar Republic after the First World War, and at the turn of the twentieth century the flamboyant Marchesa Luisa Casati (Luisa Adele Rosa Maria Amman) turned theatre auditoria into a stage for the display of scandalous costumes – for instance, attending the Paris

Opera 'wearing an entire set of white peacock feathers' in her hair, 'while blood, applied beforehand by her chauffeur from the freshly slit neck of a chicken, flowed over the pale skin of her right arm'.[28] So, too, might we think of countercultural artists in downtown New York in the 1960s and 1970s – Jack Smith, John Vaccaro, Charles Ludlam, Penny Arcade (Susana Carmen Ventura), Black-Eyed Susan (Susan Carlson), and Mario Montez (René Rivera) – or we might think of the plays of Yukio Mishima before his notorious public suicide by disembowelment (*seppuku*) in 1970, or the spectacular garments designed by Leigh Bowery in the 1980s and Hew Locke, Athi-Patra Ruga, Yinka Shonibare, and Iké Udé in the 2000s and 2010s. Theatre in the final years of the Ottoman Empire also found playwrights and essayists returning to decadence, and essayists and playwrights from Africa to the Caribbean have explicitly addressed decadence in compelling critiques of empire, colonialism and the stultification of creativity – for instance, in the plays and critical writing of Wole Soyinka and Derek Walcott. Decadence, in short, is a travelling practice. It cuts across diverse art forms and styles, and it becomes ever-more saturated with meanings and prejudices as it traverses time periods and continents.

However, this book is not looking to historicize theatre and decadence, in part because groundwork for such a project has already begun.[29] This book is also not looking to establish 'decadent theatre' as a genre or aesthetic category. Aesthetic categories have already been introduced that can usefully inform the performances that you will be encountering in the pages that follow, which I will be turning to in a moment. I am also not convinced that decadence congeals into anything like a stable aesthetic category because of the sheer extent of the styles and genres that lend themselves to its study, as the eclectic list of examples just surveyed goes some way towards illustrating. This is as true today as it was in the late-nineteenth century, when playwrights, theatre makers and theorists experimented with a range of different styles and genres, sometimes in the same work. Rachilde's play *Madame La Mort* (1891) is a case in point, which cuts across decadence, symbolism, and naturalism. I am also wary of approaches that consign decadence to concepts in circulation during the European fin de siècle, which very often found writers penning misogynistic narratives that fetishize women as sirens or victims, or that exoticize the Orient and ethnic difference (albeit often with subversive or satirical intent).[30] Decadence is not monolithic. As others have recognized, it is both a relative 'direction or tendency', and 'a characteristic mode of reception, rather than a discernible quality of things or people',[31] although this mode need not exist within or even explicitly relate to a canon of decadent art and literature inherited from nineteenth-century Europe.

Instead of cobbling together a potted history of theatre and decadence, this book presents critical frames for addressing original twenty-first-century performances in light of the specific political, cultural, and economic contexts that have shaped their production and reception. It is on this basis that I am interested in a range of associations that have informed how contemporary theatre makers and live artists have engaged with ideas and practices that are relevant to decadence as a phenomenon at odds with productivism, even if these artists have tended to work with alternative terms in describing their work.

Books like Julia Skelly's *Radical Decadence: Excess in Contemporary Feminist Textiles and Craft* (2017) and Jillian Hernandez's *Aesthetics of Excess: The Art and Politics of Black and Latina Embodiment* (2020) have made clear the extent to which the enjoyment and significances of decadence and the aesthetics of excess are ripe to be redefined in terms that would be alien to most scholars focused on the European fin de siècle, but in alignment with the kind of decadence championed by Witherspoon, for instance.[32] Recent works of decadent fiction like Shola von Reinhold's *LOTE* (2020) have also greatly enriched the range of themes and issues that we might come to associate with decadence, as have a number of cultural histories and theories by Black Studies scholars. For instance, Saidiya Hartman has offered a radical reformulation of white European conceptions of beauty, framing beauty not as luxury, but as 'a way of creating possibility in the space of enclosure, a transfiguration of the given. It is a will to adorn, a proclivity for the baroque, and the love of *too much*'.[33] This may not seem 'decadent' in the sense inherited from fin de siècle Europe, where 'decadence' (unlike aestheticism) is more likely to be associated with the defilement of beauty. Nonetheless, the will to adorn, a proclivity for the baroque, and a love of too much might still decentre understandings of decadence that insist on its meaning being tied to nineteenth-century worldviews, as important and instructive as this context has been in the theorization of decadence in art, literature, and politics. In short, rather than seeking to 'master the concept of decadence' by 'free[ing] it from inconsistency',[34] I want to explore instead *how* else decadence might be imagined, *who* else might do the imagining, and the friction that emerges when competing terms of reference rub shoulders.

Sianne Ngai's *Our Aesthetic Categories: Zany, Cute, Interesting* (2012) offers one example of an existing aesthetic category that can help with identifying and unpacking the staging of decadence (it will also become an important point of reference in Chapter 4). Ngai identifies the zany, the cute, and the 'merely' interesting as aesthetic categories that can shed light on how cultural repertoires in postindustrial economies relate to hyper-commodification, information saturation, and the compulsion to constantly perform. Of particular note is the zany, which describes an 'aesthetic of nonstop acting or doing', performed by 'an unusually beset agent [. . . and] that seems to be on a deeper level about work'.[35] Performances of the zany confront audiences with an awareness, often the product of discomforting humour, that the incessant and precarious flows of activity performed by frenzied or exhausted performers might have something important to say about the obligations and expectations that surround their own social and occupational activities.

Ngai's book is not about decadence, and zaniness is not the equivalent of decadence, but the zany nonetheless shares a concern with the augmentation of productive endeavour that is central to the present study's interest in over-identification. We might also say that the zany can *become* decadent once its useless freneticism reaches a point of abject stasis, in which performers find themselves performing exhausting routines without going anywhere or achieving anything other than the expenditure of energy, especially when that expenditure is refined and the process of refinement itself becomes a site of perverse pleasure. Frenetic standstill and the zany might also become decadent when performers disidentify with debilitating injunctions to do and achieve more and more. This might occur when artists conceive of these injunctions as symptoms of an economy in the last of its decline, indulging in languorous or slothful actions and inactions ill-suited to anything other than their own enjoyment – like the devotees reclining at the feet of Isis in Witherspoon's *Priestess of Twerk*.

The hyperactivity or inertia caused by frenetic standstill are not in themselves decadent, then, but they can become so once expressions of their experience are tied to radical forms of augmentation, disengagement, or a taste for the distasteful – an 'uncommon sense' – which the decadence scholar David Weir identifies as a quintessential characteristic of a decadent sensibility.[36] You will find this uncommon sense revealed in the work of Martin O'Brien, Julia Bardsley, Marcel·lí Antúnez Roca, jaamil olawale kosoko, The Uhuruverse, Toco Nikaido, Toshiki Okada, Ron Athey, Wunderbaum, and Hasard Le Sin. These are the core artists that this book will be addressing in the chapters that follow, and all of them, I argue, have cultivated a decadent sensibility. They each offer uncommon takes on what makes something useful or productive, finding bountiful fruit in the outmodedness and wastefulness of making theatre and performance.

If uncommon sense and a taste for the distasteful offer us a flavour of a decadent sensibility, then uncommon actions as well as inaction invite reflection on the politics of decadence as a critique of modernity – specifically the refusal of a capitalist work ethic, which played an important role in the work of many decadent writers in the nineteenth century.[37] However, the artists discussed in this book are not really concerned with modernity per se. They are preoccupied with the specificities of the contexts in which they produce and share performance: with the coronavirus pandemic and its impact on business-as-usual (Chapter 1); crisis capitalism around the time of the 2008 financial crash (Chapter 2); racial capitalism in the 2010s (Chapter 3); the lost generation in post-bubble Japan (Chapter 4); and the culture wars that raged in the 1990s, 2010s, and that have reared their head again in the 2020s (Chapter 5). Each context affects the cultivation of a decadent sensibility, just as they demand sensitivity towards the ways in which productivism has changed and developed in recent years. Hence, there is a need to account for the ways in which capitalism has evolved from a time when industrialization was novel, to a time when there seems to be no alternative to capitalism in postindustrial societies, as this must surely affect how we conceive of the relationship between decadence and the political. What has this transition done to the relevance and critical power of decadence in the twenty-first century?

Slowdown and the pursuit of busyness

What makes decadence timely and instructive in addressing the work of the artists in this book is not simply the ways in which their performances 'look' or 'feel' decadent, although decadent aesthetics feeds into what makes them compelling. It is the ways in which the staging of decadence can produce inspiring deviations from productivism's prizing of usefulness, efficiency, incessant innovation, and intensified productivity – the opposite of those features that I outlined earlier as being key to the uniquely valuable qualities of live performance. What makes decadence in performance valuable in the twenty-first century is its refusal to take productivism for granted. This section is about that refusal, and what it is that is being refused.

If decadence once served as a critique of modernity and industrialization, and the performance makers considered in this book are no longer living in a period of modernity and industrialization, then the moment in which they do live and its relationship to the past requires some clarification. Social and cultural commentators have been preoccupied with intensified productivity and speed since around 1750, although in the wake of the industrial revolution 'there followed wave after wave of diagnoses of an acceleration of tempo (of life, of the world, of society, of history – or even of time itself)', as the sociologist Hartmut Rosa observes.[38] One such commentator was Karl Marx. Industry was speeding up at an unprecedented rate by the time Marx reached adulthood in the 1840s, outstripping human capabilities and subordinating factory workers to the productive capabilities of technology. This is what prompted him to study working conditions in British factories, and the exploitative nature of capitalism in a newly industrialized world. But alongside his depiction of capitalism's means and ends, Marx chose to unfold another narrative. For Marx, the pursuit of intensified productivity and unremitting growth meant that it was only a matter of time before the inherent contradictions of capitalism would bring about a series of crises, and with those crises would come new opportunities for socialism and, thereafter, the promised land of communism. One reason is that capitalism relies on living labour to produce the surplus value it needs for growth, but it is also driven to diminish the size of the labour force through innovations in methods and modes of production. If we are to follow this narrative through to its logical conclusion, the cogs and wheels of growth and accumulation must eventually fall into a cataclysmic tailspin.

But despite a raft of crises, capitalism has proven to be extraordinarily resilient. In the 1960s, the futurologists Alvin and Heidi Toffler produced studies urging readers to prepare for a pace of life that was only going to get faster.[39] They implore their readers to adapt, capitulate, and perform: a demand that performance theorist Jon McKenzie would later identify as a logic governing the postindustrial workplace.[40] What was once vaunted as an inspiration among certain avant-garde artists, like the Futurists, as industrial modernity was establishing itself at the turn of the twentieth century, had become a prosaic reality by the dawn of the twenty-first century.

Despite a shift away from manufacturing in postindustrial societies, new machines and technologies strive towards ever-increasing speed and efficiency, even though productivity levels are diminishing in workplaces that struggle to benefit from the gains they promise. Technological development is putting increasing pressure on job markets, precarious portfolio careers are pitched as an answer to unemployment, and organizations are passing their own productivity pressures onto individual workers, as was the case in Marx's day. The difference is that these changes are now entrenched, and precarity has 'become a noisier part of the collective consciousness as traditionally secure economic and ethnic groups move closer to or into downward mobility'.[41] This affects not just those who fall out of work, but those who have found employment as well, including theatre and performance makers, who several scholars have identified as the 'exemplary' or 'ideal' posterchildren of a precarious postindustrial workforce.[42]

However, while the pace of life is *felt* by many to be accelerating, bearing the weight of projected possibilities in a frenetic present, the heydays of accelerating growth and productivity are over.[43] Even capitalism's most optimistic advocates concede that growth and productivity have been stagnating in advanced capitalist economies (post-pandemic bounce-backs also need to be read in light of longer-term trends).[44] This has not stopped demand for productivity rising, just as the gap between productivity and worker compensation widens on both sides of the Atlantic.[45] The intensity of work is increasing, alongside the demands and expectations attached to work, but oftentimes this intensification occurs regardless of actual productivity gains.[46] Personal insecurities about the precariousness of jobs are exacerbating the amount of time spent thinking about work, there is increasing social pressure to be *seen* to work longer hours, and an increasing amount of work slips under the radar of the time sheet and contract. Average employment hours may have changed little since the 1970s in Europe and the United States, but studies dwelling on the *quantity* of free time do little to account for qualitative changes in how it is experienced.[47] Auto-exploitation matched with an 'imperative to achieve' can seriously damage mental health by exhausting creativity and motivation, exacerbating rates of depression as workers come to view the interruption of work as a hindrance to self-realization.[48]

As productivity pressures intensify, so does the need for capital to sustain itself by increasing the rate of consumption. Commodities soon become or are *designed* to become obsolete, but instead of repurposing or repairing them, many of us adhere to habitual rituals of replacement. One-click purchases and same-day delivery have widened the possibilities of what we can consume to a near limitless scale (budget-depending), minimized the amount of effort and time we need to expend in the act of shopping, and given rise to what Virilio describes (in much the same vein as many other theorists of postmodernity) as an '*era of intensive time* [. . .] of *staying on the spot*, of *housebound intertia*'.[49]

Theories advocating for social acceleration by way of full automation and the surpassing of capitalism's own limits do not direct us anywhere, other than in circles.[50] More importantly, the evidence just surveyed clearly suggests that advanced capitalist economies are not accelerating at all, but stagnating, just as the myth of perpetual growth continues to foster counterproductive injunctions to produce and consume more. Productivism now forms a central part of the 'realism' of capitalism, in which a life not governed by productivism seems increasingly difficult to imagine. In short, what is at stake is a battle for the imagination.

I am not doubting or questioning the value and pleasure of being productive. Taken together, the critiques of productivism explored by the theatre makers and live artists in this book insist on the fact that there are multiple ways in which productivity might be organized and shared. In exploring these alternatives, perhaps we might conceive of how to retrieve pleasure from productivity, 'as well as other pleasures that we may wish to discover, cultivate, and enjoy', as Kathi Weeks – a key critic of productivism – puts it.[51] The pressures of productivism can be ruinous, as they can impact a subject's health and well-being as much as the sustainability of an environment. However, as Sara Ahmed reminds us, it is also possible to 'ruin what ruins' – an idea that seems to me to be of much relevance to decadent praxis.[52] With Ahmed, perhaps we might think of decadence not just as a process that leads to something decaying or falling down, but as a basis for learning about ruinous things by dismantling them, or simply revelling in acts of border crossing.

The theatre makers and live artists explored in these pages stage alternative ways of doing, being, feeling, and seeing to those mapped by productivism. These alternatives are to an extent indebted to decadents of old who explored the potential of decadence to undermine or circumvent industrial modernity and the progress it was understood to represent and propel, but not because they mirror their methods or intentions. Postindustrialism produces different contexts that embed and shape the production and reception of contemporary theatre and performance in ways that invite different calibrations of decadence as an anti-productivist practice, and who this practice might serve. This book is about such practice. With Sherwood, it is concerned with a slagheap of materials and ways of working that fall away from efficiency and instrumentality, instead favouring inefficiency as grounds for another kind of bounty – one that delights in filigree and ornamentation as much as a distasteful taste for the discarded, and incompletion. As with Witherspoon's Temple of Isis, it also concerns performances that luxuriate in time – that *take* time – and the reclamation of space as a territory of uncommon pleasures. In these spaces and times, theatre and live art focus and refine the very things that might otherwise ensure their demise, and that we would do well to retrieve and explore as their most valuable assets in contexts that know the price of everything and the value of nothing – namely, their spectacular uselessness, wastefulness, outmodedness, and unconventional productivities.

What follows

Aside from access to live performances and video recordings, in selecting case studies I have focused on work by artists and companies from countries affiliated with the Organisation for Economic Co-operation and Development (OECD), an intergovernmental organization that promotes and measures economic 'progress' on the basis of growth enhancement and productivity. I am particularly interested in member states that have suffered from stagnating growth and output per capita since the 2008 global financial crash, which brought debates about cultural value and what it means to be a productive subject into sharp focus. Companies and artists from Japan, the Netherlands, Spain, the UK, and the United States were chosen for a variety of reasons ranging from the relationship of a work to a specific set of policy decisions and debates, to what a performance can tell us about specific aspects of the broader productivist paradigm – for instance, the relationship of productivism to temporality and spatiality, technology and new media, and race, sexuality, gender, and physical capability. I also discuss the work of a Finnish performer – Hasard Le Sin – in the book's Conclusion. This is partly to wrap up with a performance staged at an event that was explicitly themed around decadence, as with the performances by Witherspoon and Sherwood discussed earlier, although it also enables engagement with work by a Scandinavian performance maker: a context that has only recently drawn attention in studies of decadence, and that is indicative of the ways in which the field has been opening up to consider twenty-first-century contexts.[53]

Much as theatre and other forms of performance can and frequently do take the realism of productivism for granted, they also have the potential to enable temporal and spatial politics of a very different kind. Chapter 1 explores that potential, with a focus on the temporal. It looks at a series of performances by the British performance maker Martin O'Brien that centre on the productive capabilities of a slow coughing body. All of O'Brien's work is grounded in his experiences of living with cystic fibrosis (CF) beyond the age of thirty, which he was told would mark the likely span of his life. He frames the years lived since as 'zombie time', with his work turning to the embodiment of the zombie as a way of exploring chronic illness, alongside temporalities and rhythms that fall and flow away from wider processes that affect how bodies come to be seen as healthy and their actions appropriate. Addressing work made before and during the pandemic, which presented an acute threat to those living with CF, I argue that O'Brien's figurations of the zombie and its stumbling slowness take on decadent qualities in their revaluation of the embodiment of sickness, a taste for abject counterpleasures, and the fostering of temporalities opposed to the compression and intensification of time in productivist societies. In O'Brien's work it is the kingdom of the sick – famously explored by Susan Sontag – as well as the temporalities of the sick that reign supreme, not least the interminable waiting and zombie time experienced by those living with chronic illness.

Where Chapter 1 considers the temporalities of decadence and productivism, Chapter 2 dwells on materiality and the scenographic. The grounding of decadence in Literary Studies has produced scepticism towards the actual embodiment of decadence. Retreat into an immaterial, imaginative domain had political potency in the late nineteenth and early twentieth centuries, when industrial modernity was in the ascendency; however, in the late-twentieth century – with the rise of postindustrialism – the immaterial domain became a prime site of capital production. I argue that the prospect and value of exploring decadent materiality and the decadent body in performance accrue special significance in the context of postindustrialism. Through detailed analyses of work by the British performance maker Julia Bardsley and the Catalan artist Marcel·lí Antúnez Roca, I look at what the performing body and what I call 'decadent scenography' has to offer to our understanding of immaterial infrastructures and cybernetic technologies before and after the 2008 financial crash, and what space there might be for imagining a time after their end.

Decadence tended to be understood in apolitical or reactionary terms in the nineteenth century, which continues to affect how it is thought about in Decadence Studies today. Chapter 3 responds by querying the extent to which it is still appropriate to approach decadence in the same terms at a time when capitalism no longer appears effective as a driver of growth and productivity. In doing so, I turn to the work of two non-binary African American artists: jaamil olawale kosoko, and The Uhuruverse. Their explorations of entropy and pessimism in performance enable us to think the cultural politics of decadence afresh by connecting these interests to both Afropessimism and Afrofuturism, albeit in ways that balance these otherwise incongruous philosophies very differently. While incorporating Afrofuturist tropes and references, kosoko's 2017 piece *Séancers* offers a nuanced study of enervation and the disposability of Black bodies. In contrast, The Uhuruverse begins with a nihilist world view – neatly captured in the punk mantra 'No Future' – as a starting point for exploring the expanded horizons and possibilities afforded by Afrofuturism. In both cases, it is not necessarily the look and feel of their work that lends itself to decadence, so much as the ways in which they speak back to neocolonial diagnoses of societal decadence as styles of social evaluation. They also invite their audiences to catch glimpses of ethereal and extra-terrestrial beings that reference and subvert the 'progress' that racial capitalism represents: awakening to the countercultural dreamings of a bygone era, and inhabiting liminal netherworlds or the infinite blackness of space as bases for intervening in racial capitalism, or prefiguring Black fugitivity.

Chapter 4 takes as its point of departure a dance form in Japan called *otagei*, which is usually performed by superfans (*otaku*) at J-pop concerts. *Otagei* is characterized by a rapid series of syncopated upper-body movements, but with the feet pressed firmly to the floor. This results in a frenetic routine that is, at the same time, static. Drawing inspiration from the *otagei* dancer's embodiment of 'frenetic standstill', the chapter considers how two contemporary theatre makers – Toshiki Okada and Toco Nikaido – have reacted to a socio-economic predicament in Japan that has been conditioned by both the fetishization of intensified productivity, and longstanding economic stagnation. Nikaido and Okada work with strategies of augmentation that lend themselves to a decadent sensibility, but they do so in very different ways. Nikaido intensifies excessive productivity to points of exuberant and messy excess, whereas Okada stages the catatonic effects of super-saturation and ceaseless compulsions to do and achieve more in less time. However, that 'decadence' is only legible in the context of specific discourses that gained momentum after a disastrous economic crash in 1991. The crash prompted conservative commentators to deride Japan as a 'decadent' society, just as a 'lost generation' of people who came of age at the time were castigated as 'decadent' because of their refusal to engage with productivist priorities. Nikaido and Okada speak back to this discourse. Neither envisages an alternative to productivism, but in estranging or exploding its apparent intractability, they call attention to its failures. They also offer a very different engagement with decadence compared with those explored in the rest of the book based not on refusal, but augmentation, exaggeration, and over-identification with the debilitating excesses of twenty-first-century capitalism.

On 14 February 2022, the co-chairman of the Conservative Party in the UK at the time, Oliver Dowden, gave a speech condemning 'woke' beliefs and attitudes as 'a dangerous form of decadence', citing planned legislation to protect free speech on university campuses that would also challenge what Dowden described as the 'Left-wing excesses' of the arts, humanities, and social sciences. Other policy consultations were also proposing to cut funding for these subjects by 50 per cent, putting them and the careers they foster in a double bind: at once dangerous in their decadence, and frivolous in their uselessness. Exploring a range of speeches, policy documents, and campaign advertising, the chapter considers the nature and stakes of a resurgent culture war – typified in Dowden's remarks – by considering previous culture wars in which art and artists have been derided as 'decadent' or 'degenerate'. This includes the condemnation of artists and performers like Robert Mapplethorpe, Andres Serrano, and Ron Athey on the floor of the US Senate, which is why particular attention is given to Athey, especially the denigration of his work and sexuality as 'decadent' at the height of the AIDS crisis. The chapter also turns to a more recent example in the Netherlands in which the Dutch theatre company Wunderbaum lampoons Dutch politicians who rationalized the erosion of public support for the arts in the wake of the 2008 financial crisis, as well as the dismissal of divisive publicly funded artworks – particularly a controversial statue by the North American artist Paul McCarthy – as 'degenerate', useless, and a waste of public money. By studying the cultural politics of decadence in historical context, I argue that we will be better placed to respond to those moments when the arts and humanities are most threatened.

The negative valences of decadence have long been used to deride – these valences have rhetorical utility – so it is unsurprising that figurations of decadence as a dangerously destructive form of decline have been making headway again in the thick of a resurgent culture war. The implications for the practice and study of theatre and performance, as well as the arts and humanities more broadly, are grave. A rhetoric of uselessness, wastefulness, outmodedness, and a perceived failure to contribute effectively or productively to economic growth and productivity has underpinned how the arts and humanities have been understood by those intent on hindering their capacity to thrive, if not on doing away with them altogether as inessential drains on the health and wealth of a nation. Productivism and submission to market stimulation and economic growth provide politicians adhering to this view with a rationale for rendering the arts – especially theatre and performance – not only obsolete but dispensable.

Rather than justifying the relevance and value of theatre and performance on the basis of the extent to which they contribute to economic growth and productivism, or on the basis of their intrinsic value per se, I call for a more uncommon breach of the frame that positions incessant economic growth, the cultish pursuit of so-called upgrades, and intensified productivity as acceptable measures of success, significance, and value. Theatre and performance *are* useless, they *are* wasteful, they *are* outmoded, and the productivities they stage are not fit for purpose in a world that strives always to accelerate into the future, regardless of the frenetic standstill that this striving has produced in the twenty-first century. That lack of a fit, that resistance to a future that is to all intents and purposes undesirable, is why we have much to learn from performances that embrace decadence in all of its glory: languishing in time, breaching horizons of taste and social acceptability, falling and flowing away from hierarchies and taxonomies, and making a spectacle of useless, wasteful, outmoded, and endlessly creative practices at odds with the ends of twenty-first-century capitalism.

1

Zombie time

Sickness, performance, and the living dead

Decadence refers to a process of falling or flowing away from an established order or hierarchy, often in ways that stylize and refine decay by luxuriating in its putrid bounty. Decadence falls and flows through time and anticipates endings, giving it a crepuscular quality – hence its affiliation with the fin de siècle. This gives decadence an apocalyptic flavour, but decadence also makes space for revelling or languishing in endings – including those things we might wish to bring to an end, cultivating a taste for their defilement – and anticipates forms of doing and not doing that might come after the end. This makes performance as a time-based art a particularly interesting forum for exploring the temporal qualities of decadence. Performance is an entropic art of making and unmaking, disappearing and haunting, ending only to be reanimated again, in one form or another, night after night.

This chapter explores the chronic qualities of decadence in performance by turning to the work of an 'artist who believes he's a zombie', as the BBC put it in a sensational headline: the British live artist Martin O'Brien.[1] How do zombies experience the passing of time? What do they have to say about 'good' uses of time – about diligence and labour, for instance, or career ambitions? Do they mind that their bodies are decomposing, and what do they make of one another's decay? Are they concerned by the apocalypse they are said to inhabit? There are a number of artist-zombies who could have been asked in exploring these questions – like Jenny Lawson and her strategies for 'becoming zombie', Claire Hind and Gary Winters with their embodiments of the dead, or any number of flesh-eaters performing in immersive zombie experiences and protests.[2] However, I opted for O'Brien because of the different ways in which his work engages with the chronic as both time and illness, and because of the relevance of his practice to this book's overarching concern with decadence and the ends of capitalism.

All of O'Brien's work is grounded in his experience of living with cystic fibrosis (CF) beyond the age of thirty, which he was told would mark the likely span of his life. O'Brien is not the first to embrace CF as a stimulus for performance. He is working in the shadow of Bob Flanagan, who died of the disease in 1996. Flanagan's creative collaborations with life partner and mistress Sheree Rose have been well-documented, particularly their use of S&M in both managing and aestheticizing Flanagan's disease – an approach that has since inspired O'Brien's own practice.[3] Rose has also collaborated with O'Brien on a number of projects, including the staging of performances that were planned by Flanagan and Rose, but unrealized in Flanagan's lifetime, including *Dust to Dust* (2015), which was presented in Los Angeles in the United States, and *The Viewing* (2016), which was shared at DadaFest in Liverpool in the UK. These performances epitomize 'the kind of queer affiliations that challenge rote and rigidly mainstream conceptions of kinship and family', to borrow from art historian Amelia Jones, given that O'Brien becomes a kind of surrogate for Flanagan, and an adopted 'son' to Mistress Rose.[4] However, O'Brien's practice also reaches beyond the caretaking of Flanagan's legacy, especially in works that centre his interest in the zombie – and it is these works that draw focus in this chapter.

O'Brien describes the years lived since his thirtieth birthday as 'zombie time',[5] embodying the zombie as a way of exploring chronic illness and a temporality that flows away from the attachments and anxieties that affect how time is experienced in work-oriented cultures and in a globally distributed marketplace. His zombies are not the bewitched slaves associated with African-diasporic zombies, which feature in some of the earliest zombie movies, like Victor and Edward Halperin's film *White Zombie* (1932) and Jacques Tourneur's *I Walked with a Zombie* (1943). Where these films trace zombies to their Haitian roots, depicting Black people dispossessed of consciousness by sorcerers and colonial masters, George A. Romero made them chomp their way through society as 'mindless engines of decay', beginning with *Night of the Living Dead* (1968), and continuing through other classics of the subgenre including *Dawn of the Dead* (1978) and *Day of the Dead* (1985).[6] Romero's zombies do not become zombies because they are bewitched, although in *Night of the Living Dead* they are mysteriously reanimated by radiation from an exploded satellite. They propagate by consuming the flesh of humans. Romero made zombies infectious.

O'Brien riffs on the sickness and infectiousness of Romero's living dead, and the subversive potential of zombies once they congregate as a horde in the ruins of capitalism. Of particular note is Romero's *Dawn of the Dead*, which finds zombies trudging through an abandoned shopping mall, unsure whether to consume the flesh of their victims or the latest fashion, as well as *Day of the Dead*, in which zombies overcome the attempts of living humans to domesticate their unusual tastes and drives. O'Brien shares Romero's interest in the zombie as a contagious entity, as a surrogate for workers and consumers, and as a powerful horde. He is also drawn to the unusualness of their desire to feast indiscriminately on human flesh. None of these characteristics are decadent in themselves, but O'Brien turns their unusual appetites into a desirable taste for sickness and decay, lusting after sickness, the sick, and abject pleasures. This is what lends his zombies to decadence, which also does something interesting to how the ruins and ruination of capitalism are imagined. In O'Brien's hands, productivism – which refers to the centring of intensified productivity as a basis for self-realization, and a panacea for ailing economies – is corrupted, crumbling into a conception of society based not on the apparent permanency and intractability of productivism, but the abject pleasures and desires of the sick. In the worlds he imagines and stages, it is the kingdom of the sick – famously explored by Susan Sontag – that reigns supreme.[7]

O'Brien's invitation to consider what might happen to desire in the kingdom of the sick has taken on fresh significance in the years since the emergence of the Covid-19 pandemic. Horror movie fans were quick to connect the pandemic with the zombie's insatiable appetite and the deserted streets of quarantined towns and cities, and O'Brien has been explicit in connecting his own interest in the zombie apocalypse with the time of the pandemic, in which the normative time of business-as-usual was suspended.[8] This is an important consideration, as his work has more to offer than a purely pathological reading allows, and it is not autobiographical;[9] it is situated within and speaks to a particular and evolving social and cultural context, inflecting his work with new meanings and significance along the way. At the same time, it would be egregious to uncouple his idea of zombie time from the chronic illness that inspired its staging. This chapter therefore traces *proximities* between zombie time and interminable waiting during the pandemic, opening out to address a much broader range of issues including the medicalization of sickness, outbreak narratives, and the prizing of ever-improved health, growth, progress, and productive capabilities.

Two concerns draw particular focus. The first is an ethical concern that has to do with the expectations that surround those living in productivist societies. This concern is linked to decadence in a pejorative sense that derides the passing of time in ways that are deemed to be a waste of time, as well as forms of productivity, capability, and desire that are seen to be somehow 'unnatural' or at odds with ever-increasing healthiness and ever-expanding growth. However, I am also interested in how oppositionality might form the basis of a more positive valuation of the same factors. This leads me to the second core concern, which has to do with futurity. What might we learn from the embodiment and enactment of practices that fall away from dominant narratives of progress? O'Brien's zombies return to different parts of this question, inviting us to query assumptions that measure progress on the basis of continual growth, the enhancement of physical and social capabilities, and the unabated intensification of productivity. In short, the challenge these zombies pose to productivism is grounded in a decadent desire to inhabit and propagate the kingdom of the sick.

Interminable waiting

One of the last performances I attended before the UK entered its first period of lockdown in the Spring of 2020 was a lecture performance at the Tate Britain in London, called *Until the Last Breath is Breathed* (2018–20). As a lecture performance, this was one of O'Brien's more reserved performances compared with his earlier actions, which tend to be very messy in their use of bodily fluids and buckets or tubs of thick green mucus-like gunge, as well as challenging in their incorporation of scarring and piercing of the body, and radical in their staging of queer desires and actions inspired by S&M practices and CF treatment regimes. *Until the Last Breath is Breathed* incorporated some familiar but less messy and resource-intensive actions from these earlier performances, including heavy pounding of his bare chest to release mucus (derived from a therapeutic exercise) and the use of an S&M breath restrictor or 're-breathe hood', as well as monologues recycled or adapted from several earlier works, including *If It Were the Apocalypse I'd Eat You to Stay Alive* (2015–17), *The Unwell* (2016), and *The Ascension* (2017). Several actions were also screened from a durational performance presented to a group of friends in an abandoned morgue in the hours leading up to his thirtieth birthday – the point at which he was told his life would end – including acts of self-cannibalism, which find O'Brien gnawing at his own joints and limbs, carving the shape of lungs onto his chest using a scalpel, and repeatedly blowing on a relighting birthday candle. (O'Brien sometimes uses the term 'endurance art' rather than 'durational performance', but the latter highlights the temporal significances of his practice).[10]

'This is the beginning of the zombie years', he tells us as the performance gets underway; 'I should be dead but I'm not. [. . .] Now I'm existing in a different time. This is the zombie time, the time of the animated corpse. I feel immortal. Death is behind me instead of in front. Zombie time is a different relationship to death, and life. It's about survival, but also infecting, creating a horde'. He daydreams about a river of phlegm that oozes through cities and villages, bubbling out of taps. People start to cough. They become diseased in a festering, viral landscape – but a luminary also preaches about a different way of inhabiting this land. He speaks of a queer zombie apocalypse in which desires fall and flow away from normative expectations. 'The virus would infect people and kill them, but they would immediately return. [. . .] What would follow, so the luminary foretold, was the end of civilization as we know it'.[11]

Although recycled from earlier works, this sermon on sickness speaks to the hopes and fears that were circulating when the Covid-19 pandemic reared its head. Television screens and radio waves made ruination and inertia hyper-present while residents of quiet streets hauled up indoors, but what was to follow seemed an open question at risk of closure. In the UK populist impulses drew many people back to a pseudo-imperialist nostalgia based on rebuilding structures of oppression from the wreckage of an economy on its knees. The popularity of Victory in Europe (VE) Day celebrations is a case in point, with street parties marking one of the few opportunities for public gatherings that were socially legitimated at the time. As Priscilla Wald suggests in an influential study of outbreak narratives, the time of a pandemic is a time in which interaction is risky, but it is also a time when the bonds of a community can be disrupted or cemented.[12] The street parties marking VE Day bore out the latter in contrast to the more radical or reformist hopes that many on the Left pinned to the suspension of business-as-usual.

Communities based on reactionary nostalgia tend to breed xenophobic attitudes, and the pandemic was no exception,[13] but O'Brien's practice imagines a different kind of community based on the queering of dominant outbreak narratives. There's no triumph of humankind over disease, no attempt to expunge sickness and the sick, and no vigilante or medical authority rescuing a nation from the peril of infection. O'Brien's vision is based on dispersal, on rivers of phlegm lateralizing hierarchies, and on coughs serving as the hallmark of a community of equals. His practice is shaped by his own experiences of a specific chronic illness, but he has also been explicit in discussing how zombie time speaks to the time of the pandemic, as noted earlier. Zombie time and the time of the pandemic are not synonymous – those fending off the prospect of death have a different relationship to mortality compared with those for whom 'death is behind [. . .] instead of in front' – although there is a proximity between them insofar as both bring time's passing into focus, and how particular acts of passing time either play into or fall away from dominant modes of imagining community.

I was due to attend another of O'Brien's performances, *The Last Breath Society (Coughing Coffin)*, at the Institute of Contemporary Art (ICA) in London the month after his lecture performance at Tate Britain, but it was cancelled once it became clear that the spread of the virus had evolved into a pandemic.[14] Its premiere had to wait until July 2021, once restrictions on social interaction were lifted and the particular risk to those living with CF was reduced – a delay that seems appropriate given this durational performance's preoccupation with death, waiting, and the passing of time.

The performance was based around the manipulation and dismantling of eight black coffins. At times O'Brien would clamber inside an upright coffin and tilt it precariously from side to side like a ticking metronome, each time getting closer and closer to a point of collapse. At others he would hang the long flat edge of a coffin's interior along his back, making it look like it had sprouted legs. He would seal himself inside coffins, he would smash them, he would pile them one on top of another. He also recorded their handling on a series of tape recorders, as well as other sounds emitted throughout the performance: the sound of laboured breathing while wearing a re-breathe hood; the sound of violent gargling after an assistant forces O'Brien to drink water poured through a metal funnel into his open mouth; the sound of him dragging a stuffed hammerhead shark along the floor with his teeth. All of these objects – the re-breathe hood, tools of domination and subordination, a taxidermy shark – would have been familiar to anyone acquainted with O'Brien's earlier practice. They ghost the work. This performance was also the first time that previous iterations of the *same* work played into the hauntology of his practice. It was structured around the sounds of previous performances being re-played on tape recorders, making this a performance not of four hours – the duration of the live element that excludes time for attending an installation beforehand – but thirty-two hours across eight days (Figure 1.1).

Actions within a single performance followed an order that was repeated in reverse in its second half. Sometimes these actions were performed in ways that seemed to be the product of methodical planning, and sometimes in clearly improvisatory ways, but they always took a long time to complete. Time stretched as we watched O'Brien's body labour through the tasks, 'sometimes pushed to the edges of its capacities and repeated with a dedicated work ethic', as performance scholar Gianna Bouchard puts it in a commentary on his earlier performances.[15] The work ethic in question, though, is not necessarily based on the achievement of a specific goal. As the philosopher Alphonso Lingis suggests, his performances – almost purgatorial in character – manifest 'a time of waiting and of convulsive effort that [does] not advance or build or accomplish'.[16] O'Brien stages a hypnotic and absorbing form of creative endeavour that makes space for reflection and the settling of affect: not the consummation of a practice in a conventionally productive outcome, so much as an opening up of possibilities that court unpredictable consequences, including collapse.

As a durational work involving a lot of waiting – a work that was also commissioned by a Welcome Trust project, 'Waiting Times', exploring

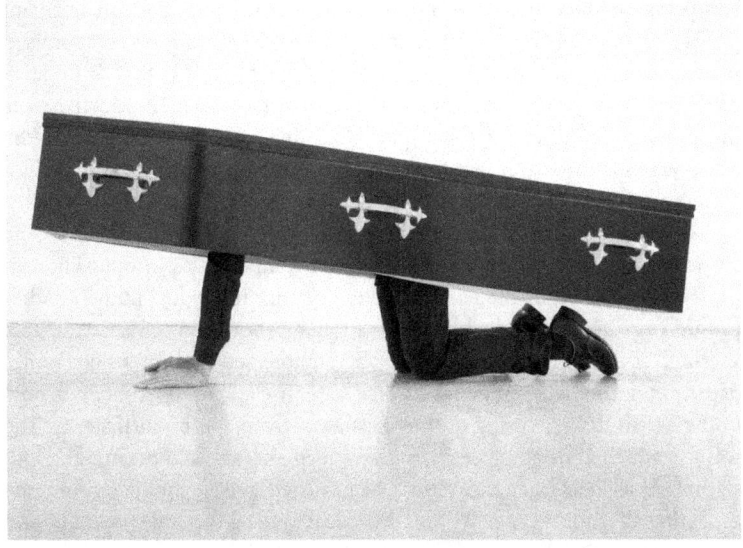

Figure 1.1 Martin O'Brien, *The Last Breath Society* (2021). Institute for Contemporary Art, London. Photo by Holly Revell.

temporal experiences and practices of care in medical contexts[17] – *The Last Breath Society* was also about cultivating a different relationship to time: an *interminable waiting* in which moments of affective intensity were interrupted by protracted periods of meditative stillness, in which nothing much happened, or in which things happened very, very slowly. The psychosocial scholar Lisa Baraitser (a joint Principle Investigator of the 'Waiting Times' project) encourages us to think about this kind of waiting as a 'suspension' of time that can 'produce felt experiences of time *not passing*': a time in which temporal imaginaries can be invoked 'that have a tangential relation to those that characterize "the capitalist everyday", thereby stilling, even if they don't manage to disrupt, modes of production based on utility or exchange'.[18] Key to this 'capitalist everyday', I suggest, is what the economic geographer David Harvey calls 'time-space compression'. Time-space compression refers to the shrinking of time horizons in a globalized world that facilitates instantaneous transactions and communication.[19] The shrinking of a world made more accessible to those enabled by capitalism, and the intensification of a time in which more and more is achievable, is a self-perpetuating phenomenon that can arouse a desire for its furthering: for instance, getting to different places quicker and more smoothly, and achieving more in less time, regardless of necessity. The taken-for-granted-ness of time-space compression is part and parcel of 'the capitalist everyday' today, and its continual enhancement underpins an important aspect of how socio-economic progress is appraised in advanced capitalist economies. It is also one of the things that distinguish productivity in general from productivism in particular. Productivism is the consequence of compressed space and time, potentially facilitating the achievement of more in less time, but more often than not resulting in a counterproductive and directionless busyness.

The queer theorist Elizabeth Freeman explores a similar idea to the suspension of time when she pitches queer temporalities in opposition to '*chrononormativity*, or the use of time to organize individual human bodies toward maximum productivity'.[20] O'Brien's production of interminable waiting, in the sense of suspending the compressed and intensified times of chrononormativity, might then read as a 'useless' use of time, but only to the extent that the using of time falls away from chrononormativity. The ways in which O'Brien passes time in performance are still meaningful and significant as 'necessary excavations of [. . .] self-agency and imagining the capability of choice from within lives deprived of these by sickness and the intense medical routines that this demands'.[21] Determining usefulness or uselessness depends on the register one uses to make that judgement, and takes nothing away from the significance or meaningfulness of how time is passed. O'Brien's work shines a spotlight on the cultural politics of designating a particular passing of time as useful or useless, in sync or at odds with the pursuit of time-space compression and the kinds of body and capability that it favours.

Suspended time has the capacity to 'still' the busyness of time-space compression, and can inspire sensitivity towards modes of chronic experience that are not based on an explicitly healthy or productive use of time ('chronic' both in the temporal sense of that word, and, as we watch O'Brien suffer for his art, physiological too). O'Brien approaches time as an (im)material, experimenting with what the art writer Stephen Wright describes as a 'fuzzy' time that is 'recalcitrant to the tyranny of real time': an invitation, perhaps, to think about the reclamation of time in terms of a temporal commons that exceeds the spatial.[22] The interminable waiting endured by O'Brien – and his audiences – is antithetical to the chronicity of the capitalist everyday. Otherwise put, the recalcitrant and fuzzy passing of time in this performance is what makes it *ana-chronistic*.

The anachronistic codification of temporal experience in *The Last Breath Society* felt especially resonant as I stood in the airy studio space of the ICA in what turned out to be a period of respite between two waves of infection during the Covid-19 pandemic. There was no shortage of time to mull over the past and to reflect on the present and the future in periods of lockdown. Days, weeks, and months seemed to blur into one another; they acquired a 'viscosity', to borrow another of Baraitser's tropes.[23] There were no social engagements to speak of other than those held online, leaving work as one of the few activities left to mark time's passing, not least for those living alone, as I was at the time, and who were neither furloughed nor jobless as a precarious freelance worker or as someone unemployed. Putting time to use lent itself to the marking of its passing during the pandemic, often in ways that risked distorting an appreciation of its mindful experience – apart from when time had been judiciously allocated for mindful reflection.

The Last Breath Society was reimagined from the ground up when the pandemic reared its head, having been commissioned before its emergence.[24] What was ultimately presented to audiences was clearly a response to the undoing of chrononormativity and its impact on sociality. Time passed in ways that were useless in a productivist sense, taken up with gestures and actions that, with time, became significant as indices of a life lived longer than expected. This was a performance about the lived experience of survival – of living with death – but it was also about the insights that emerge from the time and space of doing and experiencing nothing in particular: the time and space, perhaps, of the temporal commons.[25] It was structured around a sequence of repeated actions, manifesting '[t]he repetitively performed impossibility to reach what one is aiming for', as the performance scholar Eirini Kartsaki writes;[26] however, it was ultimately *in*action and stillness that prompted reflection on the counting of a productive use of time, and the kinds of meaning that one might derive from or attach to the use of time (Figure 1.2).

Time that is passed in ways that flow away from a normatively useful or productive spending of time need not be a waste of time. As the playwright Chris Thorpe observes in a reflection on theatre making in the wake of the pandemic, 'the biggest waste of time is the time you spent punching yourself for not being as productive as you'd been taught to expect'.[27] Thorpe advocates for the unexpected affordances of reflection, surprise, intimacy, and slow learning that can emerge from the time and space of doing nothing in particular. *The Last Breath Society* does something similar, although it is not simply about clearing mental space in order to render oneself more productive in the future; it is about luxuriating in or suffering through the aimless passing of time.

Slowness and interminable waiting, hovering between impulses to act and inertia, are what characterize this performance's decadence most of all. One of the reasons why I wanted to dive into this performance as one of the first detailed examples considered in this book is because of the ways it makes clear, from the outset, that decadence in performance need not

Figure 1.2 Martin O'Brien, *The Last Breath Society* (2021). Institute for Contemporary Art, London. Photo by Manuel Vason.

necessarily refer to immoderate wastefulness in the sense of some mindless profligacy leading to massive expenditure on material resource. There is an asceticism to this performance: discipline and sparseness, especially, but also wasting time in the productivist sense and expending energy that might otherwise be put to productivist use. This 'would seem to be the very opposite of excess', to borrow from the philosopher Karmen MacKendrick: 'a defiance even of the moderate demands of one's bodily and social selves, certainly a defiance of hedonistic extravagance. Yet it is in this *defiance* that we find not only the *pleasure* of asceticism' – what she refers to as a form of 'counterpleasure' – but 'a denial beyond all moderation'.[28] For MacKendrick, counterpleasures invoke pleasures (of the kind explored by Georges Bataille and Michel Foucault, among others) that are explicitly 'nonproductive', and that 'tend away from all sorts of teleologies. Even the aim of subject shattering' in certain kinds of submissive and masochistic practice 'can be approached only indirectly, and will destroy the pleasures if it takes them over'.[29] The asceticism of O'Brien's practice, particularly its 'denial beyond all moderation' of productivist endeavour, its improvisatory refusal of goal-oriented action, and its languishing in a recalcitrant and fuzzy time, is what lends that practice to decadence, particularly once drawn into the orbit of a taste for the abject and the counterpleasures of queer desire. It is to such tastes and desires that the next section turns.

Zombie time

Until the Last Breath Is Breathed and *The Last Breath Society* both explore zombie time, although the zombies familiar from popular cinema do not feature in either. Zombiedom is explicitly referenced in *Until the Last Breath Is Breathed*, but O'Brien appears as himself; he does not look like a zombie, at least not the campy zombies made famous by Romero in his classic films, although he does permit zombies to appear in the mind's eye in his monologues. The same is true of *The Last Breath Society*, although to a lesser extent. O'Brien presents himself as a living corpse, but there is no attempt to mimic pop-cultural zombiedom. However, the pop-cultural zombie is pulled front and centre in some of O'Brien's other works, queering these zombies in ways that are distinctly decadent.

Multiple histories have informed the development of zombiedom in twentieth-century popular culture. As noted earlier, some of the earliest depictions of zombies in cinema – including *White Zombie* and *I Walked with a Zombie* – make explicit reference to the zombie's roots in the African diaspora and slavery. Performance scholar Lee Miller defines the African-diasporic zombies in these films as 'proto-zombies': completely objectified forerunners under the influence of a colonial master or sorcerer that tend to be whitewashed in the late-twentieth-century renaissance of zombie films inspired by Romero, although it is notable that *Night of the Living Dead* cast a Black actor as a protagonist seeking refuge from an army of predominantly white flesh-eaters.[30] O'Brien's living dead owe more to the kitschy cultishness of Romero, which is an important point. Where zombies of the African diaspora were generally depicted as being controlled by a zombie master,[31] O'Brien turns to the cult cinematic zombie as a stimulus for exploring the retrieval of autonomy from a specific disciplinary regime (medicine) in a society that pushes sickness and queerness (as distinct from the mainstreaming of homosexuality) to its peripheries. The environmental conditions in which O'Brien's submissive actions take place are of his own choosing, as is the public spectacularization of more explicit acts of degradation (in a particularly memorable example he pours a bucket of his own shit mixed with gold paint over his head, extracted by means of an enema – a purgative that interested several decadent writers).[32] However, as O'Brien points out, there is also a clear 'tension between voluntary endurance in performance and the endurance of a life lived within the duration of slow death'.[33]

The constellation of themes that I will be exploring in this section – unconventional productivity, drawing sickness into the orbit of desire, antithetical relations to the quantification of goal-oriented progress, and a taste for decay and abjection – lends O'Brien's zombies a decadent edge once put into dialogue with more typical features of the zombies made famous by Romero, especially their idleness, slowness, and inertia (as compared with post-millennial 'Zombie 2.0' films like *28 Days Later* (2002), in which zombies appear as frenzied monsters).[34] These themes are especially present in O'Brien's film *The Unwell* (2016), which was made in collaboration with the filmmaker and musician Suhail Ilyas, and was originally intended as 'a strange, tongue in cheek utopia [. . .] in which only the sick can survive'[35] – although it took on weightier resonances with the advent of the Covid-19 pandemic, prompting O'Brien to re-release the film in March 2020 when the survival of the sickest was in particular jeopardy.

The film opens with a zombie labourer crawling on his hands and knees out of a woodland, his high-vis jacket glowing in the dark. He is alone, as are all of the sixteen zombies we encounter in empty car parks, squares, and industrial estates. As the film cuts to an empty highway, we hear O'Brien intoning a monologue: '[t]his used to be the most optimistic city in the world. Now the sun never rises. The shops are never open. The birds never sing. The streets are always empty. [. . .] Perhaps this place used to be beautiful, but it seems as though it has experienced an apocalypse'. A zombie staggers in an abandoned shopping mall. 'Time has ended here [. . .]. But something still remains [. . .]. Something moves slowly through the darkness. They have replaced human life. They resemble us, but they are not us. They fill the city with an unwell sound'.[36] Heavy breathing . . . Phlegmy coughs . . . Voicings of an inner creature that do not adhere to language: 'the voice of illness', demanding to be heard.[37]

Zombie time underpins a logic of futurity in *The Unwell*, a logic that is also closely indexed to the present. To paraphrase the feminist, queer, and disability theorist Alison Kafer, how one comes to understand sickness in the present determines how one imagines sickness in the future.[38] To conceptualize the absence of sickness in positive terms and the presence of sickness in negative terms is to limit how we might come to imagine sickness in the future: that is, we would be better off without, for good. For instance, bio-medical discourse understands the time of sickness as a 'curative time' defined by prognosis and the prospect of remission.[39] This discourse reads time and futurity through a progressive journey from sickness to health, or the management of occurrences and relapse. Alongside bio-medical discourse, productivism is another influence that forecloses sick futures. Productivism sees sickness as a hindrance to the maximization of productivity, or in Kafer's terms 'as obstacles to the arc of progress', unless rehabilitation positions the sick as a 'sign of progress, the proof of development, the triumph over the mind or body'.[40]

Understanding ever-improving health as an inherent good and as a necessity for productive enterprise negates the politics of sickness, insofar as the desirability of sick experiences, sick feelings, sick people, and sick capacities are assumed to be 'against nature' and beyond debate in their wrongness. O'Brien's experimentation with futurity (as with other kinds of queer and crip futurities)[41] refuses this act of foreclosure by challenging the assumptions that determine the casting of sickness as that which must be purged in a 'healthier' and 'more productive' present or future. Instead, he celebrates activities that unfold in zombie time – especially those activities that are indulged for their own sake (lingering, observing, wandering, longing) – and does so through the fabulation of post-apocalyptic worlds and scenarios in which the sickest both survive *and thrive*, drifting away from, while remaining haunted by, productive regimes 'in order to make room for pleasure'.[42]

In his filmed work, the passing of zombie time is 'mapped' more concretely in comparison with his live performances, where there is greater openness to unpredictability in live events that might, just might, go wrong, or that are guided by indefinite ends. Nonetheless, these films make space for silence and stillness, which encourages those watching to attend to the flow of zombie time. Zombies in *The Unwell* also roam the ruins of productivism. O'Brien's zombies might find themselves dressed as workers, but time is not passed by working. They feed on their own flesh, consuming themselves as if haunted by auto-exploitation, and yet their silent bodies also 'speak' to futurity – what the performance scholar José Esteban Muñoz, after the philosopher Ernst Bloch, calls the 'not yet conscious' of a future society 'that is being invoked and addressed at the same moment'.[43] Their slow stagger is not goal-oriented. They have no career ambitions. It is as if the structures and processes of zombification have vanished, leaving behind a dazed horde – only now the zombies are awakening to a new kind of potentiality.

Zombie time is not to be confused with the 'chronic' time of capitalism, which refuses to die despite perennial crises, its life endlessly extended by means of political and organizational ingenuity. For the cultural theorist Eric Cazdyn, to 'settle for the new chronic is to choose the known limits of the present over the unknown freedom of the future'.[44] In contrast, O'Brien's embrace of zombie time as an (im)material in film and performance is about a relationship to the future: an exceptional time in which death is behind and not in front (not being-*toward*-death, in its Heideggerian formulation, so much as death-*in*-and-*behind*-being), and in which acts of fabulation prefigure a strange and radically different future.[45] In this, O'Brien's zombies have more in common with what Cazdyn calls the 'already dead' insofar as these zombies suggest 'a future beyond the temporal constraints of the new chronic [. . .] informed by a certain way of living in time and space, and in relation to an unknown and unrealized future'.[46] However, it is sickness – not its 'cure' or expungement – that forms the basis for this 'certain way of living in time and space', a notion that would be quite unpalatable for Cazdyn despite his own experiences of living with a chronic illness.[47]

Sickness forms the basis of the clearest sign of life that these zombies have, as well as their clearest form of productivity. The frequent coughs that are a hallmark of CF and that punctuate the film are what remains of life – convulsive sickness animates the coughing body – and they are also symptomatic of an unconventional productivity that finds the body producing an excess of phlegm. This makes O'Brien's zombies excessively productive as a 'mucus factory' – a term that O'Brien draws from Bob Flanagan[48] – but in a way that would not be recognized as a particularly useful or valuable form of productivity in medical contexts or in the capitalist everyday given the limited ways in which physical capability is understood in these contexts. O'Brien's zombies queer 'healthy' productivity by framing an alternative capacity, which productivism recognizes as an incapacity, as a site of excessive production.

O'Brien's zombies are also driven by and drawn to an uncommon sense and a taste for the distasteful, which the decadence scholar David Weir identifies as a key feature of decadence.[49] Their kingdom of the sick is a kingdom of infection, a kingdom in which 'mortality is sexy'.[50] Their taste for the distasteful draws them to this kingdom, although it is not a taste that is cultivated in the reclusive environs of an ivory tower. Their uncommon sense is connected to an irresistible intimacy: a queer intimacy with strangers based on acts of consumption, communion, and consummation. Their uncommon sense is also not altogether 'indifferent to right and wrong', which Jack Halberstam identifies as a hallmark of pop-cultural zombies.[51] Unlike Romero's stumbling flesh-eaters, O'Brien's zombies seem to be awakening to a social consciousness of a kind that makes space for bodies and acts deemed abject or unnatural. Their behaviour is not based on an ethos, although in falling away from the normative streaming of desire and appetite they make apparent the extent to which productivism shapes desire and appetite. They are driven instead by a conflation of sickness and desire, prompting reflection on the assumptions and prejudices that stick to sick bodies in societies that prioritize the productive capabilities of the healthy.

It is important to emphasize the humour in these kingdoms of the sick. O'Brien does not want to die, and he does not want others to fall ill. These are fables told with a wry smile.[52] For instance, a monologue in *Until the Last Breath is Breathed* descends from an innocent memory of participating as an actor in a live zombie horror experience to delighting in the putrid and sloppy practicalities of sex between zombies, imagining what it must be like to be smothered by the ass of another zombie, 'with the smell of death and rotten organs emanating out of it. I couldn't help but imagine his massive, rotten gangrenous penis shooting blood and puss all over me'.[53] O'Brien's tongue may be in his cheek – or between cheeks, as the case may be – but there is also a seriousness behind the nods, winks, and abject humour. He invites his audiences to question teleological narratives of health, growth, and betterment, and the prizing of capabilities well-suited to productivity's continual intensification.

Bio-medical science and the capitalist everyday provide the clearest examples of the kind of teleological narratives of health, growth, and betterment that O'Brien's zombies refuse. However, other, particularly illuminating, examples can also be found in Marxist literature, which one might otherwise assume would be an ally of those pushed to the margins of society. For instance, György Lukács, in his essay 'Healthy or Sick Art?' (1934), finds irremediable regression in the collapsing of love into 'mere' eroticism, of eroticism declining into 'mere' sexuality, and sexuality into 'mere' phallicism.[54] He goes on:

> The man of decadent bourgeois society who stunts himself spiritually and morally not only has to go on living and acting in his crippled state; in this inhuman self-deformity, he must even seek a psychological and moral 'cosmic' justification for his condition. And he finds this justification, too, no longer basing his conception of the world on how the world is objectively constituted or how it affords a real object of mankind's revolutionary practical activity; instead he adapts his conception of the world to fit his own deformity and to provide an appropriate environment for his own crippled state.[55]

O'Brien queers what Lukács sees in this 'man'. In fact, it is not a man at all that O'Brien imagines, but an 'inhuman' zombie – a sick zombie who seeks cosmic justification for the condition of zombiedom, and who does so by basing a conception of the world not on the realism of its objective constitution, but a conception that fits his sickness, desires, and the abject sickness of those desires. The revolutionary consciousness of these zombies reacts to the reality of a society that does not accommodate their alternative capabilities and productivities, their distaste for the useful and taste for decay, or their uncommon desires. Where Lukács limits his interest in decay and ruination to their socially mimetic representation as 'unhealthy' symptoms of a decadent society that has lost sight of its monolithically revolutionary purpose,[56] O'Brien's kingdom of the sick presents a challenge to the values that codify and shape ideas of progress and regress, and that lead to the measurement, monitoring, and privileging of 'health' and 'the healthy'.

O'Brien does not regard health in teleological terms, as that which must be 'improved' and 'bettered' with time, but instead turns to his own temporal experience of sickness as a basis for thinking about and intervening within the spheres of social and cultural production, or mimetic reproduction (with Jacques Derrida, we might say that O'Brien's '[e]schatology breaks teleology apart'; it has an astonishing side to it that is alien to the achievement of a goal).[57] Progression along a legitimated path might be eased for those attuned to established arcs of progress, but, as the cultural philosopher Sara Ahmed puts it, '[i]t can be wearing to inhabit a world that is not built for you.'[58] O'Brien's zombies are ghosted by productivism's exhausting excesses, which is especially evident in *The Unwell*, but he also steers their incompatibility with productivism along a different path. The daydreams and sermons that O'Brien stages or narrates in his performances and films are always set in some unknown future, a future that is near, in which the smell of decay 'is an aphrodisiac'.[59] These daydreams and narratives prefigure alternative worlds that are at odds with regimes of progress based on teleological and contingent notions of betterment and enlightenment: the purity of a gene pool, for instance, or the integrity of a family unit, or designs upon the health and wealth of a nation and its capacity to continually grow and to produce ever-more productively and competitively in a global marketplace. In O'Brien's kingdoms of the sick, unproductive counterpleasures are enjoyed by unusually abject entities: the very monsters and nightmares imagined by societies fixated on linear conceptions of progress. Also, when he describes zombie time, it is not in the future tense; 'This *is* the zombie time. The time of the animated corpse. [. . .] It's no longer linear. It's full of breaks and ambushes. In zombie time you keep moving, but not towards anything. [. . .] No goals, only desires. No plans, only reactions'.[60] This time of the animated corpse is out of step with productivist-led conceptions of progress. It is an errant time that luxuriates in its passing.

In sum, the ways in which O'Brien conjoins sickness and desire, along with a conception of futurity that resists productivist regimes of progress, are important factors in what lends his work to decadence. He stages a decadent historicity that rejects the steering of progress towards spurious notions of betterment, growth, health, and productivity. His embodiment of the zombie and explorations of zombie time encourages us to think beyond the realism of productivism in ways that challenge its taken-for-granted-ness, just as his rejection of conventional progress narratives invites us to think beyond the myth of perpetual growth in capitalist economies condemned to perennial crises. The futures he prefigures are not based on these narratives and myths; they are based on the centring of abject bodies and behaviours, on the time of the sick, and the ruins of a post-apocalyptic world. In short, *these* zombies lend themselves to decadence. They manifest a decadent temporality at odds with both the compression and intensification of productivist time, and the positioning of productivism and its conventionally healthy stakeholders as engines and guarantors of progress.

Conclusion

What lends the performances discussed in this chapter to decadence is their conjoining of sickness, queerness and desire, a taste for abjection, their fascination with morbidity, their disruption of chrononormativity, and a conception of futurity that resists or corrupts productivism. The kingdoms of the sick he imagines are not based on the myth of perpetual growth and betterment, but sickness, abjection, and the post-apocalypse. Time flows differently in these kingdoms, away from the compression and intensification of productivist tempos and rhythms. His embodiment of the zombie also demands engagement with the viscerality and temporality of chronic sickness, desires that fall and flow away from 'healthy' attachments, and unconventional productivities – for instance, in their excessive production of phlegm.

Zombie time and interminable waiting are first and foremost about conceptualizing a different relationship to death, experiencing it not in teleological terms – not as a point one reaches – but as that which is already experienced as being both present within a body, and behind it as a subject who has surpassed their own life expectancy.[61] For O'Brien, the pandemic brought about a newly dispersed proximity to zombie time as millions of people around the world negotiated a different relationship to death and the prospect of 'gainful' employment, throwing into question what might be meant by gainfulness as a condition of living or a possibility for thriving. This makes it all the more important to resist pathologizing O'Brien's work as being 'about' his own chronic illness – his performances are not autobiographical – although experiences of the chronic clearly frame and shape each aspect of his practice, including his engagement with the kingdom of the sick. His zombies invite us to imagine these kingdoms as places where time flows differently, no longer bound to the injunctions of productivism, stretching time rather than compressing and intensifying its passing and use: a time of crescendos as much as cadences, growth as much as decay, creativity as much as ruination, and the creativity to be found *in* ruination, the aesthetics *of* decay, and an experimental relationship to futurity that refuses the myth of perpetual growth, and the cultish pursuit of more.

2

Para-sites and wired bodies

Decadence, scenography, and the performing body

An army of Plagues invade the stage, each one dressed in devilishly abject garments of disease: hand-stitched pustules and blemishes, sores and wounds, the embodiment of pestilence and infection. A tube stretches from a pregnant woman's womb to a gasmask worn about the face. They do not seem concerned by their own decay or aberrant behaviour; in fact, they relish rot. Codpieces stand erect from the groins of hermaphrodites, hips thrusting, propelling them along an apocalyptic catwalk. The pulsating beat of techno music lends rhythm to these thrusts and gyrations. They exude sensuality. If this is the apocalypse, then these Plagues are its licentious horsemen. They stand to gain everything at the end of time, or the end of time as we know it – the end of the end, where wild desires and abject pleasures reign supreme.

In Catalonia, a different vision is brewing: not the end of time, but the summoning of a mythic technoscape. Wired bodies conjure strange sounds from deep within the chest and abdomen. Androgynous Bacchants lactate, copiously, or spread milky seed over the bodies of others who stretch and climb to receive these offerings. They inhabit the belly of a vast machine, its guts and organs comprised of spinning wheels and cogs, each one dripping with organic lubricant. A Minotaur appears: their torso fleshy, their bullish head cast in gold. This is the time of the eternal cyborg, in a space of unabashed revelry and orgiastic excess.

The Plagues invaded the stage towards the end of the British multidisciplinary artist Julia Bardsley's performance *Aftermaths: A Tear in the Meat of Vision* (2009), while the Catalan performance maker Marcel·lí Antúnez Roca hosted the revelries of the Bacchants in a performance called *Hipermembrana* (2007): performances that took place in the years before and after the 2008 global financial crash. Both concern the immaterial infrastructures and systems that led to the crash, but they are more explicitly about the performing body: its fleshiness as much as its garmenting. This chapter is about the tension between these two poles: the immaterial domain, which has long preoccupied decadents of old, and the corporeality of the performing body, as well as the materiality of its trappings. These performances invite us to think about the body in the decadent imagination afresh – not as that which tarnishes its flights of fancy, but as a starting point for cultivating a decadent sensibility.

The study of decadence owes a debt to literature. Many writers associated with decadence charged themselves with its proselytization in the nineteenth century, and were first in the firing line when conservative critics parodied or ostracized their social marginality and anti-establishment proclivities. However, connecting decadence to the literary imagination has limited how decadence has come to be understood – confining its uncommon pleasures to the reader's domestic armchair – which in turn has produced scepticism about the appropriateness of engaging with these pleasures in the flesh. This is partly the consequence of its association with literary symbolism, which found writers retreating into the immaterial planes and spiritual domains conjured by the written word.

The relationship between decadence and symbolism is a hot topic, but the point that often gets missed in these discussions is that decadence, in aesthetic terms, is contingent upon and means very little without the body.[1] What, then, might a decadent corporeality or a decadent materiality *look* like? What might it *feel* like when these bodies appear in front of our eyes – in spaces where we can hear them breathe, and see them sweat? What might this 'do' to the decadent imagination, especially with regard to its long-standing opposition to the alienating and dehumanizing effects of modernity and industrial capitalism?

The last of these questions is an especially important question to ask in considering the contemporary relevance of decadence. In the nineteenth century, the mind's eye was approached as a retreat from rampant industrialization, but today – a period that has been described as 'postindustrial' – immaterial and virtual domains no longer serve as sanctuaries from the normative reach of capitalism. Capitalism in advanced capitalist economies is immaterially predisposed and dispersed, or at least gives that impression. In actual fact, the immateriality of the information economy and the service industries are based on infrastructures and technologies that are material (networks of wires and cables; energy-hungry servers in remote warehouses; the outsourcing of precarious labour, etc.), but the point stands. Immateriality is no longer a haven for those wishing to retreat or escape from productivism. Access to clouds and networks for those who are enabled to access them is now an omnipresent feature of working and social life. Transport, shopping, communication platforms . . . Even culture and knowledge production have become algorithmic, with thousands of bots editing sizeable chunks of new and existing encyclopaedia entries every day. In short, the immaterial and virtual domains are where these excesses are cultivated today, even if their effects wreak powerful biopolitical effects on the bodies of workers and consumers, and yet most people know very little about them. They have taken on an occult dimension that mystifies our ability to comprehend their complexity,[2] although the bodies that Bardsley and Antúnez Roca stage in their performances give us clues as to how the body is worked on and through in a socio-economic system that lays claim to immateriality as a site of capital production. They problematize and satirize the habitual use of technologies and the acceptance of immaterial infrastructures as immutable entities. They riff on the occultism of postindustrial infrastructures and the productivism of the technologies that support them. Importantly, they also exploit uncontainable excesses and leakages that point towards their fallibility, contingency, and the prospect of their demise.

Engaging with the performing body in their works can also help us in appreciating decadence as an embodied and enacted practice. When I think of the depiction of decadent bodies in literature, I tend to think of them languishing, or about characters that find ever-more ingenious ways to corrupt their bodies and their normatively-functioning abilities, or bodies that strive to achieve states of pleasure so intense as to obliterate their own being – if only for a moment. I think of artificial paradise. But Bardsley and Antúnez Roca present apocalyptic acts of border crossing in a different mode. In their work, the body becomes both a sign of 'the end', and a signal of its being surpassed, or its cancellation. They herald the prospect of cancelling a cancelled future.

The slow cancellation of the future is a common trope in post-Marxist writing about postindustrial society, just as it is in the punk and post-punk music that inspired it (the original title of the 1977 Sex Pistols anthem 'God Save the Queen' was 'No Future'). It forms the basis of Mark Fisher's theorization of 'capitalist realism' – which he defines by way of reference to a line of Frederic Jameson's, 'that it is easier to imagine the end of the world than it is to imagine the end of capitalism' – as well as texts by a number of other writers including Franco 'Bifo' Beradi and Paul Virilio.[3] But decadence and especially decadence in performance has the potential to give us a different take on this otherwise very bleak assessment of a present without an alternative. As a concept linked to endings, decadence invites us to consider 'the end times' not simply as the erasure of the human, although it might be read in posthuman terms, but as the end of an epoch. It invites us to imagine an end to the incursion of productivism in the immaterial domain, opening possibilities for alternative flows of desire inspired by the creativity and persistence of bodies in a shared space and time.

The next section addresses Bardsley's *Aftermaths*. Her most memorable garments (Bardsley tends to use the term 'garment' rather than 'costume') adorn the apocalyptic army of Plagues that opened this chapter. These garments and revelling in the end times initially read as nihilistic, and yet, as we reach 'the end', we also reach a moment of anarchic celebration in which weird desires and uncommon pleasures are unleashed upon a decaying civilization. Weird and monstrous bodies, as well as (in)actions conventionally regarded as hindrances to utility and productivity – inertia, decay, disease – emerge through her work and especially her scenographic practice in ways that are profoundly decadent and anti-productivist, or rather anti-productivist *because* of how decadence has been materialized in performance.

The second section then turns to the work of Antúnez Roca, focusing especially on *Hipermembrana* (2007) in the context of several earlier works that illuminate his engagement with cybernetics and the cyborg body in performance. I am especially interested in the juxtaposition of fleshy, leaky bodies with inorganic technologies and informational networks. From a contemporary standpoint, the technologies that Antúnez Roca works with seem quaintly retro, with innumerable wires protruding from exposed flesh. The uses to which these technologies are put are also 'unproductive' in a productivist sense; by today's standards, they would fall short of the challenge of 'Techno-Performance', a term coined by the performance scholar Jon McKenzie that names the effectiveness of technological strategies for avoiding obsolescence.[4] Nonetheless, they are profoundly productive in another, more decadent sense in promoting and facilitating the lavish expenditure of energy in orgiastic Bacchanals.

Broadly speaking, then, this chapter is concerned with decadence, the performing body, and what I want to call *decadent scenography*. Decadent scenography is a broad church, but in this chapter it refers to the scenographic rendering of those key concerns that have been points of orientation in its pages so far: which is to say, theatre's uselessness, wastefulness, its outmoded character, and its engagement with creative forms of productivity that are at odds with productivism. This chapter also takes inspiration from another, related notion introduced by the theatre scholar and cultural geographer Rachel Hann: that of a decadent 'scenographic' geared towards the information economy. Ultimately, my concern is with approaching decadence not in terms of a retreat from or a renunciation of technology per se, but as a perversion of its productivist orientation and codification, which has significant ramifications for how we might conceive the political potency and appeal of decadence in the twenty-first century.

Parasitical space: Julia Bardsley

Julia Bardsley's early career was initially suggestive of a directorial journey through subsidized theatre. Between 1985 and 1989 she worked with Phelim McDermott (who is now the artistic director of the British theatre company Improbable) as a co-founder of Dereck Dereck Productions. She then served as joint artistic director of the Haymarket Theatre in Leicester between 1991 and 1993, and was co-director of the Young Vic theatre in London, alongside Tim Supple, between 1993 and 1994, sharing an experimental artistic vision that they described as an 'Alternative Recession Aesthetic'.[5] However, frustrated by the institutional limitations of theatre production, and disenchanted by a tendency in the UK at the time to foreground the written text, she abandoned a potentially flourishing directorial career in pursuit of a more hybridized, intermedial practice as an auteur. Although much of her work has been presented in programmes of live art since, she still builds on her background in theatre, and rejects the distinction that is frequently drawn between the 'realities' underpinning live art's dogged pursuit of 'presence', and spectacles of representation and artifice.[6]

Bardsley's *Aftermaths* was co-commissioned by and presented at the SPILL Festival of Performance (Laban Theatre, London, 2009), Trouble #5 Festival (Les Halles/La Bellone, Brussels, 2009), and New Moves International, which produced the final and widely praised iteration of the National Review of Live Art (NRLA) in Glasgow in 2010, where Bardsley shared a programme with artists including Ron Athey, Shaun Caton, and Guillermo Gómez-Peña, among many others. It is the third instalment in Bardsley's 'Divine Trilogy' following *Trans-Acts* (2003–8) and *Almost the Same (feral rehearsals for violent acts of culture)* (2008–9). All three parts of the 'Divine Trilogy' explore transgression, transformation, and transcendence (which also serve as titles in the three-part structure of *Trans-Acts*), and the relationship of patriarchy and capitalism to the meatiness of human, animal, and monstrous bodies. The multimediality and cross-disciplinarity of each of these performances are also suggestive of an overarching interest in the relationships between material bodies and their immaterial dispersal across informational networks, which in *Aftermaths* is explored in the context of the 2008 global financial crisis and the revelation of the occulted transactions that brought it about.

The NRLA website listing for the performance introduces Bardsley as a preacher of The Doctrine of Last Things. We are told that she will emerge on an 'apocalyptic catwalk [. . .] amongst the glorious atrocities of the plagues', both summoning and animating 'a display of secreting surfaces, wounded landscapes, curtains of skin and hair, mutating bodies, fragments of meat, merchandise and money', and glorying 'in the catastrophe of End Time'.[7] It is a work presented by a prophet of profit in the year after the crash who revels in the ecstatic excesses of finance capitalism. The fervour and pseudo-religiosity of a financial market shaped and guided by faith in the prospect of infinite growth and gain are here brought into dialogue with the Book of Revelations and John of Patmos (aka John the Revelator and John the Divine).

The audience arrive wearing black at Bardsley's request, having handed over a small black object prior to the performance that they felt able to share as a sacrificial offering. The space is promenade. A black, cross-like catwalk stretches to all sides like a sacrilegious crucifix, illuminated by demonic red glowing runners. The score and live-mixed sound by Bardsley's partner and long-time collaborator, Andrew Poppy, lays harmonious string samples over the remote echoes of a synthesized piano. Attention is initially drawn up to projector screens that surround the space, each presenting an illustrated diagram of a human eye set against a pulsating fleshy mass. As the audience acclimatizes to such a visceral schematic, with the mechanics of vision diagrammatically exposed as a technology for seeing, the performance's subtitle – 'a tear in the meat of vision' – appears superimposed over the flesh, the eye fading out of sight as a new title, 'AFTERMATHS', gently floats into view. A knife slices through flesh, leaving a thick white mark as the eye diagram reappears, scarred by the tear. One by one a fresh set of words appear to the rhythmic throb of Poppy's chords: 'THIS IS THE BEGINNING OF THE END'.

Bardsley appears on screen, close-up, wearing the thick black eye shadow, moustache, and glittering gold teeth that make up her alter-ego for the evening: the Preacher we were promised, but with a hint of Madame Chantelouve too – a practitioner of the occult who plays an important role in Joris-Karl Huysmans's novel *Là-bas* (*The Damned*) (1891), best-known for its depictions of satanic ritual and the macabre eroticism of the fifteenth-century child-killer Gilles de Rais. Illuminated by yellow torches that protrude from beneath the hood of a cloak, Death-like, they stagger onto the stage using crutches. The cloak is dropped, revealing a wide-brimmed hat, long black hair, devilish hoof-like heels, and a grotesquely protruding cod piece (our host's attire for the evening was constructed by another of Bardsley's collaborators, Annabel O'Docherty). The letters 'R.I.P.' morph and fragment on the projection screens, Poppy's score transforms into an industrial soundscape, and the Preacher pulls black handkerchiefs with the same letters from their sleeve. A knife cuts through a skin-like film on the screens as a bloody hand clutching guts punches through in jerky stop-motion. It is difficult to watch, and reminds me of the feeling in my stomach the first time I saw Daniel Joseph Martinez's *Self-portrait #9, Fifth attempt to clone mental disorder or How one philosophizes with a hammer, After Gustave Moreau, Prometheus, 1868; David Cronenberg, Videodrome, 1982* (2000). The Preacher grabs a megaphone, and their voice crackles: 'It's show time! It's show time! It's shoooow tiiiime! Welcome to my para-site. Welcome to the dying room. Welcome to the black market. Welcome to end time. [. . .] I will be the eye by which you see the sight of things hidden. [. . .] Have faith in me. Believe in me. Trust me'.

Aftermaths speaks to Mark Fisher's notion of 'capitalist realism' in a number of interesting ways.[8] Capitalist realism refers to the transition from a moment where the idea of there being no alternative to capitalism formed an ideological battleground (captured most succinctly in Thatcher's attempt to *persuade* a nation that 'There is No Alternative'), to a moment in which that claim 'carries an *ontological* weight': the appearance of the only *viable* system of economic organization.[9] It refers to the ways in which capitalism scaffolds the apprehension and understanding of 'reality', and the difficulty (Fisher would describe it as a near-impossibility) of imagining a world without that scaffolding. This difficulty is problematized in *Aftermaths*, demanding instead a more radical – indeed, apocalyptic – break with that 'Real' (Bardsley riffs throughout on the etymological connection between 'apocalypse' and 'unveiling', or 'revelation'). Our Preacher *is* crisis, and the end time we are invited to celebrate addresses itself to the limits and porosity of our own corporeality as much as our capacity to think and dream. In short, Bardsley invites us to imagine the end of capitalism by way of imagining the end of ourselves.

The Preacher's church, we are told, is their 'para-site': a site alongside another, both distinct from and analogous to another para-site, the 'site' of fully dispersed capitalism (as Fisher puts it, capital itself 'is an abstract parasite').[10] We occupy these sites, but in a sense the para-site also claims us – the Preacher's congregation. The Preacher animates the technologies of finance capitalism, signified by a string of distorted words barked through the megaphone – manufacturing crisis, debt, derivatives, short trade, betting on failure, all bets are on – but the capacity 'to animate' these immaterial technologies is contingent on the material presence of our bodies feeding a ghostlike market: invoked and represented through complex symbolism and occultation. '*Give*': another injunction, this time Moloch-like with the congregation's black sacrificial offerings ritually destroyed, golden teeth gnashing on the projection screens. The tirade goes on: toxic debt, critical mass, the Lehmann has bled green.

'Bring on the Plagues!', shouts the Preacher, as Poppy's score switches to a rhythmic techno pulse: a cue for a steady invasion of the stage by monstrous entities costumed in 'garments of dis-ease' realized by Sonja Harms and Stevie Stewart. One has viral masses flopping out across their body (pestilence). Another is covered in peeling red and white skin-like fabrics (wounded and scorched by sun, hail, and fire), hips thrusting forward on crutches as if led by the virile pull of their erect codpiece. A third is covered with glowing breast-like wounds and hairy tassels (sores and boils), and a fourth wears a gold sequined dress with a gasmask that connects to their own pregnant belly (death of the firstborn).[11] If these Plagues are the progeny of Bardsley's Preacher, then they read as harbingers of an empire in the last of its decline, though without the 'indolent acrostics' or 'languid sunshine' depicted in Paul Verlaine's famous poem 'Languer' (1883).[12] Instead they dance to a rhythmic drone, delighting in the grotesqueness of their bodies, the pulse slowly fading, the Preacher squeezing out a final muddle of words: the revelation, art as cure, the revelation, the revelation, the revelation.

On leaving the space, the audience are invited to an exhibition of these 'garments of dis-ease', each Plague standing alongside abominable domestic commodities. Some seem to be gleaned from the house of serial killer Ed Gein, who used the skin and appendages of exhumed corpses (mostly female) to make lampshades, wastepaper baskets and items of clothing. The erotic fetishism of some of the materials – this furniture seems to want to be desired in all its beautified abjection – pastiches the abstract fetishism of commodities, rooting their tactility and affordances in an uncannily corporeal form. We might bid 'farewell to meat' on Bardsley's apocalyptic catwalk, but its various bodies – human and nonhuman – persist as monstrously hybridized entities.

In the third of seven theses posited in a theorization of monster culture, cultural theorist Jeffrey Jerome Cohen describes how monsters 'are disturbing hybrids whose externally incoherent bodies resist attempts to include them in any systematic structuration'.[13] Bardsley's Plagues take on something of this monstrosity. It is what makes the appearance of the Plagues at the end of *Aftermaths* so odd in the otherwise 'clean' black space in which Bardsley's Preacher invokes the occult magic of the market. Their excessive hybridization is also what links them to another of Cohen's core theses about the monster: 'The monster is difference made flesh, come to dwell among us. [. . . T]he monster is an incorporation of the Outside, the Beyond – of all those loci that are rhetorically placed as distant and distinct but originate within'.[14] The monster's embodiment of 'the Outside' – an Outside that 'originate[s] within' – can make the monster anxiety-inducing, or rather it is what makes the monster a fitting emblem for revealing a given culture's anxieties. The specific ways in which Bardsley's plagues manifest are cases in point (pestilence and contagion, the vulnerabilities of the flesh, sexually transmitted diseases, the fate of future generations), but the anxiety at stake seems to have more to do with the gaping abyss that opens up once the stultifying security of a cancelled future is replaced with an apocalyptic envisioning of the end times.

Where Bardsley's monsters depart from Cohen's taxonomical breakdown of monster culture is in how they invite us to partake in their weird revelries. Where, in another of Cohen's theses, 'the monster stands as a warning against exploration of its uncertain demesnes',[15] Bardsley's Plagues are perversely hospitable. They invite us to share the diseases they manifest, which is also what connects them to Cohen's sixth thesis: that fear of the monster 'is really a kind of desire'.[16] While grotesque, their movements and gyrations compel attention. As the pulse of a soundscape takes shape, so, too, does a desire to move with it, and with them. Like Frankenstein's monster, they allegorize 'a production that refuses to submit' to their creator; they may be hailed by the Preacher, but they are the 'hideous progeny' of the market.[17] There is a weirdly utopian dimension in their refusal, which promises the cancellation of a cancelled future, as well as their invitation for us to partake in that refusal – but strictly in the sense offered by Jameson in their invitation to conceive 'of the radical break as such [. . .] forcing us to think the break itself, and not by offering a more traditional picture of what things could be like after the break'.[18] The performance's utopianism does not extend narratives of progress by dwelling on the project of regenerating a society from the ground up after an apocalyptic cataclysm, then; rather, in Bardsley's world, the utopian moment *is* an apocalyptic moment.[19]

Cohen's study of monster culture provides valuable context for appreciating another, related field of enquiry – 'the weird', which has been associated with decadence in Literary Studies.[20] In a discussion of Bardsley's *Almost the Same*, performance scholar and live artist Eirini Kartsaki (who performed as one of the Plagues in the piece) approaches the weird

> as a place for a reformation of desire and a rethinking of norms. It is a space that accommodates what lies beyond the familiar, a desire, which exceeds the parameters of the ordinary, which in my understanding consists in normative life narratives that are concerned with notions of stability, longevity, and permanence achieved through institutions such as family, heteronormativity, and reproduction.[21]

Bardsley's design of *Aftermaths* as a 'para-site' offers just such a place. The monstrosity of capitalism is reflected in the bodies it shapes in Bardsley's performance, but these bodies – the Plagues – exceed the 'realism' of immaterial capitalist infrastructures. By embracing monstrousness as an engine of desire, desire is brought back to the body. These Plagues are alienation's aliens cut loose from the rigid structures that direct desire, ambition, and value towards a familiar 'ordinary'. Put differently, the weirdness of Bardsley's scenography pastiches the occultism of postindustrial infrastructures.

A key trait of weird fiction is the attention to detail that so often goes into the depiction of various creatures who 'do not belong', such as those you might find in most of H. P. Lovecraft's short stories.[22] That which strikes us as weird seems to arrive from outside of the field of our normal comprehension and perception. Bardsley's monstrous and weird creatures trouble the *possibility* of fixed and natural laws by exposing their contingencies on an act of faith in there being 'no alternative' to the fabricated familiar. This is also what underpins the decadence of Bardsley's scenographic practice, which is full of hybrids that are at once grotesquely unnatural in their fabricated monstrosity, and all-too-natural in their indexing of oozing corporeality. A lot of time, effort, and care goes into making these Plagues look the way that they do, stitch upon stitch contriving to detail voluptuous rot. It is what defines their decadent materiality.

Histories of decadence are primarily associated with male authors, although not exclusively,[23] and while decadent literature of the fin de siècle bears a complex relationship to feminism at best, decadence and feminism are by no means antithetical.[24] Rather, as the art historian Julia Skelly observes, 'the concept of decadence can be employed to critically examine artworks that speak to "excess" and the exceeding, or refusing, of gendered norms and ideologies, including those related to what art "is" and what it "should" be made out of'.[25] I share Skelly's interest in artworks that speak to excess along the lines that she articulates, and agree that this can play into the development of a decadent aesthetic – especially, in the context of this book, by way of exploring uselessness or unconventional use, and embracing outmodedness, the 'wasteful' expenditure of energy and endeavour, and forms of productivity that elude the injunctions of productivism. Excess is not synonymous with decadence, but particular kinds of excess can *become* decadent. The zones of strangeness and porous borderscapes that Bardsley stages are examples, and it is her use of textiles and garments, crafts stereotypically associated with women (unlike fashion, where high-profile male designers tend to steal the limelight), that encapsulates the ways in which 'excess' and 'decadence' might be folded or stitched together (Figure 2.1).

As with the various craft and textile artists that Skelly considers in *Radical Decadence* – which includes work by Shary Boyle, Rozanne Hawksley, and Allyson Mitchell – Bardsley's Plagues work 'within a framework of paradox

Figure 2.1 Plague in Pink Accident Corsets: Garment of Disease from the Apocalypse Collection. Designed by Julia Bardsley for *Aftermaths: A Tear in the Meat of Vision*. SPILL Festival, London 2009. Photo by Simon Annand.

and ambivalence'.[26] This is a common framework in feminist studies of monstrosity. The Plagues are hailed by a diseased prophet of profit, and yet, while the Plagues themselves are monstrous and abject – a pregnant figure who seems to be feeding off their own womb is one of the most striking examples – the culmination of *Aftermaths* depicts an unleashing of unrestrained desire upon the world. The Plagues are the faces that capitalism would rather hide in its reduction of reproducible bodies to that which must feed and be fed upon in order to survive, but they are also entities that emerge from an occult space into an apocalyptic carnival that places the monstrous-feminine centre stage.

The 'monstrous-feminine' has been most famously theorized by the feminist film theorist Barbara Creed. Creed warns of the risk of reinforcing phallocentric notions that position female sexuality as inherently abject, which Bardsley would seem to rebut in crafting hybridized garments as likely to feature wounded breast-like shapes as grotesquely phallic appendages. But Creed also insists that the notion of the monstrous-feminine – which we might extend to account for pangendered monstrosity based on grafting multiple, augmented, and differently-gendered sexual organs onto a single body – has the potential to disturb the pacifying power of phallocentrism's ordering and domination of the symbolic realm.[27] One example can be found in Bardsley's subversion of the archaic mother – 'the mother as primordial abyss, the point of origin and of end'[28] – encapsulated in the abject image of a Plague feeding off its own unborn child. This is not the (re)productive mother cherished in phallocentric societies, and neither is it the (re)productive mother required by capitalism. Instead, this monstrous mother makes known what Silvia Federici describes as 'the secret' of capitalist productivity by materializing the status of women 'as the producers and reproducers of the most essential capitalist commodity: labor-power'.[29] They stand in for 'a world of female subjects that capitalism had to destroy', only here dancing and gyrating at the precipice of capitalism's demise (Figure 2.2).[30]

Bardsley also offers her audiences the time and space to enjoy the intricacies of the garments that she and her collaborators create in the exhibition that concludes the performance. The ability of audiences to recognize a meticulous attention to texture and detail in this final part of the performance underpins 'the mechanics of deviance construction and identity formation' that Bardsley works with. These Plagues and their disease-ridden bodies have been contrived as stitched representations of abject bodily phenomena (we might say that Bardsley appropriates and subverts Charles Baudelaire's famous imploration to women to 'borrow from all the arts the means of raising herself above nature').[31] The audience is invited to share in this taste for deviant appearances – a taste grounded in gendered assumptions and practices – and it is this taste that tips Bardsley's staging of the monstrous-feminine into the terrain of the decadent.

In the poem by Verlaine cited earlier, 'Languer', the individual poet is figured as the synecdochical embodiment of societal decay and disintegration. Bardsley's Plagues do something similar to the extent that they materialize the end times of capitalist realism by way of imagining the end of themselves as subordinated subjects. However, there is nothing of the anti-social decadent in this vision of the end, which some have attributed to decadents like Verlaine.[32] Bardsley's Plagues revel in counterpleasures in ways that open out to others – including the audience. As I explored in the previous chapter in reference to the philosopher Karmen MacKendrick, counterpleasures refer to uncommon pleasures that are antithetical to productivist uses and economically oriented forms of production and consumption.[33] With Verlaine, we find a comparable revolt 'against positivism, rationalism, materialism, faith in progress, and the virtues of bourgeois conformity, rejecting descriptions of nature in favour of a kind of aesthetic artificiality',[34] but, in rejecting capitalist realism and the immaterial productivism it supports, dancing at the end of the world as we know it, they also point towards a perverse kind of hope: perverse in its eschatological grounding, and hopeful in what might by revealed once this world gives

Figure 2.2 Plague in Gold Restraint Gown: Garment of Disease from the Apocalypse Collection. Designed by Julia Bardsley for *Aftermaths: A Tear in the Meat of Vision*. SPILL Festival, London 2009. Photo by Simon Annand.

way . . . to something else. Something founded, it seems, on the unleashing of desire and counterpleasurable enjoyment. This is a decadence resistant to the bifurcation of pessimism and the vaunting of an artificial paradise, then; it is a kind of decadence that takes on something of both, that *materialises* both in the spaces and textures of decadent scenography.

Techno-productivism: Marcel·lí Antúnez Roca

Marcel·lí Antúnez Roca is a Catalan performance artist and founding member of the theatre collective La Fura dels Baus. The company formed in the midst of *La Movida Madrileña* (The Madrilenian Scene): a post-dictatorship countercultural movement associated with ebullient and inventive creative expression, but that 'was also strongly prone to a decadent underside' (as Sharon G. Feldman points out, the name 'Madrilenian Scene' 'was borrowed from drug culture, which used it to refer to the acquisition of hashish'; her use of the term 'decadence' would seem to imply a negative value judgement about this culture, rather than seeing it as part and parcel of the movement's experimental inventiveness).[35] La Fura dels Baus has cultivated legendary status in both Spain and the international arena. Their work is ritualistic, carnal, precarious, and spectacular; it often takes place in repurposed postindustrial spaces; and it draws inspiration from Antonin Artaud's Theatre of Cruelty and Viennese Actionism in a search for alternative forms of emotional and visceral communication and connection. What resulted was – and continues to be – a form of presentation based on abundant outpourings of physical, creative, and erotic energy after the collapse of General Franco's fascist dictatorship.

Antúnez Roca worked on their first three productions, *Accions* (1983), *Suz/o/Suz* (1985), and *Tier Mon* (1988), before permanently leaving the company to focus on his work with the cross-art collective Los Rinos, which he co-founded with Sergi Caballero and Pau Nubiola in 1985. From 1992 through to the present, he has worked as a solo artist – although the word 'solo' is misleading, as nearly all of his work is devised in collaboration with other performers, designers and technicians. From 1992 the body's relationship to technology and placing within cybernetic infrastructures took increasing prominence in his practice, situating it in an artistic context shared with other performance makers like Stelarc and Stahl Stenslie. Nonetheless, as performance scholar Eva Bru-Domínguez records of Antúnez Roca's work at this time, '[h]e remained true to the spirit and methodologies developed with La Fura, combining live performance, drawing, mechatronics, digital media, video and sound with an interest in the natural world, organic matter and biological processes', staging 'both the anxieties and hopes for an embodied existence that is increasingly dependent on and interwoven with simulacra, technology and the machine.'[36]

In what remains of this chapter, I want to turn to cybernetics – which the performance scholar Steve Dixon defines as the incorporation of participating subjects and objects as nodes within a wider communicative system of interactive feedback loops[37] – as a way of approaching and understanding what I call 'techno-productivism', which addresses the body's relationship to technology as a specific area impacted by productivism. It is related to McKenzie's concept of 'Techno-Performance', but where McKenzie's concept considers the competitive effectiveness of market-oriented technologies, techno-productivism is specifically concerned with the body's relationship to technologies that shape productivity, and that determines what is seen to count as 'productive'. If cybernetic systems are intended to mitigate entropy, and are 'never at rest',[38] then Antúnez Roca steers the cybernetic machine in a very different direction geared not towards sterile forms of techno-productivism, but counterpleasure, the exuberant expenditure of energy, and a fetishization of outmodedness. In short, the cyborgian worlds that Antúnez Roca stages in performance are not self-regulating and orderly, but decadently entropic.

Antúnez Roca – the son of a farmer and a butcher – has been drawn to raw meat and perishable materials from his earliest actions with La Fura. In his first piece as a collaborating solo artist, *JoAn, l'home de carn* (*JoAn, The Man of Flesh*, 1992), Antúnez Roca lined a mechanical doll with pigskin and cowhide – very much an 'abject body' in the vein explored by theatre scholar Jenifer Parker-Starbuck in an influential study of cyborg theatre[39] – while his collaborator, Sergi Jordà, developed a feedback system that detected analogue sound in close proximity that could then be converted into a MIDI signal to animate the robot. First presented in the courtyard of the Sala Tecla in l'Hospitalet, Catalonia, the piece embarked on a European tour, though mostly across Spain – including Barcelona's famous Boqueria Market the following year, which is an inspired location among the flesh hanging from meat stalls. As the public pass by, windscreen wiper motors propel the robot's right elbow, right shoulder, head, and – with the highest frequencies – the penis. The body, reduced to a cadaver, becomes ornament.[40]

JoAn, l'home de carn encapsulates the integration of mechanics, information technologies and organic matter that has defined Antúnez Roca's work ever since.[41] It also informed his development of 'vudubots', which he describes as 'robotic mechanisms that suggest some sort of zoomorphic form and which are constructed based on two parameters – the mechanical and biological':[42] monstrous biomachines primarily made from stuffed animal heads, small scaffolding structures, pneumatic pistons, and wheels. His interest in monstrosity came to a tee in a contribution to an exhibition called 'La vida sin amor no tiene sentido' ['Life without love is meaningless'], presented in Barcelona in 1993, which presented a series of macabre human heads made from pork that were immersed in preservative fluid in glass jars, prompting visitors to consider the compelling grotesqueness (rather than the physical impossibility) of death in the mind of someone living.

In another collaboration with Jordà, *Epizoo* (1994) – probably his best-known piece – Antúnez Roca stands on a small metal rotating platform, flesh exposed, with innumerable wires dangling from mechanical devices strapped around his skull and waist in easy reach of the body's erogenous zones: a contraption that he calls a 'muskeleton' (the mechanics were sculpted by Roland Olbeter. Antúnez Roca would later develop this technology into other, similar contraptions that he called the 'dreskeleton', and, for *Hipermembrana*, the 'joydreske'). These wires connect him to a computer operated by participating spectators, who send digital signals back to the muskeleton that manipulates Antúnez Roca's body, causing various degrees of pleasure or pain: his buttocks and pecks pumped up and down, the corners of his mouth haphazardly stretched, his nose and ears pulled back and forth. A cylindrical flame blasts from the top of his head in response to physical pain or arousal. The body-machine interface he presents is dimly suggestive of the potentialities of a body stretched beyond its 'natural' capacities, but he remains fixated on physical stimulation, pulled back to a corporeal meat sack. Technology does not serve Antúnez Roca in *Epizoo*; it invades his body.

What is most striking about the bodily tics while interfacing with the muskeleton is their utter pointlessness. From a contemporary standpoint, the muskeleton is already quaintly retro, already obsolete: the promise of a techno-futurism reduced to a plaything. It is as if Antúnez Roca is asking his audience-operators to take on the role of the nineteenth-century neurologist Jean-Martin Charcot, pursuing experiments for their own sake without dirtying their hands with a pithy excuse to provide a remedy for the cyber virus that holds Antúnez Roca in its grip. Instead, they are invited to revel in neuronal responses stimulated by mechanical movements that serve no clear purpose save for movement itself. What results is not a hyper-masculine or liberal-humanist reclamation of power from the techno-productivist machine; it is a rebuttal of the attempt to tame cybernetic excess, and the leakage of agency across informational networks.

Antúnez Roca has an ambivalent relationship with the technologies he works with, at once excited by their potential, and concerned by their biopolitical impact on the body. He embraces technology 'without fanaticism' as means of exploring 'the animal within us: sex, the passing of time, death',[43] which would seem to be born out in his use of technologies destined to become outmoded in double-quick time. Much as Walter Benjamin and Hal Foster theorized outmodedness in their theories of industrial capitalism and modern art (particularly surrealism, which, for Benjamin, fed on 'the last trickle of French decadence'), so too does Antúnez Roca present an 'accelerated archaism' of the forms of late capitalism at the turn of the twenty-first century, presenting the progress it is seen to represent either as being already obsolete and hence historically contingent, or in the form of 'witty grotesques' and 'critical perversions' that make a surreal spectacle of techno-productivism.⁴⁴

Antúnez Roca's ambivalent relationship with technology also puts me in mind of a provocation from the performance scholar Matthew Causey: that intermedial theatre is 'a thing of the past' in a postdigital age that asks us to think and feel like a machine, or else 'risk obsolescence'.⁴⁵ Causey's comment has added grist to the mill of scholars interested in how easy it is to overlook the impact of technologies on bodies on and off the stage given the extent of its ubiquity.⁴⁶ For Antúnez Roca, though, the 'embeddedness' of technology is an important reason why it is still useful to break down medial differences – even *and especially* if cybernetic entanglement, for most people, means that a body untouched by the reach of technology reads as quaint in the twenty-first century. For Antúnez Roca, bodies are neither obsolete nor something to be surpassed, although they might be modulated – their gender unleashed from a binary, sexuality becoming rhizomatic, their contours and textures and shape being subject to change. Rather, in what must have been intended as a response to Stelarc's cyborgian futurism, he explains how his practice does not deny 'the body in order to transcend it. The body is not obsolete. The body grows, enjoys, suffers, ages . . . and consciousness emerges and is transformed by these events. I work in favour of the body'.⁴⁷

The centrality of the body in performance and the primacy of its placing within immaterial and informational networks and systems reached its apogee in *Hipermembrana*, which was the second instalment of the *Membrana* trilogy, preceded by *Protomembrana* (2006), and followed by *Metamembrana* (2009). The title itself is taken from the part of a cell – the membrane – that denotes both containment and permeability, and it is this theme, through a visceral, quasi-orgiastic and messy exploration of desire and eroticism, that is brought to the fore most strongly in the performance.

Hipermembrana premiered at the Mercat de les Flors in Spain (after a preview at the Vic Institut del Theatre) as part of the Festival Temporada Alta de Girona in 2007. Antúnez Roca devised the narrative, provided drawings for the animations, and directed and performed in the show, although it was made in collaboration with Matteo Sisti (programming), Liliana Fortuny (animation), Pau Guillamet (music), and a long list of technicians, designers and performers. It is a loose exploration of Dante's *Inferno* (1320) and the myth of the Minotaur, summaries of which are narrated by Antúnez Roca over the course of the performance, although Euripides's play *The Bacchae* (405 BC) is another clear influence. Its core revolves around fifteen filmed actions, some of which were presented to a small audience while the work was still in development, and some of which were filmed for the performance alone. In one, the performer Ignacio Galilea – here playing a character called Xupament, embodying the naked white bull and father of the Minotaur – is surrounded and soon engulfed by the caresses of a circle of naked women covered in white paint: a veritable bacchanal, and a scene which is later echoed in another, this time on a wooden scaffold, Xupament writhing in the middle, and the bacchants ejaculating over him from prosthetic phalluses, breasts, and anuses, all of whom are drenched in a shower of milk and wine (it puts me in mind of Euripides: 'The earth flows with milk, flows with wine, / Flows with nectar of bees; The air is thick with a scent of Syrian myrrh').[48] In another scene, Cap de Toro, the Bacchae perform an ecstatic ritual dowsed in the blood of a bull, whose severed head they caress, lick, and rub against their bodies ('Bulls, which one moment felt proud rage hot in their horns, / The next were thrown bodily to the ground, dragged down / By hands of girls in thousands; and they stripped the flesh / From the bodies faster than you could wink your royal eyes').[49] In others, we are presented with captivating visions of excess: liquids of all hues and colours erupting from the heads of two women, a Minotaur covered in gold and wandering through an abandoned train factory, and a giant mechanical bull made from a complex array of spinning black and white cardboard discs and cogs, in the centre of which is Pasiphäe, hidden from Xupament's view.

There are only three live performers in the original performance: Antúnez Roca, Carolina Gallai as Pasiphäe, and Nico Baixas as the Minotaur, although in a later iteration Baixas was replaced by two women: Margherita Bergamo and Marina Cardona. Each of the performers controls the lighting, sound, and projected imagery by manipulating sensor mats spread across the stage, specially contrived microphones or 'scream machines', and special cameras activated by noise, the volume of which affects the sharpness and intermittency of the projections. For instance, a performer's wail into the microphone might cause their cartoon double to vomit. While there is a comprehensive technical team who support the show, the manipulation of these devices to create live intermedial interactions re-routes the act of production into a self-contained system. Production is *staged*. It is demonstrated before the performance proper begins, with performers showcasing the capacities of the gadgets they use. The rituals and orgies are mediated; only the act of production by organic bodies is shared live and in the flesh.

Hipermembrana obsessively returns to passages and liquids that collapse the divide between a body's interior and exterior: blood, shit, urine, saliva, semen, orifices, abscesses, and wounds. Prostheses that problematize this divide are also incorporated, facilitating gender modifications, erotic dynamics, and experimentation in cyborgian appearances. The bodies we find staged in this performance are extraordinarily productive – excessively so – but that productivity is of a kind that cannot be contained by the labyrinthine technologies and informational networks that are the *modus operandi* of techno-productivism (Ovid's description of the Minotaur's labyrinth seems especially fitting as an analogy, comprised of '[b]lind walls of infinite complexity' that lead 'the eye astray / By a mazy multitude of winding ways').[50] Instead, the unconventional nature of the productivity at stake in the midst of a leaky scenography is not geared towards accumulations but is rather of a decadent ilk based on the lavish expenditure of energy and organic resource. The scenography *flaunts* its materiality, luxuriating in it, and propagating its aesthetic excess within a cybernetic machine.

The decadence of *Hipermembrana* is grounded in the materiality of an embodied and highly visceral engagement with scenography, as well as the dispersal of this scenography across informational networks. This dispersal invites us to look and think beyond scenography as an art of the stage, into what the theatre scholar Rachel Hann describes as 'scenographics'. For Hann, scenographics identifies 'interventional acts of place orientation', where the intervention 'others' how we orient ourselves within or in relation to an environment.[51] A scenographic orientation pays particularly close attention to the regulatory effects that would normally be operating in a given environment – in this case, a cybernetic network – dwelling on how things and bodies are acted upon, but it also considers their capacities to act, produce or create. Importantly, scenographics reaches into the expanded field, inviting us to consider the applicability of theatrical contexts to non-theatrical contexts: for instance, cyberspace, telecommunications networks, and, more broadly, the vast immaterial infrastructures of postindustrial capitalism. A scenographic perspective, then, can help us with appreciating the political stakes of decadent scenography.

The decadent scenography of *Hipermembrana* is attuned and in opposition to techno-productivism, as well as the 'realism' that it shapes and propagates. Capitalist realism can give rise to an enervating malaise, but it does not foreclose alternative uses and creative misuses of the infrastructures and technologies that play into the construction of its apparent immutability. Here it is the body – a corporeal, leaky body – that signals the potential for cultivating a decadent counter-productivity in correspondence with a carefully selected menagerie of things and other bodies, both organic and inorganic, material and immaterial, that are both 'of' scenography and of relevance to scenographic orientation. Techno-productivism – as a constellation of material objects and organisms as well as immaterial networks and flows – is scenographic, and decadent scenography can help us in grasping how it might be read and understood in scenographic terms, and why it might be fruitful to do so. It can help us in understanding techno-productivism not just as an occult phenomenon, the complexity of which shrouds it in mystery, making it appear 'immutable'; rather, it can illuminate its contingency on *dis*orientation, on being made to trust in its relevance and necessity regardless of understanding, by permitting us to feel the effects of a very different kind of immaterial flow to flows of abstract data across informational networks.

Desire, as that which flows through and between bodies, encourages us to 'orient otherwise' by bringing us back to the embeddedness of the flesh in networks of production and circulation. This is what leads me to argue that Antúnez Roca's decadent scenography and the scenographic orientation that it inspires sheds valuable light on the occult machinations of techno-productivism by bringing us back to the body and the desires that flow between bodies, just as it prompts reflection on an aesthetic of entropy: an orgiastic and lavish expenditure of energy, and an unleashing of uncommon desires that flow, virus-like, through cybernetic networks without recourse to the mythic tropes of progress that underpin techno-productivism.

Conclusion

This chapter took as its point of departure the prospect of decadent materiality – an inversion, in other words, of the immaterial preoccupations that define decadences of the mind's eye. Moreover, it has situated decadent materiality and the corporeality of decadent bodies as a more fitting arena for exploring antithetical relationships to twenty-first-century productivism compared with nineteenth-century predecessors that were devised when industrial modernity was in the ascendency. Where imaginative retreats served decadents well in the nineteenth century, today the immaterial has been appropriated in postindustrial contexts as a domain of precarious capital production – prone, as the 2008 financial crash made clear, to fluctuations of such overwhelming magnitude as to risk the possibility of its ability to be productive at all (in terms of growth) without the intervention of governments and taxpayers upon whom capitalism has come to depend, parasitically.

Hence Bardsley's interest in the para-site, the weird and the monstrous, as well as her interest in the apocalyptic in-building of crisis in finance capitalism. The decadent scenography that Bardsley stages in *Aftermaths* might, on the face of it, seem to capitulate to the nihilist leanings of capitalist-realist critique, but it also signals another prospect: the cancellation of a cancelled future. The means by which Bardsley offers up this vision – a highly material engagement with the craft of scenography, with intricately contrived blemishes, the weaving and stitching of grotesque protrusions and weeping wounds – is also put into dialogue with a feminist coding of decadence that is relevant to the macho-patriarchal grandstanding of techno-utopians as much as the occult mystification of finance capitalism's immateriality.

Antúnez Roca is similarly concerned with the occultation of immaterial infrastructures and the technologies that support them. Not just any technologies, though, but perverse contraptions: already retro from a contemporary standpoint, and designed to facilitate and augment the lavish expenditure of energy in orgiastic Bacchanals. There is no less emphasis on the relationship between the material and immaterial domains, not least their enmeshment, and equally there is no less emphasis on the artificing of the abject – although here it is not stitches and weaves in the costuming of apocalyptic Plagues that garner attention, but the viscousness of contrived ejaculatory fluids, excreta, blood – all in vast quantities, poured and smothered over bodies who revel in these offerings as stimuli for ecstatic indulgence.

The decadent scenographies of these works are untethered from practices of renunciation. They promote escape (of energy, desire, organic matter), but not escapism. They do not retreat from techno-science – they are not technophobic – but make good on a perverse fascination with technology that has haunted the decadent imagination since the publication of its most famous ur-texts (think, for instance, of the sensory organ contrived by Jean Floressas des Esseintes in Huysmans's *À rebours*, or the necrophilic rendering of Jacques Silvert as a cyborgian sex doll in Rachilde's *Monsieur Vénus*, both of which were published in 1884). They also make good on what theatre has to offer as an art of bodies in space – and as, in itself, a kind of technology, already cybernetic, already conjoining organic and inorganic bodies across material and immaterial networks. As a technology, the theatre in these performances does not produce in ways that read as being conventionally productive under the auspices of techno-productivism – these are 'wasteful' performances in techno-productivist terms, with resources expended extravagantly and uselessly, not least by way of recourse to technologies ill-suited to cults of speed and infinite techno-scientific progress – but such considerations are also what make these performances waywardly productive, geared not towards accumulation, but the leakage of desire and the sharing and enjoyment of counterpleasure. This is key to understanding why these performances lend themselves to decadence, and it is what makes decadent materiality so compelling at a historical juncture conditioned by the occultation of the immaterial domain.

3

Alien nation

Afropessimism, Afrofuturism, and the decadent society

A Black body in a leotard studded with patterned gold sequins writhes beneath a sheet of translucent white gauze. In time this body is obscured by objects that have been stitched into its fabric: strips of shimmering golden foil, a deflated sex doll, a gigantic white dildo, a white-veiled skull, a black shackle, and white rubber masks bought from a two-bit costume store. The body struggles, becoming more and more enmeshed in its trappings, becoming indistinguishable from them, merging with them, collapsing beneath their weight. Movements beneath this shimmering mass are increasingly laboured, increasingly enervated, to the point – almost – of inertia.

Another work, another time, another place. A Black body wanders through the Northumberland countryside at dusk, sometimes dancing, sometimes not, searching for an impulse to move. This body is not the kind of body we expect to see in this place. They wear a silver headdress and steampunk glasses – part astronaut, part extra-terrestrial, part funkadelic urbanite – which makes them fantastically anachronistic in the Northumberland wilds. They also hold a camping lantern that looks as though it is taking flight, like a spaceship. This is not a performance in the sense of it being performed on a stage in front of a gathered public; it is a filmed recording of an artist residency, less a theatrical performance than an archival relic documenting a queer art of living.

Two very different works performed by artists with different takes on the staging of Black subjecthood. The first depicts a scene from jaamil olawale kosoko's 2017 performance *Séancers*. kosoko is a non-binary Nigerian American theatre maker, poet, and teacher, and the work premiered in a conventional theatre space – Abrons Arts Centre in New York – in 2017, having been developed from an idea first presented at Danspace Project's PLATFORM 2016: Lost and Found. The second describes a scene from a short film by and starring the non-binary musician and live artist The Uhuruverse, aka Uhuru Ali Moor. The film documents a 2018 Live Art Development Agency (LADA) residency in the Northumberland countryside in the north of England – titled *Unfunky UFO: 2100AD* – that was convened by the multidisciplinary artists Seke Chimutengwende and Alexandrina Hemsley.

In responding to the work of these artists, I will be returning to two core lines of enquiry. First, rather than mourning the downward trajectory of a society or nation, or the newly debilitating impact of modernity and industry, kosoko and The Uhuruverse begin from the point of view of a body that carries the enervating burden of white-capitalist progress. How they work with this enervation differs greatly – kosoko draws more explicitly on Afropessimism, whereas The Uhuruverse leans more towards Afrofuturism – although experiences of enervation and entropy form an important context for the development of their respective practices, as does a logic of fugitivity.

As David Fieni sets out in an important critique of decadence and imperialism, 'the discourse of decadence, like that of Orientalism, is ultimately a *style* of evaluating society and performing cultural adjudications'.[1] To critique discourses of decadence is to grapple with processes of social and cultural evaluation. This forms the second core line of enquiry. kosoko and The Uhuruverse resist a style of evaluating society as 'decadent' that is based on neocolonial fantasy, techno-scientific progress, and myths of past cultural attainment that have generally served the interests of the white middle-class and cultural gatekeepers. A good example that encapsulates this style is the *New York Times* columnist Ross Douthat's book, *The Decadent Society: How We Became the Victims of Our Own Success* (2020). Douthat trumpets the 1969 moon landing as the highest peak of human achievement, the laudable consequence of techno-scientific progress, whereas the progressive social advances made in the years since 1969 – especially those deriving from the civil rights movement, second and subsequent feminist waves, and the Stonewall Riots – mark a period not of progress, for Douthat, but decline. His thesis champions the crowning achievements of white-capitalist progress, while at the same time dismissing other styles of evaluating progress, especially social and cultural progress.

Douthat is only the latest in a long line of conservatives and reactionaries to diagnose societal decadence. Declinism has been thriving in France over the last decade,[2] and I explore several other examples from Britain, the Netherlands, and the United States in Chapter 5. Precursors can also be traced back to colonial and eugenicist discourse in the nineteenth and twentieth centuries, which were more explicitly racist in their vitriolic diatribes.[3] Douthat's argument is more sober and sophisticated in comparison with these other sources, although there is no recognition in the book of how the conquering of new frontiers plays into neocolonial fantasy, let alone the decadence of individuals who 'fail' to get on board with his view of progress and the productive and reproductive capabilities of a strong and healthy nation.

If Douthat represents a particular vision of decadence and 'style' of social and cultural evaluation, one that is both neocolonial and productivist, then what other visions of decadence emerge in African-diasporic performance, and what is it that makes that difference valuable? This is where Afropessimism and Afrofuturism come into their own as critical frames, particularly when read in tandem. If philosophical pessimism served as the outlook favoured by European decadents in the nineteenth century, then Afropessimism may well have something important to offer to our understanding of decadence in performance today, and in the wider sociocultural field. Equally, Afrofuturism – as a philosophy as much as an aesthetic – would seem to be at odds with the supposedly reactionary or apolitical tunings of fin de siècle decadence. But if we accept that decadence can be mobilized in contexts that bear little connection to the European fin de siècle, then Afropessimist and Afrofuturist performance have the potential to shift how we approach and come to understand decadence as a political concern, especially by engaging with the friction between them, enabling us to appreciate the cultural politics of decadence afresh.

As literature scholar Alice Condé points out, '[a]ffirmatory decadence, no less than progressive decadence, is hard to contemplate in the nineteenth-century socio-political context'.[4] This is because decadence and politics were seen to be anathema at a time when decadent writers 'were understood to be reactionaries', as the literature scholar Matthew Potolsky observes, 'marked by their hatred of modernity' – be it in the guise of anti-democratic sentiment (Charles Baudelaire), proto-fascism (Gabriele d'Annunzio), reactionary Catholicism (Joris-Karl Huysmans), or reactionary elitism (Walter Pater).[5] Of particular note was their hatred of mass culture, industrialism, and the market, retreating into cloistered environments befitting the cultivation of unconventional pleasures in place of anything even remotely resembling resistance or activism. Admittedly, the lines separating left from right in the nineteenth century were not as clear-cut as they are today (the young Baudelaire was an advocate of utopian socialism, d'Annunzio was as much a critic of the Italian state as he was its champion-in-waiting, and Huysmans and Pater were committed to 'the public role and collective nature of literature').[6] However, preoccupation with a decadent literary canon inherited from nineteenth-century Europe only considers one lineage – albeit an important one – in the discursive constitution of decadence, let alone its creative development as a practice.

Putting aside the fact that many European writers associated with decadence in the nineteenth century were clearly interested in politics and wrote political treatises (Wilde's 1891 essay 'The Soul of Man Under Socialism' comes to mind),[7] there is nothing *definitively* apolitical or *necessarily* reactionary about decadence. The countercultural significances of decadence are built on antithetical relations to modernity in the nineteenth century, but it is also worth considering those who never had a stake in the fruits of trans-Atlantic modernity in the first place, and whose exploitation provided a cornerstone for the 'progress' that it came to represent. As Condé recognizes, if we are to engage with decadence in the twenty-first century in any meaningful way, then we must recognize decadence as 'the domain of the socially marginalized'.[8] This is why this chapter will be addressing the perspectives of African American performance makers whose work is marked by legacies and experiences of alienation and enervation within racial capitalism. African American experience is no longer an outlier in the decadent imagination; it might just as well provide a starting point for its study.

Racial capitalism is a term used by Cedric J. Robinson that refers to the embedding of racism 'deep in the bowels of Western culture', and to the contingency of racism on white-capitalist supremacy as well as the white radical traditions (particularly Marxism) that oppose it.[9] Where white decadent writers in the nineteenth century were frequently empowered to abstract themselves from the machinations of capitalist modernity, if not the commercial market on which they relied, this has not been – and is not – a choice for those denied the prospect of wilful abnegation.[10] The work of kosoko and The Uhuruverse consistently returns to this denial, and does so by foregrounding the Black performing body: a body that is both subject to, and capable of resisting, its historical positioning as 'enervated' and a beast of burden, incapable of productivity and yet a foundational source of national bounty.

As the next section explores, all of kosoko's practice builds on their love of critical and literary texts, primarily but not exclusively by African American poets and theorists. In *Séancers*, they draw the work of an Afropessimist philosopher – Calvin L. Warren – into dialogue with writers and activists like Ruby Sales and Audre Lorde, who are all cited in the piece. I argue that the friction between these incongruous but carefully selected worldviews offers an instructive way of engaging with decadence as a theme of relevance to the pursuit of social justice, as counterintuitive as this may seem. kosoko situates the erasure of being (a key Afropessimist notion) at the centre of how the socio-economic 'sickness' of racial capitalism might be examined, but instead of treating the decadent society in the abstract, they pull their own Black body front and centre. This does not result in a decadent aesthetic per se, or an examination of the 'decadent society', specifically; kosoko stages the embodied impact of an energy-sapping decadence.

The second section then turns to the work of The Uhuruverse, who has mostly been working out of Los Angeles and New Orleans over the past decade. The section looks at the impact of Donald Trump's successful presidential campaign in 2016 on the evolution of their practice, in which Afrofuturism and Afropunk came to play increasingly important roles in their political activism, as well as how they present themselves in their art and day-to-day life. I am especially interested in their use of DIY materials in cultivating an Afrofuturist outlook that turns to the utopian dreamings of prior movements and musical genres – particularly the more radical arms of the civil rights movement, and the retro space-age aesthetics pioneered by musicians like George Clinton and Sun Ra (Herman Blount) – as a basis for prefiguring the futures these artists imagined. What emerges is a fascinating engagement with outmodedness that lends itself to the cultural politics of decadence: at once retrograde in its backward glance, and forward-looking in its attempt to visualize and enact the cancellation of a cancelled future.

'What beasts they are': jaamil olawale kosoko

kosoko's practice is grounded in their work as a theatre maker, dancer, poet, and teacher. All four areas are interconnected, as well as exceeded in ways that spill across various media and platforms. For instance: kosoko's live and digital projects tend to be accompanied by the publication of reading, listening and viewing syllabi;[11] their poetry places special emphasis on performance, often being shared in theatricalized readings; and poetry and pedagogy feature prominently in live performances, with the names and publications of critical thinkers and poets threaded throughout as tacit or explicitly quoted references. You are as likely to discover texts about Black joy informing their work as you are epistemologies grounded in an Afropessimistic world view. This is particularly the case in kosoko's four major performance projects devised as a collaborating solo artist (later framed under the umbrella of kosoko Performance + Studio) in the mid-2010s and early 2020s: *Black Male Revisited* (2013), *#negrophobia* (2015), *Séancers* (2017), and their ongoing multimedia and live art project *American Chameleon* (2020). This section will focus on *Séancers*.

As with all of kosoko's performances, *Séancers* is iterative, situational, and responsive to who and what is in the room on a given date, which is suggestive of an attempt to query the 'narrative bondage' that ties subjecthood to predictable and reductive representations of Blackness.[12] It has since toured nationally to Austin, Columbus, and Philadelphia, as well as internationally to Berlin, Frankfurt and Montréal, so it is worth specifying that the version I discuss addresses the 2017 premiere at Abrons Arts Centre.[13]

The performance opens with kosoko cradling a black infant doll while sitting among the audience: an allusion to their brother, who was murdered outside a 7-Eleven, aged twenty-two, only a few years beforehand.[14] They introduce the doll to a local 'Special Guest' in the audience, who this time around is the Igbo-Nigerian American performer and writer Okwui Okpokwasili. kosoko's leotard catches their eye, and they want to learn more about it – but kosoko is evasive. The leotard is skin-tight and covered with black and white totemic symbols. In light of a study of kosoko's work by the dance scholar and performer Brenda Dixon Gottschild – who also served as a Special Guest in its Philadelphia run – perhaps we might understand this suit as a reference to Èṣù, the Yoruba guardian of a liminal meeting place between the world of the living and the spirit world.[15] Èṣù also embodies the crux at which divergent emotions and forces meet: joy and fulfilment on the one hand, sorrow and ruination on the other. From the outset of the performance, then, we find a scenographic materialization of the kind of incongruity that informs the work as a whole: at once pessimistic in its recollection of trauma, and tinged with hope by virtue of the fact that kosoko is, quite simply, *there*.

Nonetheless, the piece is pervaded by pessimism. Nineteenth- and early-twentieth-century decadents were profoundly influenced by pessimism – not least 'the high priest of pessimism' Arthur Schopenhauer, as the writer Edgar Saltus dubbed him[16] – and they and the characters they created often retreated from the political arena. This is one reason why decadence tends to be regarded as apolitical or reactionary. However, kosoko's interest in pessimism is not grounded in the spin that decadents gave Schopenhauerian philosophy in the nineteenth century, which took the form of (or was critiqued as) wilful abnegation or 'wilful sadness'.[17] Rather, it is grounded in a branch of pessimism pioneered by theorists including Calvin L. Warren and Frank B. Wilderson III.

Towards the beginning of the performance, kosoko tells the audience about the convergence of Blackness and queerness and its appropriation in mainstream popular culture, drawing on Warren's notion of 'onticide' (which is also referenced in kosoko's 2021 work, *Chameleon Revisited: Morocco*).[18] Onticide frames gay Blackness as an ontological impossibility in white heteronormative cultures that validate whiteness, through difference, as an essential characteristic of being human. This hits upon the heart of Warren's Afropessimism: that is, that 'there is no way to eliminate differentiating violence without eliminating the human, since both are mutually constitutive and coterminous'.[19] For Warren, both the capacities of whites and their recognized identities as humans are contingent on the instrumentalization of Black people – 'as commodity, object, slave, putative backdrop, prisoner, refugee, and corpse' – and the ensuant erasure of their humanity.[20] In short, for Warren, to be Black is to be robbed of what it means to be human. To be Black is to exist, not to *be*.[21]

The design of *Séancers* certainly seems to have been developed with Afropessimism in mind. A shimmering sheet hangs at the back of the stage, refracting light and mirroring an array of objects: a giant white-veiled skull, a tea set, a deflated sex doll, a white dildo, a mass of white gauze. Long golden strips of foil are bundled together into wing-like pompoms, transforming kosoko's body into a protean form that re-shapes itself into innumerable configurations. There is no coherent identity amid these eclectic objects, just reflecting surfaces and half-formed things (Figure 3.1).

The theatre critic Nicole Serratore describes this eclecticism as 'a varied visual language of decadence and trash',[22] but on the basis of an interview with kosoko I am not convinced it is appropriate to do so – at least not with regard to the work's aesthetic. For kosoko, 'what someone might read as trash, to someone else is deeply important archival material. It's treasure.'[23] Trash and the trashy are not bases for an aesthetic, as they are in films by John Waters or Ryan Trecartin, for instance, which are aesthetically decadent in their own ways. Instead, Serratore's description of the piece should encourage us to think about the cultural politics of naming objects in this way, just as it prompts pause for thought on what it means to describe a performance

Figure 3.1 jaamil olawale kosoko, *Séancers*, American Realness Festival, 2017. Photo by Ian Douglas.

like this as 'decadent'. While there is something superficially decadent in the glittering surfaces that adorn the stage, it is the ideas they represent that interest me most. These ideas pertain to an objectified body that is at odds with the kinds of productive subjecthood favoured in racial capitalism. They also pertain to the utilization and objectification of Black bodies that we can trace back to the slave trade and its legacies.

Alongside the handling of these objects and materials, kosoko speaks through voices other than their own (it is a séance after all) in an effort to 'make power out of hatred and destruction'.[24] This occurs through a summoning of written and recorded texts that have inspired them – this particular quote is taken from a collection of Audre Lorde's poems, which also rests atop a table at the back of the stage – just as it occurs in acts of ritualized mourning. They mourn the death of their brother, and they mourn the passing of their parents – particularly their mother, who they embody at one point by draping an ill-fitting white dress over their shoulders, and repeating a phrase incessantly, all the while flicking the dress up and down, and gesticulating as if flows of energy take hold of their limbs: 'I tried my whole ass life to live. I tried to be good. [. . .] I swear I just woke up one morning, and I just, I just didn't want to be myself no more'. James Baldwin once observed that '[p]eople are trapped in history and history is trapped in them', which strikes a resonant chord as kosoko mediates their mother in this way.[25] They dress themselves in the trappings of history: trappings that trap, and that also serve as a gateway to personal and social trauma.

Not long after this scene kosoko leaves the stage at a point that marks one of the clearest transitional moments in the performance. Jeremy Toussaint-Baptiste's score pulsates into perceptibility – a tubular hum – and the lighting state shifts to ultraviolet, casting the white veils that shroud the gigantic skull in a strange luminescence. kosoko re-enters in a haze of smoke and light, this time clothed in a gold sequined body suit, heels, a thick silver necklace, an afro wig, and a pair of black sunglasses, microphone in hand, and singing the lyrics of one of their own poems: 'I want to fuck you with heels on'. Their voice is passed through an electronic distorter, punctuating indistinguishable words with bestial yelps and screeches – the last line of Lorde's poem cited earlier springs to mind ('What beasts they are'), as does Robinson's critique of 'the creation of the Negro, the fiction of a dumb beast of burden fit only for slavery'[26] – and conjuring the spirits of musicians like Sun Ra and George Clinton, now firmly established as Afrofuturist pioneers.

The bringing together of these two schools of thought and practice – Afrofuturism and Afropessimism – makes more sense in light of Kodwo Eshun's reading of Clinton's music as that which 'compels you to succumb to the inhuman', or an 'alien force'.[27] Afrofuturism names a form of cultural production that combines myth with advanced or ethereal technologies, and that collapses or resides in different worlds and temporalities beyond the present – the deep past, as much as the distant future. kosoko's Afrofuturism honours a specific grounding of its offshoots in Clinton's embrace of an inhuman or alien force, *beginning* with recognition of how Black people have been alienated in white society. In this part of the performance, then, we find kosoko pulling the poly-spatial and poly-temporal qualities of Afrofuturism as an 'alien force' into dialogue with Afropessimism's reading of alienation and onticide ('what beasts they are').

The skull, still enfolded in a white veil, draws the eye centre stage. kosoko sings, distantly and alone, as if lost in a space between worlds: 'I am an entertainer. Here I am, ready to entertain'. Toussaint-Baptiste's score kicks back into life, tribal drums pulsating into audibility, as kosoko picks up a white head mask depicting a doll-like red-lipped face. They pull it over their head, to the edge of their nose, unseeing blue eyes staring blankly through thick black mascara, and a frayed mass of blonde hair tumbling over their shoulders. Their head and upper torso convulse sharply forwards with a flick of the knees, then back, then forwards and back again, over and over at frenetic pace: 'spirit catching' by means of torso articulation, perhaps.[28] The relentless riff from John Carpenter's horror movie *Halloween* (1978) takes over from the drumming, subduing it, and underpinning an audio montage of performers from the silver screen, each one reciting the line 'I'm free, white and twenty-one', or a derivation appropriate to their age.[29] kosoko pulls the mask further down so that it undercuts their top jaw – cutting into their cheeks and 'dis/figuring' their face[30] – and one by one picks up a sequence of material offerings that are wrapped about their shoulders, or attached to a growing mass that hangs about them: the sex doll, the white dildo, the white-veiled skull, and the golden foil wings (Figure 3.2).

There are some playful allusions here to what kosoko calls 'the wreckage of white culture'[31] – Carpenter's *Halloween* theme initially comes across as odd in a year in which Jordan Peele's film *Get Out* (2017) was released – but the sonic contextualization of these objects also emphasizes their overbearing weight as kosoko's struggling body becomes indistinguishable from the jumble that submerges and enfolds them. The anachronistic music, which would otherwise risk slipping into a comedic vein, makes an uncanny (perhaps disidentificatory)[32] spectacle of a horror inherited from white culture, and with terrifying implications for those whose energy is sapped within it.

Warren's Afropessimism is also concerned with energy sapping. They describe how 'the interdiction on black capacity provides the very possibility for Civilization (and civil society) to exist at all because it allows the Human

Figure 3.2 jaamil olawale kosoko, *Séancers*, American Realness Festival, 2017. Photo by Ian Douglas.

to differentiate himself from and define himself against an ultimate other'.[33] In other words, rather than critiquing societal decadence in the abstract, Warren focuses their attention on the structural predication of a society on paranormal bodies: a society in which anti-Blackness becomes 'the *energy* of the human'.[34] For Warren, as for kosoko, white subjectivity builds on the enervation of paranormal shapeshifters beneath 'the wreckage of white culture'.

Although Afropessimism pervades *Séancers*, right down to the set, costume, and musical compositions, kosoko does not seem to be entirely content with its conclusions. They stay 'in the wake' of a paradox, influentially explored by the literature and Black Studies scholar Christina Sharpe, that depicts the impossibility of resolving social exclusions and socio-economic and political inequalities 'within and after the legacies of slavery's denial of Black humanity'.[35] They offer no easy answers to structural racism, and also discourage what Saidiya Hartman critiques as 'a too-easy intimacy' with the spectacle of Black suffering, refusing to permit white spectators to position themselves in place of the Black body and the histories that it carries.[36] But they also leave space for hope. For instance, towards the end of the performance the audience hears an extended audio recording of Ruby Sales discussing how Black people might be raised up 'from disposability to essentiality'.[37] For

Sales, this 'raising up' will only be possible if whites – particularly working-class whites – recognize the extent of their own (particular) alienation in postindustrial capitalism. The juxtaposition of such divergent perspectives performs 'wake work' in ways that reveal the contingency of essentiality, capacity, and humanity within *and on* the 'realism' of racial capitalism. The realism of racial capitalism affects different kinds of body in ways that produce different kinds of capacity and dispossession, enablement and oppression, and the enervating weight of different burdens – which is to say, the weight of different histories, and how those histories haunt the present.[38]

To sum up: *Séancers* has been described as staging 'a varied visual language of decadence and trash', but the work is not decadent because it is trashy. Use, instrumentality, and the harnessing of productive energy are engaged as key concerns, but not simply as a consequence of their rejection, or even, necessarily, their queering. kosoko stages the contingency of racial capitalism on the alienation of Black bodies, the refusal of their subjecthood, and the enervating demands of wrestling with the wreckage of white culture. This approach to societal decadence demands a shift from the general (an enervated form of socio-economic organization that enervates) to the particular (how racial capitalism enervates specific bodies). It also invites us to reconceive how we imagine the politics of decadence, and who we might turn to in doing so. *Séancers* neither looks nor thinks like a work of nineteenth-century decadent fiction. Instead, it encourages us to look beneath the shimmering surfaces of an aesthetic so as to better understand the cultural politics of decadence: a politics of naming, structuration, pathologization, and embodiment. It also encourages us to question the human cost of so-called socio-economic progress, so often referenced in the abstract in ways that elide with the myth of perpetual, expropriative, and exploitative economic growth.

I am, however, left with a few questions about this work. kosoko stages what Warren describes as 'interminable falling' ('[t]o exist, as black, is to inhabit a world through permanent "falling"' without ever 'becoming'),[39] which is structurally guaranteed unless racial capitalism can be reimagined and restructured from the ground up. In this particular work kosoko makes space for hope, but not much, while Warren substitutes faith in transforming the world with a nebulous faith in 'the enduring power of the spirit'.[40] How else, then, might this 'falling' be conceived and approached? What happens to decadence when the relationships between Afropessimism and Afrofuturism are recalibrated? These are questions that I address in the next section, which looks at the work of The Uhuruverse. As with kosoko's *Séancers*, I am not interested in appraising their work as 'decadent'; rather, I turn to contexts and events that commentators like Douthat have positioned as key to the relative health or 'decadence' of a society, including the space race, in an effort to better understand the subtexts that inform notions of 'decadence' and 'productive' capacity, and their impact on subjects who have been consistently denied a stake in the progress that these events are said to represent.

Alien Nation: The Uhuruverse

The Uhuruverse is a New-Orleans-based[41] multidisciplinary artist working across live art, music, dance, burlesque, film, fashion, and design. Fashion and design took precedence towards the beginning of their professional career when they regularly modelled, presented at fashion revues (e.g. 'Let Them Eat Cake', a revue honouring and queering Marie Antoinette, 2014), and worked with fashion collectives like Omega Collektiv. From these early years onward their 'creatively strange' eccentricity has come to form as much of a basis for day-to-day self-fashioning as their artistic practice.[42] In the same years that they were walking catwalks and performing in fashion photoshoots, they were also making regular appearances as a performer in cabaret, kink, and burlesque club nights across the United States, most often in their then home city of Los Angeles (e.g. Kaos Network in 2014, and Blackesque in 2015). Their growing popularity and online presence in the States soon led to commissions and residencies in the UK, including the 2018 LADA residency that introduced this chapter, a 2019 residency at]performance s p a c e [in Folkestone, and performances at Steakhouse Live in London, Take Me Somewhere Festival in Glasgow, and Salty at Home Live Art in Hastings.

Their work has always had a strong activist dimension – the Swahili word 'uhuru' means 'freedom' – and the L.A. punk and alternative scenes informed their practice from its earliest days; however, a change of emphasis was prompted in the mid-2010s with the ascendency of the #BlackLivesMatter movement, and the 2016 presidential campaign that led to the inauguration of Donald Trump as president of the United States. From this point on the kink and punk scenes were foregrounded to a much greater extent than before in the cultivation of a yet more idiosyncratic life and art aesthetic merging Afrofuturism, Afropunk, and queercore (championed by the likes of Vaginal Davis, among others).[43] The constellation of these elements – a name meaning 'freedom', an explicit commitment to social justice, involvement in a number of #BlackLivesMatter protests – suggests that their practice resides at a considerable distance from Warren's Afropessimism (for whom the very notion of 'free black' is an ontological impossibility),[44] but their bridging of punk and social justice activism is what makes their work so compelling in the context of this chapter.

As with queercore, The Uhuruverse's punk queers the genre's chequered history (for instance, by inverting the racism and homophobia associated with white power skinheads and Nazi punk). Its framing as Afropunk also chimes with the activism of #BlackLivesMatter in its reaction to a rising tide of populist and white nationalist sentiment in the United States in the years before and after Trump's presidential campaign, which appealed to America's poorest white rust belt citizenship. Their aesthetic choices are also worlds apart from the super high-tech fantasies that pepper the pages and screens of canonical science fiction, dwelling instead on the kinds of extra-terrestriality that underpinned the composition and iconography of musicians and bands that have come to be associated with Afrofuturism, especially Sun Ra and George Clinton. The ways in which The Uhuruverse brings together queercore, Afropunk, and Afrofuturism lends the work a utopian dimension that meets the punk mantra 'No Future' with the possibility of eroding or surpassing racial capitalism.

The Uhuruverse is one of the co-founders of the Afropunk band FUCK U PAY US, is founder of the 'post-apocalyptic' art collective, Afropunk band, and podcast series #SNATCHPOWER, and is a member of several other more transient bands and outfits (for instance, Negro Assassins Slaying Authority, Black Outrage Machine, and more). They have also been working as a solo recording artist since around the time of the 2016 presidential election, when they started to release tracks that would later be brought together in their debut solo album, *The Brightest Oddest Strangest Star U Ever Did Saw up Close and Afar from Planet Earth to Mars and Beyond!!* (2018), several of which were accompanied by the release of music videos and short films. In what remains of this chapter, I will be discussing one of those films – 'Bomaye! (Suspense)' – alongside their 2018 LADA residency.

These films and the filmed documentation of improvisatory performance present a retro envisioning of space travel and the future as if gleaned from 1970s B-movies, a Parliament / Funkadelic concert, or the *Star Trek* television series (*Star Trek*'s Lieutenant Uhura, played by Nichelle Nichols, was praised by Martin Luther King as a role model during the civil rights movement).[45] Such retro touchstones shape the universe of The Uhuruverse, putting their outmoded choreographies and scenographies into a productive tension with cinematography that is more akin to the rapid jump cuts and editing techniques found in twenty-first-century social media posts. They juxtapose Afrofuturism's interest in mythologization (by mythologizing the 1970s) with the 'deep remixability' of Afrofuturism 2.0.[46] The same is true of the music that underpins these films. For instance, while 'She D'evil' (ft.

Celeste XXX) is tightly produced and integrates a range of late-twentieth and twenty-first-century beats and modal patterns, it also begins and ends with the famous five-tone melody that North American scientists use to communicate with aliens in Steven Spielberg's 1977 film *Close Encounters of the Third Kind*. These works are tonally ambiguous, collapsing different timeframes and 'worlds' into an equivocal moment. Indeed, tonal ambiguity is a hallmark of The Uhuruverse's Afrofuturism as much as their DIY Afropunk.

The grounding of The Uhuruverse's costuming and design in a 1970s space-age aesthetic brings with it an important political dimension once read in light of Slavoj Žižek's insistence (after Walter Benjamin) that revolutionaries should strive to retrieve the 'hidden potentialities' of untimely utopian endeavours.[47] For Žižek, as with other radical or post-Marxists, like Mark Fisher, '*the actual history that we have is itself a kind of realized alternative history*, the reality we have to live in because, in the past, we failed to seize the moment and act'.[48] Where The Uhuruverse contributes to this discourse is in their questioning of who the 'we' is that Žižek assumes, as well as 'the actual history' that is taken to fail in its untimeliness. Where a predominantly white counterculture in the 1960s and early 1970s is Fisher's starting point for imagining an 'acid communism' – a theory based on rekindling the utopian ambitions that came out of this counterculture[49] – and where Žižek is interested in retrieving the dreams that motivated the failed socialist revolutions of the twentieth century, The Uhuruverse turns instead to the intersections between Black Power and Afrofuturism as an alternative counterculture, and as a point of departure for staging the realization of abandoned utopias that centre women and non-binary queers of colour. This is part of what makes their seemingly frivolous scenographies – full of shimmering materials and alien kitsch – profoundly political, decentring the histories underpinning social progressiveness and radicalism in fashionable Leftist thinking.

The Uhuruverse has always been responsive to the political arena, and Donald Trump's controversial presidential campaign – and its appeal to white rust belt populism – is no exception. As the *Los Angeles Times* journalist August Brown explains, writing in 2017,

> If the Trump-resistance movement has been about trying to finally organize the potential of marginalized people, F[UCK] [YO]U Pay us is about giving voice to the other side of that coin – the inchoate rage that keeps women, the LGBTQ community and people of color up at night (both before and after Trump), and offering reminders that there is still real power in that feeling.[50]

That 'inchoate rage' – which would seem to echo the 'black rage' that many felt in the aftermath of Martin Luther King's assassination[51] – is as true of The Uhuruverse's solo work as it is for FUPU and #SNATCHPOWER (the name itself riffs on the power of femme sexuality, and the appropriation of appropriated power). It is especially acute in a 2016 #SNATCHPOWER performance at Club Fist! in L.A. that incorporated costume drawing on Black Power symbology, and that made frequent reference to the necessity of violent struggle.[52] But solo tracks like '[Dis]Obey!', released in July 2016 as an advanced single, also targeted what it means to vote in a presidential contest led by two white men,[53] while 'Basic a$$ Fake White Bytch' (2017) and its accompanying film funnels inchoate rage into the relationships between racial capitalism, cultural appropriation, and the assumptions of white post-feminism.[54] 'Basic a$$ Fake White Bytch' offers a queer-punk take on conspicuous consumption among white metropolitans as much as the pseudo-decadent bling that plays into mainstream heteronormative hip-hop videos; however, at the invitation of the African American theatre maker Nia O. Witherspoon, perhaps we might also push back against perspectives that denigrate 'the first generation of Black people that talks about gold or diamonds' in popular music,[55] instead dwelling on the desirability of staging material excess not simply as a practise of conspicuous consumption, but countercultural redistribution.

The Uhuruverse's short film 'Bomaye! (Suspense)' (2019), which they made freely accessible on social media shortly after the release of their first solo album, also draws sustenance from inchoate rage. 'Boma ye' is a Bantu (Lingála) phrase meaning 'kill him', or more generally referring to a war chant. It became associated with the boxer Muhammed Ali after a Congolese crowd shouted 'Ali, bomaye' at the 1974 Rumble in the Jungle. However, 'Bomaye! (Suspense)' also reaches beyond the power of brute force, pursuing a power that looks to transcend the structural limitations imposed on Black people in day-to-day life – not unlike Ali himself, whose power was defined not just by his capacity to win fights, but charisma and the cultivation of an idiosyncratic iconography. Staging the transcendence of these structural limitations is one of the main things that distinguishes The Uhuruverse's practice from strict Afropessimism, and creative practices that subscribe to its philosophy.

The film begins with The Uhuruverse made up in green body and face paint, cheeks daubed with red and yellow spots and white tribal markings. They wear a white leotard and a large transparent globe on their head – a DIY astronaut's helmet – and they also carry a large silver sheet reminiscent of a hiker's emergency blanket. 'Greetings deep space traveller', they intone in a synthesized voice that characterizes most of their solo vocals; 'your request to incarnate the material realm has been granted'. They tell us that we (although

The Uhuruverse is primarily addressing a queer Black viewership) are free to choose a form of our own choosing – animalia, plant, fungi, protozoa – before settling, we are told, on human form. Further selections follow: gene pool, date of incarnation, time period, gender, race, and sexual orientation. In the background, super-accelerated footage of The Uhuruverse moving through suburban streets and backyards is interspersed with green- and blue-tinted shots of single-celled organisms under a microscope, neuronal patterns, the unfurling of fiddlehead ferns, and lilies shot through psychedelic filters. 'You may evolve based on your experiences in the material realm', they say. 'Your objective is to embody your highest self. [...] Upon each fatality you will have the opportunity to reincarnate and metamorph'.

While released prior to the murder of George Floyd in May 2020 that prompted widespread uprisings around the world, these comments take on poignancy in the light of a long history of police brutality and the racist targeting of Black people in the United States (and elsewhere). The synthesized mediation of these comments and the sheer rapidity of the jump cuts and sequences gives the film and the narrative it contains the impression of unstoppable propulsion into a xenofeminist mode,[56] but the frequent inclusion of photographs from the radicalized arms of the civil rights movement – including images celebrating Bobby Seale and Angela Davis – suggest that this is not simply about catapulting beyond the present, but the collapsing of a tripartite historicity delineating past, present, and future.

As the film continues, The Uhuruverse's white leotard functions as a surrogate greenscreen for the warping and filtering of psychedelic imagery. The only material unaffected by this mediation is their own Black skin, which brings into play a number of connotations implied by the terms 'material' and 'materiality'. The Uhuruverse's commentary at this point draws a clear line between access to material wealth and access to the earth's resources, critiquing the inequitable distribution of wealth and, by extension, the exploitation of African-diasporic subjects. 'There is no shame in poverty', they say. 'Consumerism and materialism oppressing underage earthlings while simultaneously not providing enough currency for their time and energy . . . That is a war, stardust! A war you will be entering on earth'. The future tense is important, as it is for the whole film, which functions as an instructional video for an extra-terrestrial entity (stardust) to become incarnated in a collapsed past-present-future. It is implicitly figuring the 'the actual history that we have', to recall Žižek, as a *contingent* future history: a history among others that may be 'seized'.

The cinematography and editing of the film are advanced, but its scenography and choreography are low-fi. They work with bright, day-glow colours, a DIY methodology, and wear a homemade astronaut outfit comprised of dime-store materials. They also reject refinement and technique beyond digital prowess, and embrace improvisatory choreographies and the spaces that house them, which are predominantly found in suburban spaces like street corners, backyards, and the back rooms of clubs. These characteristics define The Uhuruverse's futurology as 'outmoded', but they also represent the possibility of egress from racial capitalism. Outmodedness, then, as a gateway to the forgotten dreams of the past, also stands as a portal to the hidden potentialities of the future.

As with their Afrofuturist forebears, The Uhuruverse takes the 'xeno' in 'xenophobia' (the word combines the Greek *xénos*, meaning 'stranger' or 'alien', with *phóbos*, meaning 'fear') as a point of departure for staging the anxieties of a racist, homophobic and transphobic demographic, and does so by turning themselves into an Afropunk day-glow alien, and embracing that which the alien promises: egress not just from capitalist realism, but white patriarchal capitalism. They ground engagement with the futures generally imagined within science fiction not in the cultish pursuit of ever-more refined technologies – enamoured by the conquering and exploitation of final frontiers – but in a DIY aesthetic inherited more from punk and Afropunk. This is apparent, for instance, in the short film documenting their *Unfunky UFO: 2100AD* residency in the north of England. In it, we find The Uhuruverse traipsing and dancing as a glorious anachronism through the rural Northumberland landscape – future city chic in a rustic hinterland, dressed in a silver headdress and steampunk sunglasses – at one point holding up a large camping lantern as if it were a UFO. The film serves as documentation of an improvisatory performance: a record of a wild excursion through wilderness. This suggests that there is something more – or tantalisingly *less* – going on here than adherence to the fetishization of time-bound and commodifiable 'projects' in contemporary cultural production;[57] instead, there is a refusal to commit to the production of a quantifiable or even a quality 'product'.

In the background of the film, we hear the contagiously catchy lyrics of Parliament's song 'Unfunky UFO' (1975): 'We're unfunky and we're obsolete (and out of time) / And we're out of time / Gonna take your funk and make it mine'. On the face of it, this would seem to represent an Afropessimist take on the 'nothing' of Black ontology – alluding to the obsolescence of Black bodies out of time with productivism – but the phrase is repeatedly countered by the chorus: 'You've got all that is really needed / To save a dying world / From its funklessness'.[58] As the titling of the residency suggests, which is clearly inspired by this track, the film celebrates how DIY resources might be taken as a starting point for imagining a new kind of imagination – an imagination, perhaps, that heeds Žižek's warning that 'if we change reality only in order to realize our dreams, without changing these dreams themselves, then sooner or later we will regress to the former reality'.[59] In this rough and ready performance document, a retro space-age aesthetic is presented as an anachronistic platform for experimenting with playful prefiguration. This gives rise to a situation in which an outmoded view of the future is repurposed – apparently uselessly, at least in the sense in which 'use' might be read as that which adheres to the pursuit of new frontiers and technological progress. In other words, outmoded dreams are retrieved as a basis for imagining an alternative future detached from the instrumentalization of Black bodies.

In retrieving the dreamings attached to a retro, space-age aesthetic, this work-that-is-not-a-work calls to mind the art and life of an applicant to another kind of residency. Sun Ra – a key exponent of Afrofuturism – once applied (unsuccessfully) to be artist-in-residence with NASA (NASA did actually launch an artist residency programme in 1962, which is still running; predominantly white beneficiaries to date include Laurie Anderson, Robert Rauschenberg, and Andy Warhol).[60] He, too, sought to change the idea of what it means to be a 'pioneer', but not of topography so much as sonority and expanding the limits of the dreamable. And he was not alone. Around the same time that NASA launched its residency programme, a Zambian science teacher called Edward Mukuka Nkoloso launched the Zambia National Academy of Science, Space Research and Philosophy: a project that initially and purportedly involved training twelve Zambian astronauts to compete with the United States and the Soviet Union in the space race, using only the most rudimentary resources available to them (an oil drum for simulating weightlessness when rolled down a hill; climbing a rope only for it to be cut to simulate freefall; and uniforms comprised of combat helmets, satin jackets, and embroidered capes made from silk or velvet).

The project was inspired by Nkoloso's first aeroplane flight, and the frustration he felt when the pilot refused to stop the plane to allow him to walk on the clouds outside.[61] Read in light of its inspiration, this lends the Zambian space programme the quality of an experiment in radical imagination of a kind 'far beyond the conventions of our time and [its] horizons of expectation', which the author and filmmaker Ytasha L. Womack identifies as a defining feature of Afrofuturism.[62] It was an experiment focused on the thinkable and the doable. It was also deeply satirical in the context of a space race in which competing superpowers were pumping billions of dollars into a bid to be the first to put 'whitey on the moon' while many in their respective home nations were still in poverty, not least Black people in the United States:[63] a fact that many white reporters at the time seemed to overlook, apparently more content with mocking the 'insanity' and 'clownishness' of Nkoloso's enterprise. Underpinning the satire, though, was a utopianism that is beautifully captured in a 2014 short film by Nuotama Bodomo, titled *Afronauts*, just as it is implied in the context of Nkoloso's own biography, who was better known in Zambia at the time as a political agitator, trickster, and freedom fighter. The Zambian space programme refused to limit itself to the super-speedy developmental impulses of the space race, preferring instead to revel in a tonally ambiguous emancipatory imagination, and a glint in the afronaut's eye (one might also think here of the British-Nigerian artist Yinka Shonibare's series of afronautical figures created in the late 1990s and early 2000s, all of which are lovingly crafted and textured).[64]

One of the reasons why I find it fruitful to read The Uhuruverse's LADA residency in light of the Zambian space programme is because of a link that Douthat draws between the Cold War space race and the decadence of North American society. For Douthat,

> [t]he peak of human accomplishment and daring, the greatest single triumph of modern science and government and industry, the most extraordinary endeavour of the American age in modern history, occurred in late July in the year 1969, when a trio of human beings were catapulted up from earth's surface, where their fragile, sinful species had spent all its long millennia of conscious history, to stand and walk and leap to the moon.[65]

And it's been downhill ever since, he says. Gone are the days 'in which the frontier would no longer be closed', when it was possible to counter a sinful counterculture by colonizing an extra-terrestrial landscape.[66] Since the heydays of exploration, expansion, discovery, and progress typified in the Apollo moon landing, says Douthat, 'we [by which he means American society in general] have entered into decadence', understood here in several negative senses of that word as societal decline, political sclerosis, cultural exhaustion, and economic stagnation.[67]

Douthat's perspective is underpinned by his conservatism, on the one hand, and his Catholicism, on the other; but an influence that he may be more hesitant to identify with is his neocolonialism. As the cultural historian Ian Bourland recognizes, the pursuit of space 'has long been a romantic one', but 'it is also undergirded by the darker registers of territorial conquest in the United States and the former British Empire' (the mining magnate Cecil Rhodes once said that he would 'annex the planets' if he could).[68] Douthat's attempt to rejuvenate faith in socio-economic progress and the pursuit of new frontiers fails to account for this, both of which played important roles in histories of colonial expansion and violent expropriation, and which benefitted white descendants who inherited the right to reap its rewards.

The enervating impact of racial capitalism on Black bodies in particular led several twentieth-century postcolonial writers to re-frame decadence not as a consequence of white-capitalist progress having somehow lost its way, but as a consequence of it having thrived. 'A civilization that proves incapable of solving the problems it creates is a decadent civilization', writes the Martinican writer and politician Aimé Césaire in his 1955 'Discourse on Colonialism'.[69] In place of Douthat's advocacy of rejuvenating a frontier spirit, Césaire positions that same spirit as a civilizational sickness that leads people to think that the colonization of lands, bodies, and minds is par for the course of 'progress'. W. E. B. Du Bois also condemned 'the decadence of that Europe which led human civilization during the nineteenth century'[70] – which is to say, imperialism and colonialism – while Derek Walcott chastised the 'imitated decadence' of West Indian artists who sought to absorb European modernist mannerism or a romantic or avant-garde taste for 'primitivism'.[71] The literary scholar Robert Stilling shines a spotlight on many such perspectives,[72] offering valuable context for appreciating the anti-neocolonial work of The Uhuruverse.

Douthat's identification of the space race as the pinnacle of human achievement comes at the cost of realizing that an 'Alien Nation' – a queering of 'alienation' borrowed from the music writer and journalist Mark Sinker, who is sometimes credited as the first person to conceptualize Afrofuturism in all but name,[73] already lives on earth in the streets of its metropolises, and has done since the Middle Passage. 'The ships landed long ago', he writes:

> they already laid waste whole societies, abducted and genetically altered swathes of citizenry, imposed without surcease their values. Africa and America – and so by extension Europe and Asia – are already in their various ways Alien Nation. No return to normal is possible: what 'normal' is there to return to?[74]

Or, as the media theorist and sonic artist tobias c. van Veen summarizes, Afrodiasporic subjects have been citizens of an Alien Nation since slavery's programme of dehumanization.[75] Armageddon has already happened for these citizens, albeit in ways that still haunt and shape the present. It began with the reduction of bodies to absolute things and uses. The expropriative machinations of racial capitalism is built on the abduction of 'aliens' deprived of their 'humanity' (within the logic of white humanism), with the theft of that humanity in the process of their own commodification functioning as a kind of apocalypse.

In centring themselves as a citizen of Alien Nation, The Uhuruverse offers a very different valuation of 'decadence' to Douthat's, just as they offer a way of thinking about their alien citizenship 'not just as the effect of being estranged by foreign forces', to borrow again from van Veen, or of being haunted by that estrangement, 'but of strategically mobilizing estrangement towards becoming'.[76] Their work resonates with the kind of Afrofuturism envisioned by Sun Ra: a self-proclaimed alien deity. The terms 'Afrofuturism' and 'Alien Nation' might have been applied retrospectively to Ra, but his collapse of the past, present, and future into one another influenced how these ideas have been conceptualized and mobilized in the service of Black fugitivity – which refers to 'a critical category for examining *the artful escape of objectification*'[77] – and the decentring of neocolonial productivism.

Of particular note is Ra's interest in 'a slagheap of beliefs deemed irrational, obsolete, or just plain crackpot by Western religion, philosophy and science'.[78] Douthat would consider faith in obsolescence 'decadent', given its backward glance, just as he would Ra's subversive reimagining of techno-scientific progress. In fact, as the Kenyan philosopher John S. Mbiti observes, '[i]n traditional African thought, there is no concept of history moving "forward" towards a future climax [. . . There is] no "belief in progress", the idea that the development of human activities and achievements move from a low to a higher degree', and myth is of far greater significance than 'progress'.[79] While invested in the future and bound up with space-age euphoria, Ra's futurism is not techno-utopian; rather, as the political theorist Alex Zamalin notes, it is based on creativity rather than 'the goal of ruthless industrialization, automated efficiency maximization, lifeless bureaucracy, and mindless competition'.[80]

Ra's interest in a 'slagheap' of outmoded beliefs and esoteria was grounded in the wisdom and cultural supremacy of ancient Egypt, a civilization that runs counter to the West's 'claims to cultural anteriority and superiority', as the cultural historian Paul Youngquist observes.[81] In a similar vein, The Uhuruverse's citizenship of Alien Nation might usefully be read as an attempt to recalibrate the orientation of society around values that privilege dehumanizing and expropriative forms of 'exploration', 'discovery', and 'progress'. In doing so, they open up the possibility of discovering the more radical break with racial capitalism implied in past-tense references to Armageddon and the apocalypse.

In a typically layered and temporally bewildering phrase intoned by June Tyson in Ra's 1974 film (also an album) *Space Is the Place: Sun Ra and His Intergalactic Solar Arkestra*,

> 'It's after the end of the world,
> Don't you know that yet?'[82]

These words open the film, as if broadcast not just from outer space, but outer time – not so much the future as a time beyond time as we know it.[83] These words are also tonally ambiguous insofar as they seem to be referencing both the originating apocalypse of the Middle Passage, and the end of another world haunted by its legacy which, we might speculate, is the world of racial capitalism, the world of productivism, of neocolonialism, the world that put whitey on the moon. Ra does go on to make explicit reference to the colonization of distant planets by Black people in *Space Is the Place*, but these references are clearly intended as a response to the neocolonial ambitions of Cold War superpowers during the space race. The film makes no attempt to dominate space as a final frontier or to *extend* the colonialism underpinning America's role in the space race, as there is no frontier to expand for those who are already dominated and colonized. Rather, the infinite blackness of space is aligned with Black fugitivity, and an awareness of how white supremacy on earth is based on taking its 'claims to cultural anteriority and superiority' for granted.

The Uhuruverse's low-fi Afrofuturism does something similar. One way of understanding their attempt 'To save a dying world / From its funklessness' involves the unearthing of a 'hidden potentiality' embedded in the alternative space programmes devised by Nkoloso and Ra (rather than the revolutionary grand narratives and counternarratives that pique Žižek's interest).[84] The Uhuruverse's embrace of DIY scenography runs counter to the utopianism underpinning a hyper-modern space race, alongside the colonialist impulses of that race. In this, it would indeed seem 'decadent' relative to the virile productivism vaunted by Douthat in his praise of the 1969 moon landing – which arrived the second time as farce in 2021, when Richard Branson, Elon Musk, and Jeff Bezos embarked on their own private billionaire space race – but that is part of what makes it so compelling. Perhaps there is something, after all, in Douthat's otherwise spurious prognosis that no 'meaningful' change has occurred since white-capitalist progress reached a climactic point with the moon landing. Half a century later, we find comparable neocolonial ambitions enabling private entrepreneurs to make their own leap – not forwards, but sideways – in commodifying the sky.

There are three main conclusions I want to draw in wrapping up this section. First, as with kosoko's *Séancers*, I have reservations about calling work by The Uhuruverse 'decadent'. However, I do find it instructive to consider their Afrofuturism in light of dominant figurations of techno-scientific progress and the conquering of new frontiers, which is relevant to recent theorizations of the decadent society. I have been exploring The Uhuruverse's space-age aesthetic in the context of a different set of histories to the one outlined by Douthat, including Nkoloso's satirical and imaginative actions, which fell away from the grandstanding of nations caught up in a neocolonial space race. The Uhuruverse's low-fi and outmoded scenographies also contrasts with that space race, as it does with its farcical counterpart half a century later, and their work takes on decadent qualities when read in the context of the specific histories – both dominant and alternative – that make decadence meaningful in the first place.

Second, The Uhuruverse invites us to consider what values and prejudices are bound up in the identification of particular kinds of progress and progressiveness, regression and decadence. Claims around progress (particularly techno-scientific progress) and progressive or radical social advancement (for instance, in the retrieval of white countercultural dreamings) are often normative, which belie their contingency on ways of thinking and organizing that privilege some voices and bodies at the expense of others. The Uhuruverse asks their audience to engage with these contingencies, and to think and feel beyond them. They also encourage us to acknowledge the dialectical complexity of decadence and progress: how neocolonial progress implies the wasting of particular livelihoods and lives, for instance, and how decadence heralds the prospect of a new dawn.

Finally, the ways in which decadence might anticipate a new dawn informs The Uhuruverse's experimentation with Black fugitivity. While committed to punk and its attendant mantra – 'No Future' – they remain deeply invested in the prospect of social change. Their work is both retrograde and radical in its embrace of the 'hidden potentiality' of bygone utopias imagined by African American musicians in the 1970s: at odds with the productivist codification of progress that put whitey on the moon, and in sync with an Afrofuturist reimagining of the horizons of the thinkable and the doable – beginning with the belief that it might, just might, be possible to walk freely in the sky, above and beyond a world that has mocked, oppressed, and exploited the aspirations of Black people.

Conclusion

This chapter has considered the ways in which jaamil olawale kosoko and The Uhuruverse have engaged with key themes that this book argues lend themselves to decadence in theatre and performance, including the outmoded means and thematics of cultural production, and forms of creativity opposed to productivism; however, I have not been concerned in this chapter with identifying a decadent aesthetic as such, so much as the contexts and discourses that render decadence legible in the first place, and ways of thinking, appearing and doing that find themselves caught in the cultural politics of decadence. The political tuning of these themes relative to racial capitalism may – on the face of it – appear antithetical to decadence, but only so long as decadence is conceptualized in apolitical or reactionary terms. The binding of decadence to a historical period when industrialization was at its height offers too limited an understanding of decadence if the concept is to have any value or meaning in a neocolonial moment, when some of the world's richest entrepreneurs are shooting for the stars in a bid to commodify the sky, and when our understanding of racial capitalism is significantly more advanced than it was when 'decadence' had its heyday over the course of the fin de siècle.

Douthat's analysis of the decadent society is ultimately intended to rejuvenate a frontier spirit. This makes it all the more important to revisit how capitalism relates to progress, techno-scientific or social, and what it means to fold a rhetoric of decadence into a study of that relationship, paying close attention to the bodies, proclivities and beliefs that win or lose on the basis of structural inequalities that enervate, alienate, and that prop up how the health and wealth of a nation come to be recognized and understood. kosoko and The Uhuruverse demand that we recognize diagnoses of the decadent society as a style of social evaluation, and they do so by foregrounding the specific bodies – Black bodies – that are generally elided in these diagnoses, despite the fact that their exploitation played a foundational role in the production of inequitably distributed bounty.

In the first instance, kosoko and The Uhuruverse invite us to acknowledge and engage with citizenship of an Alien Nation: either as a trapping of history within a body that is itself trapped within history, or as a projection back into the hidden potentialities of the past as a starting point for stretching the imaginable horizons of the future. In this, they, too, are proposing counternarratives to productivism and the conquering of new frontiers, but in ways that at least hold open the possibility of what might lie the other side of a cataclysmic event: which is to say, the cancellation of a cancelled future. Or, to borrow again from Ra:

> 'It's after the end of the world,
> Don't you know that yet?'

4

Frenetic standstill

Decadence, capitalism, and excess on the Japanese stage

Torsos flail breathlessly. Arms grappling glowsticks carve wide arcs of iridescent light, but from the waist down each dancer remains stationary. It looks like an accelerated semaphore, with a chorus of dancers moving in super-fast synchrony. They are excessively diligent, and their gyrations are dizzying – although their feet remain rooted to the stage: frenetic and static, disciplined and chaotic, highly coordinated and yet determinedly wasteful in their youthful exuberance. What are we to make of these contradictions? Static freneticism, disciplined chaos, coordinated exuberance – these are paradoxes, and yet here they are, brought together in a type of fan-generated dance in Japan called *otagei*, which is usually performed by superfans of Japanese pop idols. What brings these dancers together, how are they seen by others in Japanese society, and what is it telling us about contemporary culture, and its wider contexts?

This chapter is inspired by *otagei*, as well as theatre makers and pop idols who incorporate or encourage *otagei* in their practice. It is also inspired by the work of theatre makers who go too far the other way in choreographing bodies that move incessantly but slowly in scenographies saturated with clutter. It is a chapter about superfluities both fast and slow, too much and too little, maximal and minimal, and that speaks to three of the core themes that have provided anchorage in this book's study of decadence so far: spectacular uselessness, the 'wasteful' expenditure of energy and resource, and the deployment of productivities that fall and flow away from productivism, which refers to the valorisation of productivity as an end in itself, and to the introjection of intensified productivity as a basis for self-realization.

The chapter begins with a consideration of two works by the theatre company chelfitsch, written and directed by Toshiki Okada:[1] *Super Premium Soft Double Vanilla Rich* (*Sūpā puremiamu sofuto W banira ricchi*, 2014), which is set in a 24/7 convenience store, and *Eraser Mountain* (*Keshigomu yama*, 2019), which is set in a more abstract 'junkspace' – a term that I am borrowing from Frederic Jameson's reading of work by the architect Rem Koolhaas.[2] It then moves on to consider Toco Nikaido's *Miss Revolutionary Idol Berserker* (*Kakumei Aidoru Boso-chan*), which has been touring in various iterations since 2013. Where Okada dwells on the insomniac temporalities of 24/7 economies, Nikaido amplifies superflat synchronicity and chronic saturation, centring our glow-stick-wielding *otagei* dancer in a messy cacophony that eludes straightforward appraisal. While their choreographies move at different paces, taken together they serve as instructive responses to the stasis produced by demands to do and produce more, and more intensely. This is the paradox of 'frenetic standstill' – which refers to a sense of going nowhere fast, and of being pulled in innumerable directions by competing demands – and it is the paradox that underpins the choreographies and scenographies of these otherwise very different styles of performance.

I will be arguing that the work of Okada and Nikaido lend themselves to decadence, but not simply because they stage excess (too fast, too slow, too much, too little). Decadence is not synonymous with excess, although bodies, things and actions that are in a state of excess can be attuned to decadence. To understand the decadence of these practices, they need to be approached in historical context. This is why I will be looking at the mobilization of decadence in Japanese cultural-political discourse at the turn of the twenty-first century, and it is why I will be reading contemporary Japanese theatre and popular culture in light of a protracted economic crisis that followed the bursting of Japan's asset bubble in 1991. The crisis cast a long shadow over the directions that productivism ended up taking in the twenty-first century, and informs the work produced by a 'lost generation' of theatre makers. These historical factors are what allow us to understand Okada's and Nikaido's work as 'decadent', as they offer a frame for understanding the cultural politics of uselessness, wastefulness, and forms of productivity that run counter to productivist enterprise.

The economic issues addressed in this chapter and that contextualize its engagement with decadence are not unique to Japan, and I have no intention of singling out Japan as a lone progenitor of 'dehumanized productivity, of dystopic capitalism'.[3] Japan's adoption of post-Fordist productivism in the 1970s and 1980s encouraged other countries to do the same, as I explore in the next section, but what draws me to the Japanese context is not so much the historical role that Japan played in promoting post-Fordism, as the nature and quality of choreographic and scenographic practice on the Japanese stage that deals with the fall-out of that role. Okada and Nikaido invite us to engage with the very different rhythms and temporalities that productivism can produce, which can have a profound impact on embodied experiences of 'frenetic standstill'. Productivism is not homogeneous, even if the expectations and demands that surround it have become commonplace. Also, while the economic issues addressed in this chapter are not unique to Japan, there are several other issues connected to the recession in Japan that demand an approach that is sensitive to the social and cultural specificities of the Japanese context. These specificities are what led to the 1990s and its 'lost generation' being labelled as 'decadent' by commentators at the time, and provide essential context for understanding the wider significance of moving fast and slow on the Japanese stage today.

Unstoppable motility: Toshiki Okada

Toshiki Okada is a playwright and theatre maker based in Japan. He co-founded the theatre company chelfitsch alongside choreographer Natsuko Tezuka in 1997, he writes and directs all of the company's work, and he has been choreographing for the company since 2004, following the critical-acclaim of *Five Days in March* (*Sangatsu no itsukakan*, 2004) and *Air Conditioner* (*Kūrā*, 2004). What makes Okada's work with chelfitsch relevant to this chapter is the extent to which it is seen to represent the so-called 'lost generation' in Japan, which refers to a generation who reached maturity in the 1990s: a decade overshadowed by a devastating recession. Many of those entering the workforce in the 1970s and early 1980s benefitted from Japan's reconfiguration of itself as an 'enterprise society' (*kigyō shakai*), which Tomiko Yoda defines as 'a society under the powerful influence of productivity principles and the institutional structures of large corporations'.[4] Wealth poured into the country, and it became a talisman for those championing the virtues of neoliberal and post-Fordist enterprise, especially regarding the case for deregulation, flexibility, and just-in-time production. However, the gains of this transition also came at a cost. Intensified and highly rationalized labour productivity rose at an 8.1 per cent annual average between 1975 and 1985, significantly outstripping other OECD countries, but working hours for middle-aged male workers also increased by a staggering 40 per cent, hours for sleep fell by 23 per cent, and annual paid leave averaged nine days, which was a third of that in France and West Germany at the time.[5] Also, while productivist principles propelled Japan's 'economic miracle', a booming yen eventually forced the Japanese state to introduce inflation adjustment policies that fuelled a monstrous asset bubble. The bubble burst at the tail end of 1991 under the influence of a deregulated financial sector, enhanced speculation on the stock market, overvalued house prices, and increases in the cost of living, marking the dawn of a protracted recession in which the lost generation came of age.

Okada turned eighteen when the recession hit, and he has returned to its personal and social impact throughout his professional career as a theatre maker. It was a time when the value of land was plummeting, banks became insolvent, real-term wages were stagnating (in part because employment contracts became increasingly precarious with the rapid development of flexi-workers, or 'freeters'), unemployment levels were rising along with levels of inequality, and government debt was skyrocketing in light of perennially ineffective pro-investment policies under the almost continuous leadership of the conservative Liberal Democratic Party (LDP).[6] By 2008, total national debt to GDP hit 194 per cent, 64 per cent higher than Greece in the same year – a startling figure in light of the looming Eurozone debt crisis – which was only set to worsen as the country sought to deal with a declining birth rate, declines in projected tax receipts, and the difficulties of caring for an ageing population.[7] The introduction of so-called 'Abenomics', which was associated with Shinzō Abe when he returned to power as leader of the LDP between 2012 and 2020, did what it could to level out debt but remained unable to appease rates of growth, which remained stagnant. The point in all this is to stress that the context in which Okada matured as a theatre maker was shaped by productivism, despite its demonstrable inability to relieve economic stagnation.

Okada's work expresses productivism through a 'fidgety' choreographic style that often contrasts with dialogue, inspired to some degree by the 'Quiet Theatre' that Oriza Hirata was pioneering with his theatre company Seinendan in the 1990s.[8] It is as if Okada's performers are completely unaware of their bizarre, somnambulistic movements: arms that weave outward as if to reach an imaginary object, only to be retracted almost as soon as the gesture is expressed, in search of something new, something other. Thighs slowly rise and calves gently kick, fingers make little waves, and bodies flow through a continual stream of compulsive movements. An unceasing flow of half-formed gestures unfurl across otherwise static stances, like a minimalist, slow-motion *otagei* routine, endlessly in search of an outlet for movements that no longer have anywhere to go, or that serve any clear purpose (Figure 4.1).

Okada's 2014 performance *Super Premium Soft Double Vanilla Rich* is one of the best examples of this choreographic style, and one of the most exemplary as a work by a 'lost generation' director. It was first presented at the KAAT Kanagawa Arts Theatre in Yokohama in Japan before embarking on a two-year tour to theatres in Finland, France, Germany, Italy, Lebanon, Mexico, Portugal, Russia, Switzerland, Thailand, and the UK. As with the malaise that followed

Figure 4.1 chelfitsch, *Super Premium Soft Double Vanilla Rich*, National Theater Mannheim, 2014. Photo © Christian Kleiner.

Japan's ecstatic period of productivist bounty, it expresses frenetic standstill not through acceleration, or density, but agitated slowness. Store workers and consumers move in a catatonic state, oblivious to their own limbic movements. Nonchalant shoppers kick their feet hoping to find fulfilment in the release of a newly improved ice cream, only to have their hopes dashed when it fails to meet expectations, prompting the resignation of a store worker overcome by a crushing sense of responsibility. Panicked staff worry about sustaining the metabolism of stock replacement, investing the store with a corporeality that supersedes their own. A proud manager dances his way through the inventory, and delights in the redundant standardization of handing over change to customers, only for the new method to be retracted by head office. Each of these workers are prone to the kind of auto-exploitation critiqued by the philosopher Byung-Chul Han, in which the interruption of work comes to be seen as a hindrance to self-realization despite targets and metrics that fly in the face of any tangibly productive outcome.[9] They embody and enact 24/7 temporality, all set to the hypnotic scales of J. S. Bach's *Well-Tempered Clavier*, and reminding us that the intensification of working life is not heading anywhere particularly productive in its hubristic commitment to the short-term gains that once catapulted 'economic miracles' in societies like Japan.

I watched this performance via a live stream hosted by Munich Kammerspiele in April 2020, during the first of the UK coronavirus lockdowns. I was reading a book by dance scholar André Lepecki at the time in which he explores what he calls the 'unstoppable motility' of modernity, and how this unstoppable motility was expressed through choreographic practice in Europe and the United States in the 1990s and early 2000s.[10] I remember thinking that Okada's choreographies present us not so much with the exhaustion of dance, as a space that houses insomniac choreographies: a space in which exhaustion is inexhaustible, always open to the replenishment of consumed goods and burnt-out labour. I had also been to see an exhibition held at London's Somerset House only a few weeks prior, just before it was closed with the introduction of strict social distancing regulations. It was themed around Jonathan Crary's book *24/7: Late Capitalism and the Ends of Sleep* (2013), and featured fluorescent images of model office workers sleeping by their computers in Alan Warburton's *Sprites I and IV* (2016), a cartoon fox lying content in a sea of static in Ed Fornieles's *Sleeping* (2015), and a drone-like toy helicopter hovering above the head of a sleeping man in Roman Singer's *BETT, 5. Dezember 1996* (1996).

The store workers and shoppers that Okada stages share the somnambulism of these works. They seem to be experiencing something of the 'static redundancy' that Crary finds in 24/7 always-on-always-available societies, which is perfectly encapsulated in the 7-Eleven store chain in Japan. For Crary, 24/7 and 7-Eleven are not simply vacuous catchphrases and brands; they tell us something about how 'the rhythmic and periodic textures of human life' are shaped in productivist societies.[11] In the nonspace of the 7-Eleven, the time of work and consumption is not ordered by opening hours but boundlessness, and that boundlessness is what stimulates the compulsive movements of Okada's store workers and shoppers. It is what produces the catatonia behind their smiles, their dazed drifting from one place to another, as if to serve some purpose or carry out a task, without quite knowing what that task may be, or why it seemed important in the first place.

Okada's interest in 'lost generation' experiences of frenetic standstill has only become more focused with time, especially with regard to the influence of productivism on embodiment and behaviour in the nonspaces of capitalism. I am thinking in particular of *Eraser Mountain*, which was a collaboration between chelfitsch and the scenographer Teppei Kaneuji that was first presented at the Kyoto Experiment performing arts festival in Kyoto in 2019. Kaneuji litters the stage with abstract objects, arranged according to a vaguely defined geometry that eludes symmetry or order because of the extent of the clutter: lines of yellow balls arranged in a grid on the floor; bottles of luminescent blue water; a large domestic fan that emits a constant hum; rectangular video projection screens relaying images of various performers on stage; a bright purple car tyre; pieces of pine timber, some balanced precariously upright, others tilted at angles; a small garden fountain in a faux rock tub; yellow tubes connecting one abstract shape to another, each one looking as though it had been cast by a faulty 3-D printer; and a bright green cement mixer that turns incessantly, generating a rhythmic, grinding clank. Over the course of two and half hours, and three parts, a group of six performers move these objects from one place to another, as if they have some project in mind, as if these objects have a use, but of a kind that they seem to have forgotten.

The work lends itself to a new materialist reading given the hotchpotch constellation of found objects that populate the stage, some of which seem to move of their own accord, others by manipulation. Theatre scholar Peter Eckersall offers just such a reading after experiencing it at New York's Skirball Center just before the first coronavirus lockdown in that city.[12] The company's own framing of the piece as an apprehension of environment 'through a new relationship between people and objects' supports Eckersall's reading,[13] but it put me in mind not of new materialism so much as a postmodern junkspace occasionally animated by unproductive or pointless activities amid the debris of over-production. There are moments in which the 'lost generation' seems to be directly referenced: for instance, in Part 3 a character called the 'GHOSTS OF PITIFUL PEOPLE' tells us of a sense of abandonment, of a feeling of sudden change, and the production of new sources of worry. 'The actual consequences of what they called flexibility', he says, 'is happening to us. That is how we were abandoned'. But it is not the narrative, so much as the clutter and the choreography that speaks loudest in a piece that deliberately drags without going anywhere, punctuated always by the aimless moving of objects with a forgotten use.

The insomniac qualities of *Super Premium Soft Double Vanilla Rich* and *Eraser Mountain* give them a hauntological character in two different respects, neither of which are linked to the forgotten dreamscapes of the 1960s that occupies Mark Fisher's attention in his study of hauntology, although it is Fisher and not his predecessors who inspired me to follow a hauntological line.[14] First, all of Okada's work since 2011 has been haunted by the Tōhoku earthquake and tsunami of that year, and the ensuing Fukushima Daiichi nuclear disaster. Theatre scholars Kyoko Iwaki and Sara Jansen describe the resulting style in terms of being 'post-Fukushima', underscoring the profound impact of these related events on how theatre makers were approaching their work in a society rocked by catastrophe. What makes this hauntological is connected to what Jansen describes as a 'sense of loss of possibility for the future', and 'an overwhelming sense of anxiety' that still renders those lost possibilities *felt*.[15] The second way we might understand these works as hauntological has to do with Japan's longstanding socio-economic insecurity, and it is this sense that is most relevant in this chapter. Japan, as with all advanced capitalist economies experiencing economic stagnation, is haunted by productivism as a virtuality – what Fisher calls a 'spectral causality'[16] – that no longer affects the goals it set out to achieve (productivism is presented as a driver of growth and wealth creation – this is how it is made to appear – despite a demonstrable failure to produce either in the twenty-first century). This hauntology manifests most explicitly in Kaneuji's scenographic junkspace, and a choreography based on a '"compulsion to repeat", a fatal pattern'.[17] The latter produces what Okada describes as a 'noisy corporeality':[18] a visual 'static' fit for the expression of frenetic standstill.

Eraser Mountain is haunted by a virtuality that is no longer capable of being realized. It is this virtuality, which is biopolitical, that possesses the compulsions of choreographed performers, and affects how these performers approach and manipulate the detritus of Kaneuji's junkspace. Where Kaneuji's scenography litters the stage with inert objects with a forgotten utility, Okada's choreographies reveal just how unproductive productivism can become. Those who inhabit this junkspace are unable to abandon what Franco 'Bifo' Beradi describes as 'the point of view of productivity, the expectation of acquisition and of control'.[19] What is presented is a temporality not merely of slowness, but enervated rhythms driven by the directionless compulsions of productivism, and a sense of futurelessness. There is a decadence to this enervation and futurelessness, but in a negative sense of that word, shorn of any 'anti'. Rather than being antithetical to productivism, Kaneuji and Okada stretch out the effects of frenetic standstill in a catatonic performance of unstoppable motility.

The ways in which the movements of bodies and objects unfold within nonspaces and junkspaces is what lends these performances to decadence: overburdened by expectations and pressures on time, on the one hand, which results in strange limbic movements and compulsions; and by a saturated commodity space, on the other, in which objects appear as clutter, apparently having 'forgotten' their purpose or utility as they drift from one place to the next in a series of hypnotic but pointless displacements. Be it with regard to bodies or objects, or bodies lost in a sea of commodities, these performances lend themselves to decadence because of their choreographic and scenographic qualities: relational qualities contingent on unstoppable motility, but with nowhere particular to go.

Theatre as explosion: Toco Nikaido

Where Okada offers measured studies of 24/7 somnambulism and the catatonic effects of unstoppable motility, Toco Nikaido ramps up productivist velocities in ways that lead nowhere fast. In 2008, Nikaido established Banana Gakuen Junjo Otome-gumi (Banana Academy Pure-Hearted Girls' Group) with support from the scriptwriter Norihito Nakayashiki, but it was not until 2011 that the company made their mark on the Tokyo arts scene with two performances in the same year: *Banana Gaku eyes ☆ Gei-geki Big Big Big Big Big Strategy* (2011), staged in July at the Suitengu Pit Studio in the heart of Tokyo, and *BANAGAKU ★☆ Super Spunky Sports Autumn Grand Tournament!!!!! ~ Tokyo Edition* (2011), staged in October at Theater Green's Big Tree Theater in Tokyo's Ikebukuro district. These works theatricalize a phrase that the artist Tarō Okamoto popularized in 1968: 'Art is Explosion'.[20] Projectiles fly from the stage in all directions, lights flash and colours burst, exuberant bodies jump and swoop in an idiosyncratic form of 'hyper dance',[21] and the pips and wails of J- and K-pop anthems play at a super-accelerated tempo. In Nikaido's hands, theatre is explosion.

The timing of these performances is significant. Okamoto's preoccupation with art as explosion came off the back of the Hiroshima and Nagasaki bombings, whereas Nikaido's performances occurred only a few months after the 2011 Fukushima nuclear power plant disaster. As Iwaki explains, '[t]he concept of '*hisaisha no tachiba* – literally "from the standpoint of the afflicted people" – was employed in post-Fukushima Japan like an unquestionable ethical slogan'.[22] The code of *wa*, or 'harmonious integration', 'became the unwritten law of the immediate post-catastrophe society', giving rise to sociophobic fears of ostracization for stepping out of line and 'an occultation of reason [that] caused many to adopt an uncritical position: they conformed to a moral blueprint that freed them from the responsibility of deciding how they should behave'.[23] The explosiveness and visceral excesses of Nikaido's early performances certainly disrupted the disciplinary dimensions of 'harmonious integration', but it is also important to situate her work in light of the broader socio-economic history surveyed so far in this chapter, having grown up in a period – like Okada – that was defined and shaped by the legacies of commercial and speculative excess. The principle of 'harmonious integration' may have been acute post-Fukushima, but a comparable 'moral blueprint' had already been exerting disciplinary pressure through the adoption and introjection of post-Fordist productivism.

In some respects, Nikaido's practice is related to what theatre scholar Nabuko Anan calls 'girls' aesthetics'. Girls' aesthetics references an obsession with 'purity' and 'heterosexual inexperience' in performances made by Japanese theatre makers that refuse 'stereotypically defined female maternal bodies'.[24] However, the sheer raucousness of Nikaido's work – especially its super-fast speed – sets it apart from the theatre companies that Anan associates with the genre, including YUBIWA Hotel, NOISE, and Takarazuka Revue, as well as the dance troupe KATHY. YUBIWA Hotel's early club performances in the 1990s perhaps come closest to Nikaido's own work, which were decidedly punk, often featured on the same bill as hardcore bands, and incorporated various messy liquids and secretions;[25] however, the advent of twenty-first-century media capabilities and aesthetics are reflected in Nikaido's work in ways that deliberately fracture attention across multiple screens and sites, each replaced by new interests almost as soon as they emerge. The deliberate fracturing of attention and sheer speed of her performances is what sets them apart from her contemporaries, just as the perpetual and very messy undoing of images in her super-fast choreographies both references and disrupts the gendering of commodity cultures in contemporary Japan.

The group disbanded after *Banana Gakuen Big Big Big Big Big Big Graduation Ceremony ~ Farewell Banana* (2012), which was presented at the Ouji Small Theatre in Tokyo's Kita-ku district in December 2012. This was partly in response to controversy after audience members took to social media to protest uninvited interaction, which in at least one case appears to have involved groping. It is unclear whether this was a cack-handed attempt to drag audience members on stage, or the result of reprehensible opportunism on the part of a male performer. There is a need for greater clarity as to the culpability of the rogue performer, as well as a review of safeguarding procedures. Nonetheless, disbanding the company offered Nikaido the chance to embark on a new venture that sought to learn from and mitigate the risk of performers taking advantage of audience members by further enhancing the control of Banana Gakuen's trademark chaos: Miss Revolutionary Idol Berserker. Miss Revolutionary Idol Berserker is the title of the group, and also tends to form part of the performance titles as well, including *Ms. Berserker ATTTTTACKS!! Elektro☆Shock☆Luv☆Luv☆Luv☆Shout!!!!!* (2013), *Miss Revolutionary Idol Berserker: Noise and Darkness* (2014), and *Miss Revolutionary Idol Berserker: Extreme Voices* (2016). Nikaido describes these works as examples of '*ohagi live*' (*ohagi* is a sweet and sticky rice cake that can be difficult to swallow), in which *otagei* dancers perform 'in a frenzied, chaotic space, albeit with meticulously-rigid controls'.[26] She employs a rotating cast of professional and non-professional performers for each performance (around twenty-five when touring), but she also works with a core group of three. Masami Kato and Eri Takamura have worked with Nikaido since Banana Gakuen, and Amanda Waddell (originally from the United States) joined with the formation of Miss Revolutionary Idol Berserker in 2013.

Various iterations of *Berserker* have toured internationally to countries including Australia, Austria, Germany, Poland, and the UK between 2013 and the outbreak of the pandemic. While the show is often re-titled or tailored to each location – for instance, *Crazy Girls Save the World* (2017), which toured China, Israel, and South Korea – the basic framework of the performance is maintained, albeit in ways that build on Nikaido's hunger for reinvention. I attended the *Extreme Voices* run at the Barbican Centre's Pit Theatre in London in 2016, which was presented as part of the London International Festival of Theatre. We were invited to put on rain macs under the guidance of translator Kyle Seiya Hogue, and given that the seats were covered in plastic wrapping, it was clear that things were going to get messy. Akimi Miyamoto's kaleidoscopic projections covered the whole of the stage area and offered information about the show and warnings about noise and liquid projectiles, although guidance was soon overtaken by a strobe-like stream of anime graphics and bubble-gum colour washes. Nikaido stormed the stage sporting a velvet crown and delivering a spoken tirade at a pace so fast as to elude meaningful translation, before retiring to a tech desk where a barrage of instruction marshalled her team with the occasional punctuation of a whistle. Performers wearing kimonos and clutching parasols traded places with flailing dancers as a stream of idols erupted from the thick of a hyperactively pulsating crowd of cheerleaders, homogeneously uniformed regardless of gender, and each taking turns over the forty-five-minute performance to sing along to an accelerated series of J- and K-pop anthems. A chorus line chattered snippets of text that were incomprehensible in a cacophonous fast-forward simultaneity. Others picked up glow sticks to perform *otagei* routines. Navy swimsuits and traditional headbands, a turquoise wig in the style of the iconic virtual idol Hatsune Miku, military fatigues, rainbow-coloured school uniforms, and pompoms were all put on, cast off, and thrown into the audience with machinic syncopation. Endless confetti rained from the rafters, reminiscent of the showers of cherry blossoms featured in countless paintings and anime films in Japan, as much as the deathly rose petals that the Roman Emperor Elagabalus is said to have showered upon his guests. The audience was also compelled to make way for performers as they clambered over seats, all the while dodging sweat, buckets of water, *wakame* seaweed, and viscous tofu. And yet, most of us, at the end of the night I attended, still welcomed an invitation to join the stage and dance as the performers took our seats, enthusiastically applauding our efforts (Figure 4.2).

As theatre critic Lyn Gardner writes, *Berserker* has 'a magpie tendency to alight upon the shiny shards of western culture that have taken over the Japanese brain like knotweed' – for instance, the sugary melodrama of *Les Misérables*' 'One Day More' (1985), and the interlacing of Disney songs with its J- and K-pop playlist.[27] Dancers sporting Union Jack flags and face paint emerged from showers of confetti, with touristic Brit-trash standing as

Figure 4.2 Toco Nikaido, *Miss Revolutionary Idol Berserker: Extreme Voices* (2016). Festival Theaterformen, Braunschweig. Photo by Andreas Greiner-Napp.

indices of nationhood drowned in hyper-enhanced *genki* (roughly translated as vigour or pep). *Berserker* is aligned with the production and display of bodies and subjectivities fit to perform the unstoppable motility outlined by Lepecki, only here the performance extends and intensifies 'a pure display of uninterrupted movement',[28] conducting performers and audiences entranced by *otagei* glow sticks, and pushing kinetic subjectivity to points of agitated excess.

Nikaido's strange homage to British culture in this example is typical of her approach whenever she brings *ohagi live* to countries outside of Japan, although the work is more explicitly invested in Japanese pop and underground idol traditions. As Yuji Sone notes, the 'idol' in Japanese popular culture initially referred to mainstream female pop singers in the 1960s and 1970s, but in the 1980s and 1990s the focus of the term 'shifted from talented individual singers to young female TV personalities within popular TV variety shows' – often drawn from high schools – with fans increasingly accepting 'that a female idol is created and understood as a "product" to be consumed'.[29] Major advertising companies like Dentsū came in on the act, which sought to bypass talent shows by introducing idols via TV commercials, using their appearances 'to raise the profiles of stars and sell them back to TV as performers, actresses and variety show personalities'.[30]

While the feeding of the pop idol industry via commercials is relatively unique in Japan, the factory-like production of pop idols through TV talent contests is now a globalized platform indebted to the rise of Japan's cultural influence as the second-largest music market in the world.

Some of the best-known idol acts include AKB48 and Morning Musume, the latter being put together through a TV talent contest led by the male singer and producer Tsunku (Mitsuo Terada), who also wrote many of their songs. The group's members actually lost the contest but were guaranteed a record deal if they could find a way of selling 50,000 copies of a song produced by Tsunku in five days – which they accomplished. Tsunku did little to hide his capitalistic paternalism in offering the group a contract. 'It was just after the [economic] bubble burst', he says. 'People were no longer interested in one another's welfare. Before, men used to spend money on women (and vice versa) but afterwards people just spent money on themselves. [. . .] I just saw a gap in the market and threw a ball right into it. Morning Musume made the audience want to spend money on them'.[31] In other words, the group succeeded in a recession because of their willingness to commit to a spectacularization of excessively diligent and highly gendered labour, if Tsunku's comments and the terms of the group's record deal are anything to go by. (Another idol act worth noting is Kasōtsūka Shōjo, which roughly translates as 'Virtual Currency Girls'. Each of the eight members represents a different cryptocurrency identifiable via a brand printed at the front of Mexican *lucha libre* wrestling masks adorned with fluffy ears. The lyrics of their debut single – *The Moon and Virtual Currencies and Me* (2018) – sets out advice on cyber security, sound investment principles, and the risks of online fraud. They embody the technology and transformative potentialities of virtual currency in a spectacular and apparently sincere performance of over-identification).

Where acts like these operate within the regimented parameters of the idol industry, Nikaido exaggerates (further still) its productivist excesses, augmenting the extremities of intensified productivity, gendered consumerism, and the corruption of a commodified and deeply problematic beauty myth that fetishizes – and eroticizes – adolescent 'cuteness'. Saccharine and coquettish 'cuteness', or *kawaii*, underpins the formation and marketing of many pop idol acts, much more so than a capacity to sing well. *Kawaii* also pervades *Berserker*, but in a grotesque form that upstages the stylized sincerity of mainstream idol acts oriented around the interests and desires of male superfans. There is an indexing of innocence, meekness, adolescence, nasal and high-pitched vocal intonation, and so on, which are all affiliated with *kawaii*, but each is either heightened to a point of exuberant monstrousness, or is replaced almost as soon as it emerges. Teeth chatter, smiles stretch across faces, voices strain, and poses are struck one after another as if watching an accelerated sequence of GIFs. There is little opportunity for these endlessly recycled signs of cuteness to play into the possessive psychosexual fantasies that have affected other, male-dominated communities of superfans, and there is no attempt to hide the fact that pop idols serve as interchangeable image commodities. Rather, as Lyn Gardner notes, the aspirations of pop idols are celebrated while mercilessly sending up the 'vacant heart' of a manipulative industry.[32]

It would be tempting to link Nikaido's staging of 'the cute' to the cultural theorist Sianne Ngai's work on its aesthetic categorization, but it is another of the aesthetic categories that Ngai identifies as being key to the cultural repertoire of post-Fordist economies – the zany – that is most relevant to the performance's 'decadence'. The zany refers to the 'physicality of an unusually beset agent' who adopts 'a strenuous relation to playing that seems to be on a deeper level about work'.[33] The zany also concerns how this unusually beset agent commits to a 'succession of individually distinct actions' that transform 'into a blur or stream of undifferentiated activity'.[34] The connection of zaniness to work is less tenuous once we learn of its derivation from the Commedia dell'arte's stock character *zanni*, who was an itinerant servant seeking temporary work in wealthy Venetian households.[35] To be zany, for Ngai, is to intensify physical exertion *as work* in ways that often produce an aversion to performances of excessive productivity.

Nikaido's work is in this sense 'zany', crossing an unsettling threshold between ecstatic joy, and a sense that things might just be spinning out of control, however meticulously planned each element of the performance may be. In this context, 'zaniness' offers a particular aesthetic tuning of decadence, not because decadence 'is' zany – for one thing, decadence is more usually associated with languidness and inertia – but because of how Nikaido choreographs zaniness in ways that pervert, by augmenting, the pointless intensification of productivity, as well as the abundantly wasteful expenditure of energy and the spectacularly useless orientation of objects and actions.

This understanding of decadence as a perversion of productivity, wastefulness, and utility needs to be understood in historical context. Decadence has multiple connotations and ties into various historical threads in Japan, although one starting point can be found in the Meiji era (1868–1912), in which the Japanese government cultivated a national imaginary based on 'enlightened' progress and productive endeavour. An important influence at the time was the cultural entrepreneur Yukichi Fukuzawa, who condemned 'useless arts' (*yūkanteki gakumon*) – his shorthand for art and literature – on the basis that they were not pragmatic or socially relevant.[36]

This kind of utilitarian thinking had a lasting influence on productivist initiatives throughout the twentieth century, but it also inspired various 'schools' of decadence associated with Japanese writers like Jun'ichirō Tanizaki and Yukio Mishima, united in the main by a persistent fascination with the expenditure of energy (including sexual energy), and opposition to the instrumentalism of the kind promoted by Fukuzawa.[37]

'Zaniness' in *Miss Revolutionary Idol Berserker* does not simply extend this 'decadent' heritage. It is a far cry from the introversion that is often attributed to decadent subjectivities. Also, histories of decadent literature and culture in Japan are too multiform to accommodate a coherently linear genealogy of decadence, not to mention the fact that *Berserker* is not a literary work, but theatrical. Nonetheless, a preoccupation with the relationships between decadence and productivism that cuts across Japan's various schools of decadence is still relevant, not because Nikaido strives to elude the frenzy of work or urban life, which is usually the case in Japanese decadent literature – for instance, in Tanizaki's writing on the chiaroscuro play of light and shadow that the electric lights of modernity threatened to erase[38] – but because of how she asks her performers to over-identify with unstoppable motility. This is why Ngai's theorization of zaniness offers a useful framework for understanding Nikaido's take on *otagei*, as her dancers – torsos flailing, feet rooted to the ground – embody and enact the decadent stasis that defines frenetic standstill. Her performers move incomparably quicker than Okada's, but both are pulled in different directions by forces that compel productivity, without actually going anywhere in particular.

Aside from its codification in twentieth-century literary fiction, there is another, alternative history of decadence's mobilization in the cultural-political arena that informs Nikaido's work. Neoconservative commentators were quick to diagnose the 'decadence' of Japanese society in the wake of the 1991 economic crash, describing the period that followed in terms of 'decadence', 'malaise', and 'disease'. A number of other factors also affected these diagnoses, including a devastating earthquake that rocked the city of Kobe and its environs in 1995, and, in the same year, a deadly nerve-gas attack on the Tokyo subway by the doomsday cult Aum Shinrikyō.[39] However, it was not just a period that was seen to be 'decadent', but specific groups of people – especially the lost generation's *otaku*, which are at the heart of Nikaido's *Berserker*.

'*Otaku*' literally translates as 'you' or 'your house', although since the 1980s it has been used to describe fan cultures and hyper-consumption of specific media, particularly manga and anime, but also computer games, toys, fashion, and pop music (*otagei* dances at pop idol concerts are usually performed by *otaku*). As the artist Takashi Murakami points out, whose work is inspired by these subcultures, *otaku* tend to be 'obsessed with personal taste and individualism' while at the same time seeking allegiances in communities of shared tastes that are cultivated to points of excessive refinement.[40] Such obsession with individualism and hyper-refined tastes will be familiar to readers interested in the portrayal of decadent subjectivities in fin de siècle literature, especially given the fact that *otaku* taste can often be unusual or transgressive before its more sanitized entry into the mainstream. However, in what follows I will be situating the 'decadence' of *otaku* culture not so much in relation to these traits, as the ways in which *otaku* sensibility has positioned itself against a blind adherence to productivist enterprise.

Although it is less the case now that *otaku* cultures have entered the mainstream, the *otaku* label had a derogatory edge when the 1990s recession was at its height. Disenchanted *otaku* neither conformed with nor accepted conventions and expectations based on work and family, prompting older critics to condemn their independence as indicators of social decline. Condemnation of young people is of course by no means unique to Japan. Young people all over the world have long been criticized for pursuing alternatives to traditional values and institutions, lured by hedonistic and ephemeral pleasures. Ross Douthat's book *The Decadent Society: How We Became the Victims of Our Own Success* (2020) is an example, as is the cultural theorist Stephen Bertman's critique of 'hyperculture', in which 'a society of "busy bodies"' struggle to find value and meaning in a society defined by transience and a lack of care or concern for either the future or the past – or so runs the caricature.[41] However, the denigration of *otaku* in the 1990s needs to be understood in a local context of moral panic that was developing in Japan in the so-called 'decadent' period that followed the 1991 crash, following well-publicized reports of violent crimes, promiscuity and prostitution among teenagers,[42] and concerns over a rising tide of 'acute social withdrawal' (*hikikomori*).[43]

The rising popularity of *otaku* culture in the 1990s was regarded as a moral issue, then, as well as a sociocultural one. But it was also – and quite fundamentally – a socio-economic issue. Attitudes towards the 'excessive' fandom of *otaku* and the consumption practices that go with it need to be read in light of resurgent nationalist sentiment, which produced what the anthropologist Marilyn Ivy describes as 'virulent critiques of consumerist hedonism and the decadence of wealth'.[44] Note especially the distinction here between consumerist hedonism, and a commitment to work; an excess of the former and a lack of the latter is what these critics were addressing. The normative role for male workers in workplaces that marginalized women in the Japanese enterprise society also tends to take its idealized form in the rationalization of the productive 'salaryman' (*sararīman*) – but *otaku* were rejecting this ideal in the wake of the crash, and with it the patriarchal bedrock that supported the security of older male workers. *Otaku* were consequently seen to threaten the realism of productivism and the security of those who subscribed to it. They deviated 'from the ethos of productivity', and sought to 'escape from reality in a society where production *is* reality'.[45]

Nikaido's staging of excess reacts to the *otaku*'s retreat from productivism by performing an augmented and perverted form of the productive labour that their critics expected of them. They play up to what cultural critic Akira Asada calls 'infantile capitalism', which describes a 'frenzied capitalism' that fetishizes adolescence.[46] According to Nikaido, the school-issued swimsuits and rainbow-coloured uniforms worn by her mixed-gender performers are reflections of infantile capitalism in Japan, but they also re-frame its more problematic aspects and the darker side of some male-dominated *otaku* subcultures, like the popularity of Lolita imagery in fashion and pornographic manga.[47] Unlike the prevalence of Lolita imagery in the manga and fashion industries, there is very little that could be said to be sexually suggestive in *Berserker*, let alone erotic (this is also what distinguishes *Berserker* most explicitly from Nikaido's earlier work with Banana Gakuen, which was more audacious and controversial in its strategies of representation and interactivity). Rather, it enlivens a spirit of play reminiscent of Keisuke Sakurai's theorization of the child's body (*kodomo shintai*) in contemporary Japanese dance. Here, though, it is not so much globalized dance techniques that are 'misused' in the work's celebration of anarchically young bodies, as the industries that shape the perception of those bodies.[48] What results is a joyfully childish art of the sensorium that amplifies productivism to points of ecstatic superfluity, while at the same time undermining the possessive gaze that can sometimes haunt male-dominated *otaku* communities.

Bertman, Douthat, and Nikaido all approach hyperculture as a threat to traditional conventions and institutions, but react to that threat in ways that reveal their socio-political convictions. For conservatives like Bertman and Douthat, traditional values relating to an individual's moral compass, the nuclear family, religion, nationhood, and diligent work are threatened by a thirst for immediate gratification. They mourn the loss of what they see as fulfilling paths to self-realization that have tended to benefit the demographic group that they occupy. Nikaido highlights and deliberately exaggerates the 'threat' ascribed to young people in Japan, supposedly bedazzled by transient hypercultural pleasures, which results in a flattened and condensed experience of time reflective of increasingly multi-screen/multi-demand lines of 24/7 work and leisure, presenting in live encounters what Ryan Trecartin and Lizzie Fitch achieve in their frenetic films (a more familiar touchstone in West-leaning visual arts discourse). What makes this so interesting, in light of the moral, sociocultural, and socio-economic issues just mapped, is the way that she both references and augments the supposed 'decadence' of an infantile society fixated on transient pleasures and consumerist hedonism, while populating the stage with the 'busy bodies' who tend to be scapegoated for bringing about societal decadence given their refusal of a productivist regimen. The work also generates and involves its own dedicated *otaku*, moving beyond the representation of a cultural-political field towards direct intervention within that field.

Nikaido's work is clearly grounded in and responds to a very specific set of historical and contemporary contexts – economic, social, and cultural – and an aestheticization of time and speed plays a crucial role in that response. It is what preoccupies Nikaido's attention. What results from the frenetic pace of the performance, with its onslaught of images and sounds and sensations, is a 'superflat' time, as opposed to the 'superflat' appearances that have piqued the interest of other commentators on contemporary Japanese performance.[49] The term 'superflat' is most closely associated with Murakami's work and writing as a visual artist, who uses it to refer to social and economic factors (e.g. a recession-ridden society, press restrictions, the doorways of one-room apartments, mindless adherence to harmonious integration),[50] as well as aesthetic considerations (e.g. computer graphics, monitors and screens, information and data, manga and anime).[51] Nikaido's work is 'of' this superflatness, but it also explodes it outwards, augmenting the temporal dynamics of productivism in the moment of the performance's unfolding. It works with material processes and contexts based on saturation, over-abundance, and speed. However, and importantly, it also refuses to find contentment in what Nikaido describes as 'that sense of loneliness or void' in a digital marketplace that (misleadingly) seeks to maximize possibility in ways that affect how money and time are spent.[52]

Berserker makes a messy spectacle of what happens when the 'temporal commons' – which refers to a 'shared conceptualization of time and the set of resultant values, beliefs, and behaviors regarding time' in a given culture[53] – is appropriated and distributed by market stakeholders in the name of efficiency. It calls into question how 24/7 superflat rhythms and intensities are valorised, and what being pressed for time is doing to its experiential and social quality. Rather than approaching time productively spent as an intangible 'asset', Nikaido's organization of chaos puts a spotlight on the pressing of thought and action in a flattened temporal commons.

Despite the tightly rehearsed precision of *Berserker*'s choreography, the intensification of the performers' labour in this superflat time comes across as a self-propelling phenomenon. The result, like the performance's staging of zaniness and *kawaii*, is grotesque: full of contortions and grimaces, as if twentieth-century biomechanics were struggling to keep up in an age of digital processing. Constructivism without anything particularly constructive. Non-utilitarian utility. *Decadent* utility, in which the instrumentalization of people and objects is pursued for its own sake, rather than for the sake of anything useful. Productivism appears drawn into a future that is always *almost* within touching distance. Even when a six-minute digital countdown timer reaches zero towards the beginning of the performance, what occurs is not a climactic moment so much as the propulsion of fresh chaos. There is no climactic moment. Each moment marks the beginning of an end.

The decadence at stake here is of a very different kind to that which caught the attention of Japanese decadent writers in the nineteenth and twentieth centuries, who defied 'what labor means to capitalism and the bourgeoisie', as the literature scholar Ikuho Amano points out, uprooting it 'from the circuit of profit-making and the abstraction of human energy'.[54] Nikaido does no such uprooting. Regardless of the spotlight she shines on a pressed temporal commons, her work can hardly be said to retreat from the exploitation of human energy and the introjection of a productivist work ethic. Each performer is expected to respond to 'excessive notes' at the end of each performance – often overnight – in an effort to rejuvenate the work as an endlessly evolving project.[55] They are generally not paid, or receive only limited remuneration through additional promotional activities.[56] Non-core members also pay a small participation fee to cross-subsidize expenses – touring costs are expensive given the size of the group – and they are expected to pay for the (albeit cheap) props used in the show themselves.[57] This is common practice on the *Shōgekijō* scene, and is an issue with the scene more than the practitioner, but the labour intensity that Nikaido demands of her performers is nonetheless unusual.

However, it is also important to recognize that Nikaido is working in a context that still tends to allocate opportunities to male peers. Her calculated authoritarianism within the working conditions available to her, while clearly compromised, still confronts paternalistic discourse that bemoans the 'excesses' of maternal culture in Japan, sending up the 'excesses' of an empowered *mamagon* ('mummy monster').[58] Rather than resigning herself to an excluded or subordinate position, Nikaido insists on perfecting her work despite the patriarchal pedantry of cultural gatekeepers, which is relevant as much to the pop idol industry as it is to *Shōgekijō*. The work is shaped by these affordances and compromises. It is produced both in and through a limiting set of material constraints, over-identifying with those constraints in ways that appropriate productivism's gendered injunctions. What results is a discombobulating and politically thwart mess – an ordered disorder – characterized as much by the discipline and diligence of highly dedicated performers as it is by joyful exuberance and a riotous affirmation of subcultural sociality.

As should be clear from the foregoing analysis, I have mixed feelings about the value of augmentation as a 'decadent' strategy for redressing productivism's own excesses, and another factor contributing to these mixed feelings has to do with its excessive use of material resources. As set out earlier, decadence and excess are not equivalents. To spend and use lavishly can 'immolate' the energy of performers in ways that are incompatible with 'what labor means to capitalism and the bourgeoisie', as evidenced in the passionate amateurism of many *otaku* communities, or resource can be spent and used lavishly on the replenishment of new material commodities, which takes on added repercussions in a climate emergency. For Tom Wilson, a sound technician who worked on the Barbican run of the show, 'the clean-up felt like the most labour-intensive part of the work', considerably more than usual and with several runs of the show each night.[59] Very few of the materials that were catapulted across the stage and auditorium were reusable. Paper projectiles turned to pulp because of the water that was tossed over the heads of the audience, and single-use plastic confetti stuck to the plastic-wrapped chairs, which had to be re-wrapped every couple of days. Seaweed and tofu that had been mangled together with other projectiles, and had to be dumped into large trade waste bins each night, which became full of smelly mush. The consigning of each material to obsolescence and disposal after fleeting moments of revelry seems a fitting reflection of the in-building of disposability in contemporary capitalism, but the relationship to that orientation, in this case, is less critical distance than capitulation.

A final reservation that I have about this piece has to do with its tyrannical approach to audience involvement. As scholars from Jean Baudrillard to Nicolas Bourriaud and Mark Fisher have pointed out, the spectacle discussed by Guy Debord in the 1960s has long been superseded by a society of co-opted sensation, participation, and tactility. 'The spectacle subjected us to image', writes Fisher, but the tactile system 'solicits our participation, enjoins us to join in'.[60] *Berserker* has a role to play in this system, locking audiences into a 'hyper-bright instant [...]. There is no continuous time in which shadows can grow', none of the pensive chiaroscuro vaunted in Tanizaki's aestheticism, 'only a time that is simultaneously seamless (without gaps: there is always "new" content streaming in) and discontinuous (each new compulsion makes us forget what preceded it)'.[61] Nikaido orchestrates just such a hyper-bright instant as she marshals her performers and the lights that flood the stage, just as we, the audience, are eventually corralled into position, enjoined to join in.

The work's politics is as messy as its staging. It gives the impression that those caught in the slipstreams of productivism must continually improvise despite the choreography being thoroughly mapped out. But equally, the drill of its choreography is what I find so appealing in its staging of frenetic standstill. It reveals the absurdity of a logic that fixates on intensified productivity as a panacea for capitalism's stagnant realism. Nikaido's performers over-identify with this logic, but a surplus explodes out the other side, another paradox, an unproductive productivism that is made to morph into something excessively useless, fun and brazen in its subversive intent. We are not offered a depiction of a world beyond the economic – the performance is *excessively* economistic – but we are, nonetheless, confronted with a kind of decadence attuned to histories shaped by stagnation, the castigation of youthful exuberance, and the emergence of subversive subcultures. It is these contexts and influences that 'speak' to the work's decadence as much as its compromises and capitulations.

Conclusion

This chapter has considered two very different stagings of productivist tempo: one that expresses unstoppable motility through catatonic choreographies, and one that augments the rhythms and intensities that twenty-first-century capitalism recognizes as bases for self-realization and fulfilment. Taken together, they refract the velocities of productivism, which is not simply defined by ever-increasing speed and acceleration, but by ceaseless impulses and compulsions that can be much more somnambulistic in character. The chapter has also looked at the spaces in which these tempos and rhythms are performed, and the objects that are caught in their slipstreams: the nonspaces of 7-Elevens containing objects with a forgotten use, and abstract junkspaces in which bodies and things drift with no apparent point or purpose; but also the cluttered and cacophonous stages that fail to contain Nikaido's riotous spectacles, spilling into the audience, dowsing them in gunk and confetti as if they were guests at Elagabalus's banquet. It is neither possible nor desirable to untangle these choreographies and scenographies. They are developed in ways that are relationally co-dependent. We need the arrangement or disarrangement of objects, bodies, and things to get a sense of the works' tempos and the playing out of unstoppable motility, just as we need to appreciate the pace and directionality of their movements to apprehend their lack of utility and purpose.

Okada and Nikaido share an interest in over-identification, although a study of *Miss Revolutionary Idol Berserker* opens up more ground to consider the gendering of productivism. In no small part, this is due to the pop- and subcultural references that provide the performance's controlled chaos with a frame of legibility, especially its engagement with Japanese pop idols, and their committed *otaku*, who elude utilitarian and paternalistic social mores while at the same time sustaining the pop idol industry through gendered practices of production and consumption. *Berserker* makes a messy spectacle of the values, beliefs, and behaviours that derive from the gendered realism of productivism, not least with regard to the pressing of time, embodied and enacted expressions of productivism, and the sociality of producing and consuming. Moreover, it does so by staging an aesthetic well-suited to a context that has found decadence and related concepts deployed in cultural and political discourse to make sense of a protracted recession and its impact on Japanese culture and sociality.

Okada and Nikaido make work that hinges on the embodied effects of policies and attitudes that valorise productivism regardless of its effectiveness in remedying a protracted period of economic stagnation. They make work that stages the symptoms and detritus of a way of life that outpaces human capacity, riffing on a form of capitalism that pursues forward momentum by stretching utilitarian and productivist values to extremes, just as they pastiche the decadence that conservative critics find in the 'excesses' of young consumers. In experimenting with moving fast and slow, with minimal and maximal configurations of useless or wasteful abundance, and with the augmentation of productivist superfluities, they also draw attention to superfluity itself. Neither offers us a glimpse of utopia, the apocalypse, or the cancellation of a cancelled future, as we have seen in earlier chapters; rather, their critique is 'of' a superflat 'real' that is less eluded than estranged or exploded. Nonetheless, in estranging or exploding this apparently intractable 'real', they also call attention to its contingency on the preservation of a defunct and damaging mode of social and economic organization, just as they call attention to the imagined and subcultural communities whose competing perspectives are either cemented or dismissed in its service.

5

'A dangerous form of decadence'

Decadence, performance, and the culture wars

The end of history is a distant memory. The fall of the Berlin Wall in 1989 and the widespread prevalence of political centrism in the 1990s did not bring about ideological consensus. Liberal democracies in the twenty-first century have been characterized by political polarization and fragmentation, and they have also been faced with recurrent geopolitical conflicts. The cultural arena has played an especially important role in dividing societies based on fundamental disagreements about tradition and revision, universality and relativism, nature and nurture, freedom of speech and expression, scientific enquiry and critical theory, faith and secularism, the list goes on. The centre has not held.

Today, these democracies are embroiled in a culture war that has roots stretching deep into the twentieth century. Cultures are defined by the ideas, beliefs, values, and institutions that inflect the interpretation of societies and environments, the establishment of identities, and the attribution of meaning and significance. Everyone has a part to play in the production of culture, although some institutions and platforms, together with the ability to access and make effective use of them, tend to be more impactful in shaping cultures. Examples include arts and heritage institutions, broadcast media, journalism, literature, education providers, and online platforms, as well as influential community groups and lobbyists. Culture wars are stoked by these institutions, platforms, and groups, together with the politicians who are meant to represent the interests of their constituents. For the political scientist Jim George, what results is a battle 'for cultural hegemony – for the hearts and minds of the great majority of people and for the levers of power by which the dominant culture might operationalise its images of the "good" life'.[1] In short, culture wars concern what we think, feel and imagine, how we are influenced to think, feel and imagine in particular ways, and what we think, feel, and imagine about that influence.

Culture wars also involve the deployment of tropes and narratives that riff on a set of common themes: for instance, the relinquishment of the cultural domain to destructive forces that threaten the bedrock of a nation – its moral fibre, tastes, traditions, and values – or the nascent priorities of new political stakeholders. It is perhaps unsurprising, then, that 'decadence' rears its head in discourse that is either concerned with or that actively participates in a culture war, if decadence is connected in some way to ideas of decline and the cultivation of a taste for things that others might regard as depraved, regressive, or counterproductive.

The Civil Rights movement and countercultural experimentation in the United States in the 1960s and 1970s are frequently cited as important cornerstones in the history of the culture wars. For instance, several of the most vociferous voices during the culture wars in the United States in the 1980s and 1990s, like Patrick Buchanan, point the finger of blame for cultural division at the proliferation of radical and progressive advances in the late 1960s: second-wave feminism, Black Power, anarchism, radical socialism, Stonewall, the decline of the nuclear family, and the diversification or rejection of faith.[2] The National Endowment for the Arts (NEA) was established in this period, in 1965, and for commentators like Buchanan and influential Republican senators like Jesse Helms, it came to represent everything that was wrong about radical and progressive social advances, which they regarded not as advances at all but as the consequence of an insidious decadence polluting normal, hard-working families. For Buchanan and Helms, art meant radicalism, radicalism meant transgression, and transgression meant decadence and the decline and fall of a healthy, pious, and productive society.

The perception of societal decline and its linking to radical and progressive causes and the funding of art may well be ringing a familiar bell. Attitudes towards identity politics, social justice activism, campus culture, and cultural production in museums, galleries, theatres, and broadcast media have become especially topical in recent years, including in the UK, my home country. It was what prompted Oliver Dowden – a former culture secretary (2020–1) and co-chair of the Conservative Party (2021–2) – to launch a scathing attack on so-called 'woke ideology' in the days just prior to the Russian invasion of Ukraine in 2022. For Dowden, a new breed of left-wing orthodoxy dominates the cultural arena, and that domination begins with the teaching of arts and humanities subjects in Higher Education. The result, for Dowden, is 'a dangerous form of decadence' that threatens the nation's integrity and security, beginning with its sense of unity, identity, and purpose.[3]

Both of these examples pull debates concerning morality and the social contract into the orbit of debates about the funding of cultural institutions and practices. What appears to be an issue about decency, tolerance, or freedom of speech is often just as much about how 'the levers of power' are pulled, including the allocation of public funding. This makes times of economic crisis especially illuminating in a study of culture wars. For instance, in countries around the world, the 2008 financial crash provided fodder for conservatives to attack the legitimacy of subsidizing the making and sharing of art and performance on the basis of their being illegitimate recipients of public money relative to the instrumental value of essential services like healthcare (in countries that benefit from publicly funded healthcare). It is therefore unsurprising that arts funding was closely scrutinized in the wake of the crash in countries like the Netherlands, rousing deep-seated sentiment about the social relevance of practices and professions linked to the arts, relative to other practices and professions like medicine and engineering. Debates such as these touch on some difficult questions about the 'necessity' of art and performance, not least when these questions get caught up in the instrumentalization of a crisis to advance an agenda against big government or social progressiveness.

This chapter considers the unfolding of culture wars across all three of these examples: the United States in the 1980s and 1990s, the Netherlands in the late-2000s and 2010s, and the UK in the early 2020s. Ultimately, I will be arriving at a theorization of the utility of a culture war and the discourses of decadence that attend to it in the context of specific cultural and historical moments, addressing two related continuities: an anti-woke agenda that regards the pursuit of social justice as a symptom of societal decadence, and an anti-arts agenda that regards the arts as fundamentally useless and for that reason dispensable. This chapter, then, is about how decadence and related concepts have been mobilized in political discourse and rhetoric in the late-twentieth and twenty first centuries, how this mobilization has been – and still is – bolstering the supremacy of productivism, and what this means for the making and reception of art and performance. However, it is also concerned with reclamations of decadence, advocating for the value of theatre and performance not on the basis of their utility, but their uselessness, wastefulness, outmodedness, and alternative productivities.

The next section maps how the culture wars in the United States in the 1980s and 1990s were inflamed by the work of artists like Robert Mapplethorpe and Andres Serrano, coming to a tee in a controversy surrounding the North American performance artist Ron Athey's *4 Scenes in a Harsh Life* (1993–6). The AIDS crisis underpinned much of the ire of Republican politicians and commentators at the time, including Buchanan and Helms, although their homophobia was thinly veiled in debates that purported to be about the funding of artworks deemed to be in some way transgressive. Arts funding came to be viewed as a form of decadent and immoral profligacy, and queer artists, especially, were derided as vectors transmitting both moral corruption, and a deadly disease. This makes the US culture wars in the 1990s an especially instructive example for appreciating how the phantasmatic qualities of a culture war, in which issues emerge from and largely circulate within political, media, and civic circles, can have real-world consequences. Value-laden representations of real-world concerns shape the societies in which we live, and who gets to thrive – and in some cases survive – within them.

The section after that then turns to a statue depicting Santa Claus by Paul McCarthy in the city of Rotterdam, which was installed in 2008, seven years after it was initially commissioned by the municipality following public outcry about the fact that Santa appeared to be holding a gigantic butt plug in his hand. Inevitably, debates concerning freedom of artistic expression and the appropriateness of using public funds to subsidize the work came into play after the 2008 financial crash wreaked havoc on the economy. This leads into a discussion of a performance by the Dutch theatre company Wunderbaum, who took McCarthy's cause célèbre as a point of departure for their 2010 performance *Looking for Paul*, especially the ways in which Dutch politicians were citing North American funding models as a solution to the erosion of public subsidy in their own country. Juxtaposing a reductive and austere aesthetic in the performance's first two sections, with a McCarthy-esque abomination in the final scene, *Looking for Paul* invites us to reflect on decadence not merely as that which might be suffered as a slur, but as that which anticipates a future beyond utility and the purely economic.

The final section then turns to speeches and sources that have informed a resurgent culture war in the UK, including Dowden's condemnation of 'woke ideology' as 'a dangerous form of decadence'. I will also be considering an example that epitomized the Conservative Party's approach to cultural and educational policy at the dawn of the 2020s: a controversial campaign designed to deter young people from pursuing a career in the arts by championing the prospects and possibilities of a career in cyber. In response, I make a case *for* the relative uselessness and inessentiality of the study and practice of art and performance. While charged with negative valences, making or experiencing 'inessential' and 'useless' art and performance takes on vital importance in societies that know the price of everything and the value of nothing, and that co-opt productivity in the service of divisive and debilitating forms of economic recovery and growth. This does indeed imbue decadence with a kind of 'danger' by encouraging audiences to confront a reductive economic logic that reduces things, people, and practices to their utility and economic value – but a danger we would do well to welcome.

'We should not subsidize decadence': Ron Athey

This section looks at how the culture wars in the United States in the 1980s and 1990s spilled from headlines in local newspapers to debate on the floor of the Senate, in which a rhetoric of decadence, decline, and degeneracy was deployed in an attempt to quash freedom of expression in art and performance, as well as the public visibility of queer artists and performers. Numerous commentators have explained how debates purporting to be about freedom of expression at the time were really about justifying and advancing economic reforms that would do away with arts subsidy.[4] However, the elision between these two poles of the culture wars – freedom of expression, and economic reform – are intimately linked by a rhetoric that consistently returns to decadence and related concepts, like uselessness, wastefulness, and degeneracy. For Republican critics of publicly subsidized art during the culture wars of the 1990s, wasting public money on decadent art made by decadent artists risked laying a society to waste. Appeals to 'decency' in the face of challenges to conservative mores threatened more than the viability of staging challenging ideas and representations; it targeted the legitimacy of queerness as a 'decadent' orientation – in other words, a profoundly *illiberal* reaction to self-determination and freedom of personal and cultural expression.

The culture wars have been bubbling away in the United States at least since the 1960s,[5] although two events in the twilight years of the twentieth century turned a Republican bugbear into a national controversy: Republican Senator Alfonse D'Amato ripping up an exhibition catalogue depicting Andres Serrano's notorious photograph *Piss Christ* (1987) on the floor of the Senate on 18 May 1989, and a retrospective exhibition of works by the photographer Robert Mapplethorpe, *The Perfect Moment*, which opened in Philadelphia in 1988, and was set to tour cites across the United States, including Chicago, Washington DC, Hartford, Berkeley, Cincinnati, and Boston the following year. Serrano's photograph depicted Christ on a plastic crucifix immersed in a vial of the artist's urine, which was doomed to raise the hackles of conservative Christians, but the majority of the photographs in Mapplethorpe's exhibition were striking but nonetheless fairly innocuous portraits, floral compositions, and nudes in a Grecian-sculptural style. However, it also included two adolescent nudes and five highly stylized photographs depicting exposed penises and men in S&M bondage. Furore around the alleged indecency of these photographs prompted the Corcoran Gallery in Washington DC to retract its commitment to present Mapplethorpe's exhibition on 13 June 1989 – three months after his death from AIDS-related illness – although it went ahead anyway, as the nearby

Washington Project for the Arts took it on at short notice. Events came to a tee in 1990 when a grand jury issued two criminal indictments against the Cincinnati Contemporary Arts Center (CAC), and another two against the CAC's director, Dennis Barrie, 'for pandering obscenity' – although Barrie and the CAC were acquitted on 5 October 1990, the prosecution unable to convince a jury that the exhibition was artless.[6]

Patrick Buchanan, a Republican columnist, politician, and spokesperson for the evangelical Right, was not amused. 'We should not subsidize decadence', he said, in a phrase that cast a shadow over Republican debate and policy in the years ahead.[7] Buchanan's usage of the word 'decadence' is a far cry from the 'beautiful decadence' that others found in Mapplethorpe's exhibition.[8] For Buchanan, 'decadence' meant corruption. Figurations of the arts as a corrupting influence on society can be traced back to Plato, but Buchanan is not concerned with metaphysical or epistemological takes on the negative effects of the arts; his take on their decadence owes more to Puritan pamphleteers of the early modern period, who viewed the arts – and especially theatre – as a contagious entity capable of spreading moral corruption.[9]

Decadence has rhetorical power, particularly its negative valences – as profligate, useless, or perverse – and hard-line conservatives like Buchanan knew how to exploit these connotations in condemning challenges to the more austere tastes and values held by conservative Christians. Buchanan was also aware of how easily those valences could be merged by drawing the 'perversity' of artistic practices by queer and/or progressive artists into dialogue with the supposed profligacy of spending public money on 'useless' artworks (Mapplethorpe's exhibition was partially funded by a $30,000 grant from the NEA, and Serrano's work received $15,000 in funding from the Southeastern Center for Contemporary Art in Winston-Salem, North Carolina, which was the beneficiary of a $75,000 grant from the NEA).

Buchanan's condemnation of Mapplethorpe's 'subsidize[d] decadence' conjures a dark history, particularly his call to expurgate 'cultural trash [. . .]. Just as a poisoned land will yield up poisonous fruits, so a polluted culture, left to fester and stink, can destroy a nation's soul'.[10] Adolf Hitler also condemned the 'cultural decadence' of artists who embraced transgression and experimentation in their work,[11] although his agenda was not Christian. Instead of seeking to silence the artists (although many were murdered by the Nazis), the Nazi Minister of Propaganda Joseph Goebbels ridiculed them by employing Adolf Ziegler to curate an exhibition of confiscated 'Entartete Kunst' ('Degenerate Art'), presented in Munich in 1937, that mocked the supposed primitivism, madness, and childishness of modernist and avant-garde work by artists including Max Beckmann, Otto Dix, Vincent van Gogh,

Henri Matisse, and Pablo Picasso, among many others – including a room dedicated to Jewish artists. Flagging the cost of these works was deemed 'particularly relevant for items purchased during the Weimar Republic years, still fresh in the minds of all Germans. While the average German had struggled to put food in their mouths during the Great Depression, the "artist elite" spent millions buying the works now on display and mocked for their amateurishness and crudity'.[12]

For the literary and cultural historian Michael St. John, '[i]t is difficult to imagine a more politicized definition of decadence than that attempted in the *Entartete Kunst* exhibition. It is also difficult to imagine a more powerful warning of the dangers involved in defining anyone or anything as decadent for overtly political reasons'.[13] However, it is equally the case that '[t]he charge of decadence is now and has always been a potent weapon in the hands of political élites',[14] which makes the staging of a similar event only a few decades later less surprising, although no less shocking.

As the art and literature scholar Linda S. Kauffman records, Republican Congressman Robert Dornan sponsored an exhibition of 'degenerate art' at the Rayburn Building in Washington DC on 27 June 1995, which was organized by The Christian Action Network (CAN), and was explicitly intended to mock and demean the 'unnatural' work of artists sponsored by the NEA.[15] It was not just their work that was called into question; queerness was vilified in the darkest years of the AIDS crisis. The choice of a death certificate was a particularly reprehensible frame for CAN to use when handing flyers to passers-by outside of the exhibition:

> *Decedent's name:* NEA. *Sex:* Anything unnatural. *Father's Name:* Lyndon Johnson. *Mother's Name:* Jane Alexander. *Decedent's occupation:* Attacking religion, tradition, morality. Funding left-wing causes. Promoting homosexuality. Lying to the media and Congress about its activities. *Cause of death:* using taxpayer funds to depict Christ as homosexual, a drug addict, and a child molester.[16]

Dornan and CAN's attempt to curtail the activities of the NEA for sponsoring 'anything unnatural' chimed with Buchanan's mission. As Buchanan put it in a speech delivered at the 1992 Republican National Convention in Houston, a war 'for the soul of America' was at stake,[17] with roots stretching back to the 1960s (and their 'beat' precedents in the 1950s) when New Left activists and agitators, as well as artists and community leaders, were innovating 'a new America, a nation more open to new peoples, new ideas, new norms, and new, if conflicting, articulations of America itself'.[18] In its wake, those values and principles that critics of the New Left believed were intrinsic to the greatness of America (in short, those aligned with conservative Christian institutions, traditions, and beliefs, as well as hard work) were seen to be at risk of degenerating into a state of moral anarchy.[19] As the legal scholar and judge Robert Bork put it, '[t]he rough beast of decadence, a long time in gestation, having reached its maturity in the last three decades, now sends us slouching towards our new home, not Bethlehem but Gomorrah'.[20] For moral crusaders like Buchanan and Bork, the roar of this 'rough beast of decadence' was getting louder by the day, *necessitating* an antediluvian agenda fit for combatting, and reversing, the social and political gains made by liberals and the radical and progressive Left in the 1960s. This is also what defines Buchanan's *paleo*conservatism, with the prefix implying (for its advocates) a return to 'timeless' conservatism untainted by twentieth-century progressivism, and (for its detractors) a regressive, puritanical traditionalism shaped by a declinist view of society.

Alongside Buchanan, one of the most important Republican voices in the culture wars at the time was the Republican Senator Jesse Helms, who spearheaded attacks on the NEA's role in promoting 'cultural decadence' after CAN, and a related organization, the American Family Association, sent out a 'declaration of war' to key political figures – including Helms, who they saw as a potential ally.[21] Like Buchanan, Helms was profoundly concerned by anti-establishment politics and sexual and social experimentation. He opposed Civil Rights legislation, defended the constitutional rights of the Klu Klux Klan to march against racial desegregation, mocked feminists, and lambasted gay men.[22] As Susan Sontag has pointed out, in their dealing with metaphors of punitive judgement and a 'plague' of moral bankruptcy, '[p]rofessional fulminators' like Buchannan and Helms connected the negative connotations of a 'decadent' society with 'unnatural' sexualities, gender roles, freedom of expression and social liberties.[23] Their culture war was waged to preserve, not to innovate, conjoining notions of decadence and degeneracy with what many would regard as their antitheses: which is to say, social, cultural, and political progress. And their battleground was not just the idea of America, but the human body – how it looked, what it did, who it loved – including the spectacle of the *performing* body.

For Helms, the performing body's occupation of a space shared with unassuming audience members exposed the general public to contagious beliefs and practices that were, in his eyes, dangerously decadent. Alongside Mapplethorpe, he reserved some of his staunchest criticism for the performance maker Ron Athey, who binds together the imagery and practices revered by political conservatives and conservative Christians with the objects of their opprobrium: namely, queerness, and a rejection of reproductive futurism (defined by Lee Edelman as the hegemonic affirmation of heteronormativity and the prescriptive attachment of hope to the rearing of children).[24] Ron Athey and Company's ritualistic and partly autobiographical 'Torture Trilogy' is a case in point. Comprised of *Martyrs & Saints* (1992–3), *4 Scenes in a Harsh Life* (1993–6) and *Deliverance* (1995–7), it built on performances that Athey had been developing at Club Fuck!, a weekly Los Angeles club night that ran from 1989 until it was closed by the LAPD's Vice Division in 1993, and featured regular collaborators Divinity P. Fudge (Darryl Carlton), Pigpen (Stosh Filia), and Julie Tolentino, among others associated with the S&M and queer club circuits. The presentation of vignettes from *4 Scenes* in a truncated version called *Excerpted Rites Transformation* (1994) is particularly significant in the history of the culture wars, as it is the performance that prompted Athey to be seen as a dangerous renegade in the eyes of a wider public than was previously the case.[25] It is also the piece that led to Athey's being unofficially blacklisted by the North American arts establishment (although not by the club venues in which he cut his teeth), having been accused, erroneously, of exposing audiences to his own HIV-positive blood in a scene that Athey dubs the 'Human Printing Press'.[26]

Excerpted Rites was presented at Patrick's Cabaret in Minneapolis on 5 March 1994, catapulting Athey from the pages of niche gay and punk magazines into the public eye, largely because it received a measly $150 in sponsorship from the publicly funded Walker Arts Center.[27] However, documentation of an earlier version presented at the L. A. Center Theater on 15 October 1993 is most readily available online.[28] In it, we find Black body-modification artist and drag performer Divinity P. Fudge straddling a weight-lifting seat with their naked back to the audience. Athey leans over so as to apply betadine to their skin through gloved hands, before taking out a scalpel and making careful but firm incisions into Divinity's flesh (Divinity's having consented to this ritual, along with their longstanding friendship with Athey, must be taken into account when considering the sexual and racial ethics of masochistic submission and its depiction in performance, as well as congruence with the leather scenes that contextualize and inform the work). The hiss, hum, and whir of industrial music can be heard as Athey dabs paper towels over the markings, each one pegged to a clothesline, and winched over the heads of the audience. This is not the only example of blood-letting in the piece; several of the performers end up pierced, marked or scarred in some form or another, including Athey, who in one scene becomes a St. Sebastian figure (key throughout his *oeuvre*) with a punctured forehead and hypodermic needles inserted up his arm in reference to his heroin addiction in the 1980s, although this particular 'martyrdom' occurred at some distance from the audience. It was the audience's proximity to the blood-blotted sheets in the 'Human Printing Press' that attracted the most vitriol.

AIDS serves more as a contextual element than a focus for the 'Human Printing Press', although it is explicitly addressed in a later scene that pays homage to the death of Athey's friend Butch by juxtaposing pensive reflections on queer kinship with loud, orgiastic revelry. But the very presence of blood – specifically the blood of a gay man – was enough to elicit a rationale for the assessment of risk from a sponsor. In a letter sent to the progressive Democratic Senator Paul Wellstone, the governing board of the Walker Arts Center noted that they 'took all appropriate precautions as developed by the U.S. Centers for Disease Control and provided to the Walker by the Minnesota AIDS Project. The Minnesota Department of Health has publicly concurred that appropriate precautions were taken [having also] confirmed this position'.[29] This was not enough to appease those critical of the very idea of such a work receiving public funding, however slight, adding fuel to a fire that was intended to undermine the NEA as an institution. The *Minneapolis Star Tribune* published a report on its front page that 'amplified the unfounded claim that Athey's performance put Walker audiences at risk of contracting HIV', the Southern Baptist Minister Pat Robertson commissioned posters of Athey as the antichrist, while a supposedly progressive gay magazine, nervous about their status in light of the ongoing AIDS crisis, shunned support.[30] Athey became a public enemy, as well as a scapegoat in a long-standing campaign to scrap the public funding of art in America.

The strange marriage of a neoliberal attack on public subsidy and values associated with the Christian Right came to a head in the summer of 1994, when Helms proposed to Congress that:

> none of the funds made [. . .] to the National Endowment for the Arts may be used by the Endowment, or by any other recipient of such funds, to support, reward, or award financial assistance to any activity or work involving:
> (a) human mutilation or invasive bodily procedures on human beings dead or alive; or
> (b) the drawing or letting of blood.[31]

This was not the first time that Helms sought to pass a decency clause. Amendment No. 991, the so-called 'Helms Amendment', was tabled on 7 October 1989 in response to the controversy surrounding Mapplethorpe's *The Perfect Moment* – a month after Helms penned an article condemning the 'decadence' of artistic freedom.[32] The amendment proposed '[t]o prohibit the use of funds to promote, disseminate, or produce materials that are obscene or depict, in an offensive way, sexual or excretory activities or organs'.[33] Both the 1990 and 1994 amendments were defeated, but enough pressure was applied to ensure a 2 per cent reduction in the NEA's budget (equivalent to $3.4 million), as well as the approval of a vaguely worded decency clause that was controversially enforced to rescind individual artist grants in the mid-1990s (most notoriously with the NEA Four).[34]

Somewhat ironically, the censorship that Helms pursued so vehemently ended up ensuring that the work of Athey, Mapplethorpe, and others was widely reproduced and publicized, offering a platform that may have remained relatively marginal were it not for Helms's intervention (particularly in Athey's case). Helms and his peers were on a warpath opposing 'disgusting, insulting, revolting garbage produced by obviously sick minds'.[35] And not just sick minds. In what reads like a pastiche of Max Nordau's diatribe, *Degeneration* (*Entartung*, 1892), Helms displaced HIV infection from the bodies of artists suffering or dying from the disease to the body of works that they produced, which risked contaminating 'an otherwise clean American culture'.[36] Otherwise put, obscene art was made by artists who indulged obscene desires, and both warranted eradication.

For Helms, queer subcultural pleasures were synonymous with decadence and degeneracy. He rejected the legitimacy of Athey's work as 'art', in a mode reminiscent of the criminal indictments raised against the CAC and Dennis Barrie in 1990, viewing it instead as a symptom of sickness produced by 'homosexual or otherwise perverse mentalities'. But '[t]he broader issue', for Helms,

> is the sober realization that for the past two decades, an unmistakable decadence has saturated American society. A furious assault on the traditional sensibilities of the American people has taken its toll. So many have become afraid to stand up and declare the difference between right and wrong, what is ugly and what is destructive and what is noble and what is degrading. No wonder [. . .] there has been a cultural breakdown.[37]

Helms was not alone in specifying decadence as a scourge in want of purgation, as the commentaries by Buchanan and Bork cited earlier go some way towards illustrating. Robertson also condemned 'the moral decadence that has invaded the heart of America' when the Mapplethorpe controversy was unfolding in 1989.[38] However, what is worth emphasizing in Helms's speech is how explicitly he connects decadence to 'homosexual or otherwise perverse mentalities'. The threat of what queer theorist Tim Dean calls 'viral consanguinity' was very real for Helms, only for him it was not practised as 'a new, experimental form of (gay) kinship that turns "strangers into relatives"'. Instead, the threat of a stranger becoming an unwelcome relative through contagion formed part of a 'viral dramaturgy'.³⁹ As Athey says of the furore surrounding *4 Scenes*, '[w]hat it came down to was the polemic of blood in that minute – the belief that all blood is HIV-positive; that, against science, it could be airborne'.⁴⁰

Decadence clearly had a part to play in the critical reception of Athey's work by the Christian Right, who came to see it as symptomatic of cultural decline, but Athey also stages his own attack on the 'decadence' of a reified moral code and stagnant institutions, especially monogamous marriage, reproductive futurism, and the Church. The work itself *does* make use of an aesthetic that appeals to a decadent sensibility, so long as decadence is understood as a crafted or refined taste for uncommon desires and ways of being and seeing – for instance, in Athey's queering of hagiographic imagery. The work is not simply decadent because of its supposed participation in cultural breakdown, then; it is decadent because of its conscious crafting of an uncommon sensibility. It is also decadent in its spectacular refusal of reproductive futurism, and a conventionally productive or reproductive expenditure of energy.

Athey's embrace of physical intensity and excess stage a clear counterpoint to the behavioural and moral austerity of the Christian Right. The word 'austerity' implies severity, strictness, and difficulty, all of which require discipline. Athey's work, too, explores multiple kinds of severity, strictness, and discipline (S&M, the endurance of pain, the crafting of performance), but of a kind that does away with reserved expenditure – not of money, but energy. Athey's *4 Scenes* is profligate, but not because of the $150 it received indirectly in state subsidy. It is profligate in the excesses and extremities that it stages in a mode reminiscent of that celebrated by George Bataille in *The Accursed Share: An Essay on General Economy* (1949), which I will be returning to in the next section. It is this specific coding of profligacy as a spectacular, exhausting, and profoundly creative expenditure of energy that lends the performance's physicality a decadent edge.

Art, outrage, and austerity: Paul McCarthy and Wunderbaum

The scandal surrounding Athey's work in the 1990s goes some way towards illuminating the political opportunism that tends to accompany the waging of a culture war, including the implementation of economic and cultural policies with far-reaching consequences for the practice and study of art and performance, as well as the ability for minorities to express themselves freely and openly. However, the contemporary relevance of this example outside of the United States is limited by the centrality of religion in the US context. Religion can play an important role in how culture wars unfold – the Catholic Church was dubbed 'New York's hottest club' in a controversial article for the *New York Times* exploring decadence and the culture wars that was published in August 2022[41] – but in culture wars in other countries, particularly in Western Europe, religion is not nearly as influential as the size and shape of the economy, for instance, or the social relevance of a practice or pursuit. In the wake of the 2008 financial crash, especially, the allocation of diminished public wealth formed a key battleground in debates over economic policy and in the cultural arena, and it is this context that pulls focus in this section.

The Los Angeles-based visual artist Paul McCarthy is no stranger to controversy. His films and installations divide opinion, often prompting debate about the ethics of subsidizing 'perverse' or 'useless' artworks. Examples can be found in a series of publicly funded artworks incorporating ribbed, cylindrical objects that tend to be referenced as trees in titles and descriptions, but that more closely resemble enormous butt plugs. These include: a gigantic bright green inflatable work that popped up, briefly, in the Place Vendôme in Paris in October 2014 (despite the protests and vandalism that led to its deflation only two days after its installation, it apparently led to a surge in Parisian butt plug sales);[42] a series of inflatables installed in Antwerp's Middelheim sculpture park and Utrecht's Botanical Gardens; and a piece called *Santa Claus* that was commissioned by the city of Rotterdam in 2001. *Santa Claus* was intended to stand in Rotterdam's Schouwburgplein (Theatre Square), although it was never installed there because it was deemed offensive by local residents. It took another seven years before the sculpture found a permanent home in Eendrachtsplein on 28 November 2008, after public outcry prevented its installation in the city's Museumpark and main shopping street.

At first glance, *Santa Claus* looks innocent enough: a large bronze sculpture of St. Nicholas holding a bell in one hand, and something that could be a rounded pine tree in the other hand, but the tree's features make it look a lot more like an enormous butt plug, giving it the nickname Kabouter Buttplug, or 'The Gnome Butt Plug'. The timing of its permanent installation is significant, as it coincided with the 2008 global financial crash, and the introduction of austerity measures by the Dutch government. In this context, the Gnome entered into debates not just about freedom of artistic expression, but the sustainability of public arts funding at a point in time when dominant strains of mainstream discourse insisted that there were limited funds to distribute. It became a fulcrum for debate about aesthetic and moral value, as well as the extent to which public expenditure on a 'perverse' sculpture with no clear use could be at all justified when economic sectors were understood to be at risk.

The Dutch theatre company Wunderbaum took the controversy surrounding McCarthy's sculpture as source material for their 2010 performance *Looking for Paul*, which ruminates on the ways in which right-wing politicians in Holland were framing the American funding system as a favourable alternative to European models of state subsidy at the time. What drew me to this performance is its juxtaposition of an austere aesthetic consisting of little more than the reading out of emails documenting the company's relationship to McCarthy's source material with an excessively messy embrace of abjection and disgust towards the end, in which potentially useful things – a pencil, a toilet, and a bed – are steered towards explicitly unproductive and debauched ends, as if imagined by McCarthy's critics in the delirious heights of a fever dream. This lends the performance a decadent quality that references and pastiches the castigation of art as degenerate or extravagant, inviting reflection on how competing understandings of decadence rely upon one another for meaning. It also invites reflection on what decadence and related concepts and practices can reveal about the prejudices of those who use these terms. What, then, can the cultural politics of decadence tell us about freedom of expression, how forms and avenues of expenditure come to be seen as necessary or dispensable, and how art and performance come to be seen as useless and inessential?

Wunderbaum has been working out of Rotterdam, Jena and Milan since 2001, and is comprised of five devising performers – Walter Bart, Wine Dierickx, Matijs Jansen, Maartje Remmers, and Marleen Scholten – and one scenographer, Maarten van Otterdijk. Text plays a central role in the company's practice, although experimentation with the dramaturgical and scenographic composition of theatre is routinely pulled to the foreground. They regularly work with non-professional actors, and explore the ambiguities of 'reality' and 'authenticity'. Sometimes – as with their long-term project, The New Forest (2013–16), which was comprised of theatre events, discursive forums, and a film – their exploration of ambiguous realities aligns with what performance scholar Tony Perucci calls 'reality friction': 'political and aesthetic interventions that do not simply blur the boundary of theatre and "the real," but rather alternatively mark themselves as specifically being either "theatre" or "real".'[43] But other performances by the company sublimate fiction without any attempt to reveal contrivance. *Looking for Paul* is an example, which was originally devised in 2010 as part of a three-week residency at California Institute of the Arts, LA, before going on to win a Total Theatre Award at the 2014 Edinburgh Fringe Festival. The audience is led to believe that it was made with and inspired by Inez van Dam: a bookstore owner living in Rotterdam, who is actually played by company member Maartje Remmers. The performance and production credits present Inez, quite convincingly, as a real person, extending the hinterland between reality and fictionalization that cuts across the representational strategies employed throughout. They also involved the producer and performer John Malpede, in one iteration, and the cultural ambassador and performer Daniel Frankl, in another, who played himself when it went on tour (this is the version that I will be commenting on in what follows).

The performance is split into three sections. The first takes the form of a lecture by Inez, who presents an endearingly earnest introduction to the city of Rotterdam illustrated by a Powerpoint presentation filled with selfies of major and less salubrious landmarks. The presentation reaches a climax when we learn that the Kabouter Buttplug – which she inadvertently helped to fund as a Dutch taxpayer – is situated directly opposite her bookshop, where she lives and works in the flat above (there is actually a bookshop there called Van Gennep, but store worker John van Tiggelen lived above it at the time, and apparently quite liked the statue).[44] After a chance encounter in a pub with Bart, Inez is promised the chance to hold McCarthy to account in Los Angeles, his home city, by participating in a performance that would out him as an irresponsible fraud. The performance's much longer second section then moves on to document creative differences that beset the company's devising process and Inez's involvement within it, or so we are led to believe, as they found themselves struggling with the responsibility of putting their $20,000 funding to good use, which was secured from the City of Los Angeles Department of Cultural Affairs' Cultural Exchange International Program, and the Foundation for Dutch Artists Abroad. This part of the performance features nothing more than the company members, plus Inez and Frankl, sitting down on a row of chairs reading emails sent to one another and to their producers over the course of the creative process. There's an austerity to it, stripping back the theatrical machine, with the company failing to fulfil their obligations to be productive as they deteriorate in fits of artistic in-fighting. Bart is determined to seek the involvement of McCarthy, Frankl is worried about Bart's idol worship, Jansen wants to capitalize on their European avant-garde credentials, Scholten demeans Inez and her 'provincial' story, and Inez gradually realizes that the group has no intention of confronting an artist they clearly admire. What emerges is a scathing attack on censorship, a critical reflection on the irony of travelling to America to make work about arts funding in Holland, and a playful challenge to the piety of artists who express social commitments while exploiting intended beneficiaries, poking fun at the hypocrisy of their own conspicuous consumption in LA while they're at it.

The performance's final section is an homage to McCarthy that disrupts the austereness of the preceding scenes. Stagehands remove the chairs and microphones to reveal a crude set: little more than a bed, projection screens, and a toilet contained within scaffolding. Jansen enters wearing a long white shirt, stuffed rubber gloves with grotesquely elongated fingers, and a pair of enormous ears that protrude from a blonde wig – all drawn from McCarthy's video performances. Jansen heads for the toilet, apparently to defecate, which he then 'cleans' with a realistically shit-like substance. Scholten stumbles onto the stage, looking inebriated and dousing herself in alcohol, and drags Inez – wearing pigtails and a McCarthy-esque mask – by means of a leash. Finally, Frankl, dressed as a chef, wheels in a trolley carrying ketchup, mayonnaise, chocolate sauce and a bowl of spaghetti (all McCarthy staples), semi-methodically squirting or flinging each about the stage, or stuffing them into pants. Jansen smothers his surroundings with shit before thrusting a giant red pencil into the toilet, throwing the toilet onto the bed, and mock-fucking its bowl. By this point the stage has become a noxious site of utter degradation: noses pressed against sodden backsides, and bodies stumbling in a dazed stupor (Figure 5.1).

The final section is the most relevant to the study of decadent aesthetics, but its political resonances are incomprehensible without the preceding scenes, which ruminate on the US culture wars and the introduction of

Figure 5.1 Wunderbaum and camera team, *Looking for Paul* (2010). REDCAT, LA. Photo: Steven A. Gunther.

austerity measures in Holland. In one of the email exchanges read aloud in the second section, Frankl explains how he understands the former:

> I'm kinda worried how the audience will receive a bunch of fancy Europeans telling us [that our funding system is] wrong. [. . .] We ended up getting national arts funding before we put a man on the moon. And things went okay until the Reagan Republicans totally freaked out when they found out they funded Mapplethorpe's photo of the bullwhip stuck in his ass [. . .]. It seems like a better idea that you can learn how we got fucked in our country, and then try to prevent it in your own.

He builds up to this passage by suggesting that the company explore something more tasteful and less antagonistic towards McCarthy – like Pina Bausch, he says – letting slip his own fetishization of 'fancy Europeans'. He also expresses frustration at the inability of the company to make progress, revealing his expectations around what constitutes 'productive' creativity, which is to say, a demonstrably productive process accountable to its backers. What he worries about is indolence, and potentially offensive transgression.

One of the most important issues that the show explores centres on the legitimacy of a nation spending €180,000 on McCarthy's statue that was seen by some to offer limited benefit to the local community. Debates over the legitimacy and value of state support for the arts were exacerbated after the 2008 global financial crash, the Eurozone crisis – which prompted the *New York Times* columnist and author Ross Douthat to describe the European Union as 'a case study in decadence itself'[45] – and the ascendency of the pro-business and right-wing People's Party for Freedom and Democracy (Volkspartij voor Vrijheid en Democratie, VVD), which took control of a coalitional cabinet in 2010 under the leadership of Mark Rutte. The Netherlands became a vocal advocate of austerity across Europe under Rutte's leadership, which was struggling to decrease the size of its national debt despite the introduction of tax increases that disproportionately affected lower-income groups already encumbered with rising levels of unemployment, poverty, inflation, and personal debt. Unsurprisingly, the arts were targeted in the austerity programme. On 10 June 2011, the Dutch state secretary for Culture, Halbe Zijlstra, sent a letter to arts and cultural organizations based throughout the Netherlands titled 'Meer dan kwaliteit: een nieuwe visie op cultuurbeleid' ('More than Quality: A New Vision on Cultural Policy'), which announced plans for a €200 million funding cut, including a 50 per cent cut to stipends and working grants for artists, with the performing arts being particularly badly hit.[46]

In an open letter titled 'A New Dark Age for Dutch Culture' (2011), leading Dutch artists and curators explain how Zijlstra and the coalition he served regarded 'traditional art [as] merely the superfluous ornamentation of a society. Contemporary art is labelled as alienating, and even, although no one actually says it out loud, as "degenerate art".[47] In other words, art – and artists – were shifted into a pejoratively decadent dimension, helped along by their being pitched as anti-productivist drains on an ailing economy. The far-right leader of the Party for Freedom (Partij voor de Vrijheid), Geert Wilders, had previously argued that '"hardworking Dutch citizens" should not have to facilitate the needs of artists who, in practicing their subsidized or "left-wing" hobby, feign work thanks to state injections'.[48] Wilders's attempt to undermine not just the viability but the legitimacy of work in the arts *as work* might have been dismissed as the ranting of an extremist were it not for the Party for Freedom's political gains at the time – they came third in the 2010 election – and Zijlstra's support of Wilders's comments. Also, when there seems to be no alternative to austerity, it is easier to convince a beleaguered public – not least those working in manual, low-paid, and/or precarious jobs – that practices and livelihoods not explicitly bound to productivity enhancement are expendable, or parasitic: decadent expenditure to fund decadent lifestyles. (There are resonances here with the essays of the modernist architect Adolf Loos, who argued against ornamentation in favour of a crafted object's function; he understood 'healthy' art to be the consequence of efficient creative means, cost-effectiveness, utility, and aesthetic austerity).[49]

Looking for Paul engages with the view that arts funding can read as profligacy when publicly funded artworks antagonize a community's 'austere' tastes, despite the economic contributions of the cultural industries to GDP, which ought to appeal to those of a productivist mindset. However, it also challenges the legitimacy of that view, opening out to the oppositional potential of a decadence that revels in revolting acts of physical expenditure. For instance, the gigantic pencil thrust into the bowl of a toilet, aside from being a nod to McCarthy's video performances,[50] magnifies the perceived uselessness of artistic endeavour, lampooning perceptions of contemporary art as the pastime of artists suffering from an 'infantile disorder'.[51] To borrow from the art critic and curator Ralph Rugoff, we might see this as a nod to McCarthy's Rabelaisian 'theatre of regression', which is a somewhat decadent turn of phrase.[52] In the context of a performance about arts funding, the final scene of *Looking for Paul* also lampoons perspectives that view public support for the arts as wasteful, and artistic practice as a pastime unfit for serious adults. Wunderbaum appropriates and inverts the negative valences of decadence as profligacy, uselessness, or perversity, then, revelling in the cultural, social, and economic ruination of which they and McCarthy stand accused.

Throughout this book I have been making recourse to a definition of the decadent sensibility furnished by the literature scholar David Weir, who defines it as 'a subjective principle [. . .] more a matter of sensibility than rationality [. . .] not a "common sense" but something more refined, an uncommon sense' that delights in disgust, or 'in things that people who have normal taste react to with revulsion'.[53] This is a helpful way of thinking about how the performance's cabal of McCarthy-esque characters interact with their environments, although I suspect Weir would be suspicious of the work's deliberate lack of refinement. Nonetheless, the performers delight in human and culinary waste, cultivating a 'kalliphobic' uncommon sense akin to McCarthy's own. The art critic Arthur C. Danto describes 'kalliphobia' as a distaste for the conventionally beautiful,[54] and it is the cultivation of a taste for the distasteful that connects most clearly with Weir's reading of the decadent sensibility.

The decadence of an uncommon sense in the last scene of *Looking for Paul* is not simply linked to messy wastefulness, or excess per se. Physical energy and materials are expended in ways that are unproductive in an economic sense, but tremendously productive in a creative sense that eludes or subverts utility and instrumentality, *luxuriating* in waste and wastefulness. As with work by Athey, this puts me in mind of Bataille's account of the poverty of organisms invested in the myth of perpetual growth. 'Minds accustomed to seeing the development of productive forces as the ideal end of activity', he writes, 'refuse to recognize that energy, which constitutes wealth, must ultimately be spent lavishly (without return)'.[55] What ensues affirms dissipation, and an entropic use of physical and material resources, 'sending [them] up in smoke' in ways that 'go against judgments that form the basis of a rational economy'.[56]

There are several factors that lend this performance to decadence, then. First, the work riffs on the condemnation of art and the subsidization of art as a form of decadent profligacy. In this instance, 'decadence' is to be understood in a two-dimensional sense of that word, in which the concept is hollowed as a generic term referring to anything deemed wasteful or useless, especially with regard to the 'failure' of an occupation or the work of an artist to contribute to economic recovery and growth. Second, the work parodies perceptions of artists as indolent slackers unfit for purpose in a society oriented around intensified productivity. Third, *Looking for Paul* draws on the castigation of particular kinds of artwork not merely as useless, but distasteful – and it is here that the more rounded connotations of decadence can be glimpsed. Although the point of departure for the performance was the offensiveness provoked by McCarthy's statue in the eyes of its critics, who read the work as a distasteful affront to their moral and aesthetic sensibility, the final scene luxuriates in a kalliphobic uncommon sense that delights in disgust. Rather than transcending the everyday, which characterized arguments in support of the intrinsic value of art in the nineteenth and early twentieth centuries,[57] Wunderbaum explore boundaries of taste and the shaping of values. They deliberately cite these boundaries – concerning 'good' taste, for instance, or 'acceptable' behaviour – in order to breach them. Theirs is an art of transgression, not transcendence. Hence, the ways in which *Looking for Paul* stages the cultural politics of decadence need to be read across these three areas – economic, ethical (in the sense of adhering to or falling away from a productivist ethos), and aesthetic – as well as the specific vectors in which the decadent imagination is performed and transmitted, be it in the media, public debate, or on a stage.

As the playwright and theatre scholar Dan Rebellato observes, 'the enjoyment of what other people's bodies can do [in performance] is an excitingly decadent thought. There's a kind of politics in that, as well; it's a glimpse of a world beyond the purely economic'.[58] Wunderbaum enables us to catch a glimpse of this world, although, like the process of its making, that 'glimpse' (deliberately) fails to materialize into a clearly packaged message. *Looking for Paul* stages a creative act without a goal, an act untethered from the instrumentalization of productivity and the utility of creative endeavour. It is a spectacularly useless performance that seems unable to move much beyond the negative and hollow valences of decadence that it might otherwise critique, despite its attempt to share and propagate a taste for the distasteful. There is therefore a need to dig deeper into this 'uselessness', and the sending of forms of creative productivity that fall and flow away from productivism 'up in smoke'. This is because the debates that this performance references and stages are rearing their head again in a fresh culture war that has pulled 'decadence' into the foreground even more explicitly, inviting closer examination of what the risks and potential value of the cultural politics of decadence might be in the twenty-first century – as the next section explores.

'A dangerous form of decadence': The war on woke

On 21 January 2021, the UK government published a letter to the Office for Students, England's Higher Education regulator, outlining funding guidance for the 2021–2 financial year. The letter proposed to cut spending for non-prioritized subjects by 50 per cent, with further reductions in future years, redistributing savings to 'high-value subjects that support the NHS

[National Health Service] and wider healthcare policy, high-cost STEM [Science, Technology, Engineering and Maths] subjects and/or specific labour market needs' (specifically medicine, pharmacology, dentistry, nursing, veterinary science, engineering, and IT).[59] These cuts were part of an attempt to effect a wider shift in how different lines of work were understood to be useful or useless, economically viable or wasteful, during the coronavirus pandemic, the implication being that some subjects and occupations fail to offer meaningful social or economic benefit – including (and especially) those that fall under the umbrella of the arts, humanities, and social sciences.

The proposals were shored up in February 2022 when a policy consultation was proposed in response to the Post-18 Education and Funding Review led by Philip Augar (a former investment banker who has also written books on banking, capitalism, and crisis). The consultation document makes over one hundred references to the 'quality' of course provision, deriding courses with 'poor graduate employability, and poor long-term earnings potential', and championing 'job-facing' degrees in medicine and STEM as well as skills-based Higher Technical Qualifications that are 'aligned to the needs of the economy and society more broadly'.[60] The report goes on to describe the teaching of subjects that do not fall into these categories as 'perverse'.[61] The writing was on the wall for theatre makers, musicians, dancers, and performers in general who tend to favour work satisfaction above economic gain, not to mention those working across the arts and humanities more broadly. Against the new criteria, the study and practice of art and performance were framed as a dead end for deadbeats, neither 'job-facing' (an idle pastime rather than a useful or productive occupation), nor meeting 'the needs of the economy and society'.

These policies raise some troubling but important questions: Is funding for the arts – not least theatre and performance given their resource intensity – a form of decadent expenditure? How are quality and value calibrated in policies like these, and what other values are involved in that calibration? If we accept that the performing arts are not as socially 'useful' (in normative terms) as nursing, say, or medicine, does it necessarily follow that they are disposable when 'difficult decisions' need to be made in times of crisis?

Aside from the consultations, one of the things that got me thinking about these questions was a controversial media campaign led by the CyberFirst programme in October 2020, which falls under the remit of the UK government's National Cyber Security Centre. 'Re-skilling' formed an important part of Prime Minister Boris Johnson's 'New Deal for Britain',[62] led by a Delivery Taskforce dubbed 'Project Speed'. What made the campaign controversial was an advert featuring a picture of a ballerina tying her ballet shoe, above which, emblazoned in white, we read:

Fatima's next job could be in cyber.
(she just doesn't know it yet)
Rethink. Reskill. Reboot.

The advert was widely ridiculed on social media, as members of the public took issue with the implicit framing of Fatima's skills as useless and outmoded relative to the merits of working in information technology and security (dominated in no small part by male workers) (Figure 5.2). The photographer was also 'devastated' that their image was appropriated in this way, having been downloaded as a stock image (I include their original photograph as follows, with the photographer's consent).[63] Nonetheless, however cackhandedly, it epitomizes how an economic crisis might be turned into a political opportunity by encouraging those lured by subjects and careers at odds with productivist values to reconsider how they think about their potential and ambition.

Ballerinas were just one of several careers targeted in a longer-running campaign alongside retail assistants, baristas, flight crew, and others.[64] However, several members of the cabinet at the time, as well as their advisers, had been vocal in their disapproval of the performing arts as a worthwhile or viable career option. For instance, when asked in an interview for a national television network about a lack of support for those working in the cultural sector during the pandemic, Rishi Sunak – who was serving as chancellor of the Exchequer at the time – deferred to creating 'a fresh and new opportunity for people' in other sectors.[65] Shortly afterwards, in a bid to succeed Boris Johnson as prime minister after Johnson was forced to resign amid a sea of scandal, Sunak 'vowed to phase out university degrees that do not improve students' "earning potential"'.[66] Johnson's Chief Advisor Dominic Cummings is also alleged to have said in a cabinet meeting that 'the fucking ballerinas can get to the back of the queue' in receiving financial support during the pandemic.[67] Various newspapers and online sources also satirized the appointment of Nadine Dorries as culture secretary, after a cabinet reshuffle, as 'Secretary of State for the Culture Wars'.[68] Like her predecessor, Oliver Dowden, Dorries publicly embarked on a war on woke, condemning 'Left wing snowflakes [who] are killing comedy, tearing down historic statues, removing books from universities, dumbing down panto, removing Christ from Christmas and suppressing free speech'.[69] For ministers serving in or close to Johnson's cabinet, the war on woke and support for supposedly 'useless' arts and humanities degrees and the careers they foster were part and parcel of the same culture war – and this despite the fact that the majority of those serving in Johnson's cabinet just before the Covid-19 outbreak studied humanities and social science subjects at university.[70]

Figure 5.2 Krys Alex's original image that was adapted for the CyberFirst campaign. Only the dancer on the left could be seen in the adapted version, with campaign text appearing to their left. Photography by @Krysalex.

The speech by Dowden referenced in this chapter's opening, in which he castigates 'woke ideology' as 'a dangerous form of decadence', is a particularly relevant example. It was delivered on 14 February 2022 at a right-wing think tank based in the United States called the Heritage Foundation. 'The enemies of the West', he suggests, 'are finding fresh confidence in their eternal battle against liberty':

> At the precise point when our resolve ought to be strongest, a pernicious new ideology is sweeping our societies. [. . .] In Britain, its adherents sometimes describe themselves as 'social justice warriors'. They claim to be 'woke': awakened to the so-called truths of our societies. [. . .] But I tell you, it is a dangerous form of decadence. Just when our attention should be focused on external foes, we seem to have entered this period of extreme introspection and self-criticism, and it really does threaten to sap our societies of their own self-confidence.[71]

Russia is one of the 'enemies of the West' that he cites – Russia invaded Ukraine ten days later – and he worries that a sapping of energy and resolve threatens the downfall of Western nations like the UK. For Dowden, if we are to combat the enemies at the gates, then we need to tackle an enemy within: a cabal of 'social justice warriors' who have lost sight of the 'real' dangers threatening liberal democracy today.

Dowden points the finger of blame at universities, particularly the attempts of its staff and students to decolonize curricula, and what he sees as an unscholarly privileging of an emotive 'identity politics' above rational enquiry. 'Universities', he says, 'from which so much of this unthinking revisionism has emerged, have, of course, for decades been prey to Left-wing excesses. [. . .] But this ideology is now everywhere'. Statues are toppled, genders are up for grabs, jokes and locker room talk are treated as if they were lethal weapons . . . And universities are where these 'excesses' are kindled. They fail to produce hard-working citizens equipped with skills that are relevant in the real world, he says. Instead, they have produced a generation of activists who 'are not interested in real scholarship or nuance, or in explaining the context of the bad things that our ancestors did, alongside the good'. They are complicit in cultivating what Douthat has critiqued as 'the decadent society', which, for Dowden, refers to a sapping of 'the vitality of our values and the strength of democratic societies'. A woke society, he claims, is a decadent society.[72]

Many of those reading this book will work or study in universities, most likely in arts and humanities subjects, which are Dowden's primary targets along with the social sciences. The narratives we propagate, he argues, 'almost guarantees demoralisation and despair', which is why the Conservative Party at the time was planning legislation 'to protect free speech on campus. We will stop the sinister phenomenon of academics or students who offend left-wing orthodoxies being censored or harassed',[73] regardless of the fact that an earlier Joint Committee on Human Rights inquiry, while sympathetic towards some of the issues he raises, 'did not find the wholesale censorship of debate in universities which media coverage has suggested'.[74]

There are several aspects of Dowden's speech and the policies and consultations that underpin it that are worth highlighting. First, he regards 'woke ideology' not as a symptom, but as a cause of societal decadence. Decadence is coded here as being synonymous with decay and decline: the sapping of a nation's 'vigour', and the erosion of its values. Second, Dowden connects the decadence of critical theory to urgent geopolitical issues that are for the most part unrelated to social justice activism (the conflict between Russia and Ukraine has little to do with queer theory, transgender rights, feminism, or the legacies of the slave trade). Third, his comments on free speech are primarily concerned with 'cancel culture'. He does not comment on other freedoms of expression, such as freedom of expression in art and performance, which might risk offending the sensibilities of those gathered to hear his speech. In other words, for Dowden free speech is to be defended at all costs, but on freedom of expression more broadly, including freedom of artistic expression, he remains silent. Fourth, he offers no historical context for his participation in a culture war, aside from a brief nod to Margaret Thatcher. Instead, he presents himself as a modern Prometheus tasked with saving the nation – and the West – from its 'decadence'.

Dowden had only recently given up his role as culture secretary when he delivered the speech, a role that found him mounting comparable attacks against cultural organizations that supported decolonial practices and minority visibility and interests, jeopardizing Arts Council England's 'arm's length' principle in the process.[75] There were ten different culture secretaries under Tory rule between 2010 and Dowden's speech in 2022, and thirteen if you count the additional three secretaries under New Labour's leadership between June 2007 and May 2010. The role has long been viewed disparagingly by politicians as the 'Minister of Fun',[76] where 'fun' is viewed as connoting a lack of seriousness (where it is assumed that this is a bad thing), in-building prejudice against culture within the political system by positioning it as frivolous and hence dispensable. In other words, a sense of decadence as useless frivolity is embedded into the political system and harnessed in political rhetoric in ways that aim to justify the erosion of support not just for the study of the arts, humanities, and social sciences in universities, but their being practised in the professional arena as well.

The Johnson cabinet's anti-woke/anti-arts agenda came off the back of a rising tide of literature that proved popular in conservative circles in the 2010s and early 2020s. For instance, several high-profile authors launched passionate defences of the progress achieved under the banners of classical liberalism and the enlightenment, progress that they believe is threatened by identity politics and postmodern cultural relativism.[77] Steven Pinker's book *Enlightenment Now: The Case for Reason, Science, Humanism and Progress* (2018) is an example. Pinker suggests that reason, science, humanism, and progress have been unthinkingly and dangerously dismissed as symptoms 'of a decadent, degenerate civilization' by left-wing academics and activists, which for Pinker ignores how these achievements have enabled us 'to fight back the tide of entropy' that defines the human condition (not least with regard to health and human longevity).[78] A group of scholars also banded together to launch a coordinated attack on critical theory and arts and humanities scholarship by publishing hoax articles intended to 'out' poor standards of peer review,[79] while others have condemned identity politics as 'a cyclical phenomenon of social decadence' based on a disconnection between an individual's aims and the collective values of a society; if decadence 'is the growth of aimless dissatisfied individualism [...after] an extended period of material affluence, social stability and personal anomie', they assert, then it is 'a perfect match' for identity politics, with the result being the proliferation of 'non-optimal, non-productive and deleterious activity'.[80]

The common denominator across these perspectives is the view that postmodernism has morphed from a pessimistic rejection of universal truths and meanings into an intolerant orthodoxy in which cultural constructivism is accepted, but identity and the oppression of historically disenfranchised groups are reified as an objective part of reality.[81] The irony is that the online domain – which lends itself to a postmodern sensibility – has also become an important weapon in the arsenal of those condemning the so-called 'woke agenda', just as it has become a platform for social justice advocates.[82] Online echo-chambers fuel click-bait algorithms, and those claiming to represent the silent majority have been granted a platform for hyper-vocality. Each plays a part in the phantasmatic construction of societal decadence, albeit a phantasm that haunts the bodies and minds, lives and livelihoods, of real people in real-world contexts.

There are two connected issues that are worth highlighting in this brief survey of the arguments underpinning conservative policy and rhetoric in the UK in the late 2010s and early 2020s: an anti-woke agenda that regards social justice activism and scholarship as a symptom of societal decadence, and an anti-arts and anti-humanities agenda that regards them as fundamentally useless and to be discouraged for that reason, especially where the allocation of public subsidy is concerned. The latter is used to justify the erosion of support for the practice and study of the arts and humanities, however erroneous the assessment of their supposed 'failure' to contribute 'productively' to a society.[83] The culture wars today pivot on the axis between these issues, suggesting a close relationship between an ideologically driven cultural-political battle, and the implementation of economic policies that are presented as 'common sense' necessities, but that are no less ideologically driven.

One 'common sense' response to this situation, as far as the performing arts are concerned, would be to sell their merits on the basis of the extent to which they align with and contribute to the economic health and wealth of a nation: for instance, their capacity to boost economic recovery, growth, and fledgling productivity. However, I advocate for a more uncommon sense, a more 'decadent' sense that understands the value of theatre and performance not on the basis of their utility or instrumentality, but their relative uselessness, wastefulness, outmodedness, and alternative productivities. In this I am in agreement with Nuccio Ordine's assessment of the arts and humanities as 'useless', if we understand that uselessness as being 'free of any utilitarian end'.[84] Understood in this way, the social value of performances that lend themselves to decadence is to be found in their capacity to disrupt or transgress discourses and practices, infrastructures and institutions, that champion the cultural supremacy of economic value above alternatives that have little to do with the intensification of productivity and the enhancement of growth. As mentioned earlier, this is not merely about advocating for the intrinsic value of the arts, or 'art for art's sake'. Unlike aestheticism, decadence feeds off the borders and limitations, boundaries and reified structures, that shape the capitalist everyday in order to breach or undo them. Also, as Sara Ahmed remarks, the issue at stake is not necessarily with the notion of 'use' per se, but with the distribution of usefulness *as a requirement* – which will always position some things, activities, and people as 'useful', while others are discarded or passed over as 'useless'.[85]

To describe theatre and performance as 'useless' is not to evacuate value and significance from what they have to offer to society. Rather, seizing on the uselessness of artistic practices may have the potential to prefigure futures that are not oriented around the merely useful.[86] A lack of utility only becomes scandalous in contexts that assign value and significance to usefulness, which may well be extrinsic or alien to a given practice, like performance. Hence, in appealing to the enjoyment of uselessness, unconventional expenditures of energy, the recalcitrance of art designed to be shared in space and time, and the alternative productivities that theatre and performance both stage and inspire, we might come to appreciate what it is that can lend these art forms to 'decadence', and why this decadence might be worth pursuing.

I am suggesting that we need to move away from a rhetoric of necessity and essentiality in framing what it is that makes theatre and performance valuable. As with so many crises, Covid-19 pulled the judgement of work and leisure as essential or inessential, useful or useless, into the forefront of governmental and popular discourse. As Caridad Svich demonstrates in a series of interviews with UK- and US-based theatre makers that were published during the pandemic, times of crisis can reveal just how *beneficial* and *meaningful* theatre and performance can be for many people. For instance, in one of the interviews documented in the collection, playwright James Graham observes how 'nothing has proven better the mental, social and emotional benefits of storytelling and art than the pandemic. It is what got millions of people, across class, ethnic and cultural divides, through the trauma'.[87] But the benefits and meaningfulness of theatre and performance do not make them necessary or essential, much as the systemic issues affecting its production and consumption (systemic racism, for instance, or ableism) demand redress. Rather than rationalizing the 'necessity' or 'essentiality' of theatre and performance, which is a fool's errand, I am suggesting that we should celebrate their inessentiality, especially the ways in which theatre and performance can offer us 'a glimpse of a world beyond the purely economic'.

The value of appreciating how theatre and performance can lend themselves to decadence is based on understanding the usefulness of their uselessness, which strikes me as an especially appealing uselessness as we come off the back of a global pandemic: a time scarred by millions of deaths, redundancies and joblessness, isolation and humourlessness, and temporary commitments to community support groups and Big Society volunteerism at the cost of more sustained infrastructural transformation. The uselessness of which I have spoken in this book is not, therefore, without social or personal benefit and meaningfulness; it is potentially of tremendous social and personal value and significance. It is incumbent on those who care about theatre and performance and the arts and humanities more broadly to become better-versed in appreciating that value and significance for what it is: spectacularly useless, potentially wasteful in productivist terms, forever at risk of simply 'illustrating' the advances of science and technology, at odds with the valorization of productivity as an end in itself, and for these reasons all the more timely, significant and worthwhile.

Conclusion

Arguments condemning the profligacy of arts funding and the uselessness of the arts – or more accurately arguments that refuse to recognize uses and forms of productivity that are not primarily or exclusively oriented around economic interests – demand that we learn from historical precedent, especially examples that, with hindsight, expose how easily ideological motives and goals can elide with appeals to 'common sense' and 'economic necessity'. The victimization that Athey endured was informed by the specificities of the AIDS crisis and a rising tide of religious fundamentalism adhered to by Buchanan and Helms, but the controversy surrounding his work was also used to justify the erosion of the NEA's resources and the legitimacy of the NEA as an institution. Cultural factors and political interests were instrumentalized to effect changes in the operation of government and the economy, and comparable processes underpin both the CyberFirst campaign in the UK context, and the debates that played out over the funding of McCarthy's sculpture in Rotterdam. The viability of the arts as a basis for a worthwhile career continues to be called into question, routinely castigated as an unproductive and useless pursuit of an idle class. In the process, public funding for the arts comes to be seen as being somehow complicit in societal decline: a decadent expenditure fuelling a decadent society. However, the denigration of artistic practice and study as decadent on the grounds of their being useless and inessential also raises a compelling question: are uselessness and inessentiality necessarily 'bad'?

The works of Athey and Wunderbaum invite us to consider the cultural politics of decadence not just as a slur levelled against economically backward or transgressive performance practices, and the communities those practices are seen to represent; they also invite us to consider the potential value of a practice that refuses adherence to an ethos that instrumentalizes productivity in the service of economic recovery and growth. Although economic recovery and growth can be desirable (for instance, by enhancing welfare support, health care, and education where a progressive tax system is in place), these goals can also be instrumentalized in the service of political aims with a more extensive agenda of economic reform at heart. In such cases, growth-led productivism can exert a debilitating and counterproductive pressure on the ability of 'hard-working citizens' to either work effectively, or enjoy the act and fruits of their labour.

Athey and Wunderbaum work with an uncommon sense to expose the contingencies of misleadingly common-sense views and solutions, and invite us to consider decadence within and beyond the rhetorical utility it offers to the likes of Buchanan, Helms, and Dowden. Decadence in the more positive senses explored in this book is turned against mindless utilitarianism and the conventionally productive, subverting forms of moral and economic austerity that de-legitimize support for the arts as well as the study of the arts and humanities. Perhaps, then, we might turn to decadence so as to better understand those moments when the arts and humanities are most threatened, when their legitimacy is questioned, and when utility and productivism have elided with a dominant sense of what constitutes the valuable, the necessary, the beautiful, and the worthwhile. Decadence can be reclaimed, and the very grounds upon which theatre and performance are dismissed as inessential or disposable – their uselessness, wastefulness, outmodedness, and harnessing of alternative productivities – also provides us with an excellent starting point for considering their significance and worth.

Conclusion

29 July 2022: a humid night in the height of summer, the kind that makes the eyelids heavy and the body slow. Subdued revellers languish beneath canopies and umbrellas outside a venue called Iklectik, globe lights flickering into life above their heads as the sun sets somewhere on the other side of an industrial estate in a secluded part of London.[1] Mist trickles through an open door leading into a performance space dressed with garlands of artificial roses and wildflowers, plush velvet drapes hanging haphazardly about the walls, and pink and blue lights dancing an absorbing *pas de deux* in the midst of the vapour. The stage is set. Hasard Le Sin – a performer from Helsinki known for their provocative 'boylesque' – makes their entrance wearing a shimmering velvet cloak with silken coverings about the arms, their head crowned with antlers, silver ferns, and diamanté sparkle. Their movements are coquettish – dandyish, even – and piece by piece their garments slip to the ground to reveal a corseted body studded with golden petals and strings of pearled gems, here playing the role of pubic hair dripping from two fabric phalluses protruding from their groin, like the pistils of an orchid: a begemmed deity in a sensuous hinterland, immersed in smoke that swirls with each flick of the wrist, only to dissipate, slowly, as they finish their act, disappearing into the darkness beyond (Figure 6.1).

This performance arrived late, both in the sense of starting later than expected, and arriving late in the process of writing this book. It arrived at 'the end', which is to say, at a time when I was thinking about new beginnings, and speaks to various overarching concerns underpinning the preceding chapters. As I explored in the Introduction, the study of decadence has been thriving over the past three decades or so, especially recently, although scholarship has largely been focused on the written word. The prospect of encountering decadence in the flesh often reads in this scholarship as a betrayal of its transgressive potential, where the mind's eye is preferred to beguiling spectacles and the corporeal presence of another who might, just might, ask something of us in return. This is unsurprising given the nature of literature, which lends itself to the comfortable retreat of an armchair. Theatre and performance also appeal to an imaginative terrain, especially when enjoyed in the darkness of an auditorium, but seated audiences are still forced to confront the corporeal presence of another. The stakes are raised in spaces where the distinction between stage and auditorium is not so clear-cut, when mist confuses just

Figure 6.1 Hasard Le Sin, *Fairy Boudoir*, Iklectik Arts Lab, London, 29 July 2022. Photo by Emma Jones.

who is performing for whom, and when the bodies of others press up against your own as they peer over shoulders to catch a glimpse of what lies beyond. In spaces like these, decadence is nothing if not felt, embodied, and enacted.

Hasard Le Sin shared a bill that night with the cabaret starlet Coco Deville, who introduced the acts; a drag king called Sigi Moonlight; and the cultural anarchist Oozing Gloop, here paying homage to the Roman

Emperor Elagabalus, showering the audience in a deluge of rose petals as live performances segued into communal revelry on the dancefloor, where those inclined could also watch a film by the multidisciplinary artist Miss HerNia. The film, as with all of Miss HerNia's work, draws inspiration from a colossal 'fatberg' – 250 metres long and weighing 130 tonnes – that clogged London's sewers in 2017, comprised almost entirely of discarded cooking oil, grease, wet wipes, and sanitary products. Their costume was covered in cotton pustules and skin-like bags – fabricating the corpulent excess of such a monstrous blockage – and they appeared, reclining, in front of a kaleidoscopic greenscreen depicting swirling stars and galaxies, like an abject glamour queen drifting nonchalantly through the cosmos. Each of these artists embodied and enacted decadence in their own, very different ways by foregrounding the undoing of gender binaries with an eye on the refinement of their delightful corruption, for instance, or by taking a decadent archetype like Elagabalus as inspiration, or by allowing mist to perform as a performance material that could be shaped according to the sensuous movements of a twenty-first-century dandy.

Mist is a fascinating performance material in the context of a book about decadence. It shapes space and atmosphere, but it is also an entropic medium that dissipates unless replenished. For the cultural theorist Mieke Bal, who has written at length about the Belgian artist Ann Veronica Janssens, vapour and haze can make the boundaries of bodies appear indeterminate. Bal's description of experiencing one of Janssens's famous mist rooms is especially resonant. She remembers how vision in these works became 'a slowly granted and slowly developed privilege', with perception 'wavering in its location, siding alternately with the subject (me) and the object – the unstable sight that I was beginning to see'.[2] In a similar way, as I glimpsed Hasard Le Sin emerging through the mist as a horned creature, I, too, felt a siding between me and 'the unstable sight that I was beginning to see': neither human nor animal, conventionally male nor conventionally female, in unity with nor entirely separate from my own feeling body, and losing the distinctiveness that gives shape to binaries in the first place. What this performance enabled, in other words, was a vicarious encounter with decadence.

Decadence is an art of border crossing.[3] Decadence relies on borders in order to breach them – for instance, by staging the undoing of gendered types and binaries, as all of the performers that night made clear, or by transgressing the mores that shape the horizons of social acceptability, especially where sexuality, taste, and demeanour are concerned. The mist in that room, that night, also made palpable the importance of recognizing the publicness of decadence in performance as a spectacle that flirts with the kind of border crossing identified by Bal. Where decadence in the nineteenth century has generally been imagined as a rather solitary interest, both atomized in its enjoyment and atomizing in its effects,[4] the mist in Hasard Le Sin's performance drew attention to the publicness of the event. Half-seen faces could be discerned through its penumbral wafts and waves, eyes occasionally meeting, or relishing the licence to enjoy another's sensuality, 'siding alternately with the subject (me) and the object'. Experiences like this make decadence palpable as a publicly performed act, encouraging us to imagine decadence not as an atomizing or anti-social practice but as a social practice of border crossing in which the boundaries between bodies, and between cultural markers and orientations, become porous, if only for a moment.

These acts of border crossing are subject to social negotiation. A border cannot be undone if the mode of its transgression ignores the interests and desires of those involved in feeling out where these borders exist, as this will only ever lead to the reinforcement of a boundary that might otherwise have been dismantled – not to mention the very real risk of harming those involved where risk is not courted, but imposed. Also, while decadence might and frequently does involve the cultivation of a taste for decay and delight in disgust – a key feature of decadence identified by the literature scholar David Weir, which has furnished this book with an important touchstone[5] – the enjoyment of a taste for the distasteful in the performances addressed in this book is not intended to propagate physical detriment or harm to oneself or others, unless pain or humiliation is actively desired in a negotiated relationship. As I explored in discussing work by Martin O'Brien, Julia Bardsley, and Marcel·lí Antúnez Roca, a taste for decadent practice is always connected to pleasure, or at least curiosity. This gearing of decadent taste, then – in my interpretation, which departs from Weir's – is about probing the horizons of social acceptability and aesthetic sensibility, and challenging oneself and others to question these horizons. The enjoyment of a taste for the distasteful – or rather that which arouses anxiety about the horizons of an aesthetic sensibility – might also have something to teach us about our own dispositions, proclivities, and desires.

If Hasard Le Sin's performance lends itself to a decadent frame, if it appeals to decadent taste, then its abundant sensuality suggests that it might also bear a connection to aestheticism. However, the relationship between decadence and aestheticism is thorny at best. Oscar Wilde furnishes readers with one of many mantras associated with aestheticism in his famous preface to *The Picture of Dorian Gray* (1891). 'All art is quite useless', he writes.[6] According to aestheticism, the primacy of beauty and the sensuous enjoyment of an artwork or work of literature should take precedence over any moral message or utility, which are seen to lessen or demean the appreciation of art for its own sake. The decadent imagination comes into play when the prizing of superlative beauty is questioned. Where aestheticism looks to transcend the everyday by means of an artistic or literary encounter with beauty, decadence looks to transgress borders and boundaries that categorize, hierarchize, and distinguish, and often does so in ways that deliberately appeal to those things that are considered too obscene or ugly to represent in 'beautiful' art and literature. Wilde's *The Picture of Dorian Gray* makes just such an appeal – it is 'nothing if not decadent',[7] full of stylistic flourishes that relish the evocation (more often than the depiction) of depravity – but the ultimate fate of its protagonist still reads as a paean to beauty, a beauty that is forever vulnerable to abuse at the hands of those intent on the enjoyment of transient pleasures, whatever the cost.

Aestheticism is hardly apolitical – Terry Eagleton makes a convincing case for 'a whole alternative politics' in the aestheticism of Friedrich Schiller, particularly with regard to 'suspending social hierarchy' among a 'disinterested fraternity' – but it frequently veils its politics behind an aestheticist veneer.[8] Similarly, decadence and politics open seductive ground for experimenting with 'a whole alternative politics', not least when distinctions between decadence and aestheticism are taken into consideration. Decadent performance has a habit of veiling its political commitments, like aestheticism, but it does not take much to lift the veil and relish what we find underneath. We might say that the politics of Hasard Le Sin's appearance as a horned deity hangs somewhere in those beaded gems that droop from their groin. The sensual realm in which the work resides flirts with a beguiling politics that elides pleasure with a taste for the undoing of beliefs and prejudices that masquerade as authorities on what constitutes essentiality and appropriateness. This does not betray the mantra that all art – all performance – is 'quite useless', but it does inflect that uselessness with political significance. It recognizes that acts of border crossing might be relished for their own sake, but as acts of transgression – as opposed to transcendence – they become imbued with deeper and more provocative political meaning. Recognizing the porosity or breaching of borders, then, and relishing this kind of discovery and activity, offers one way in which we might come to understand the politics of decadence in performance.

Something similar is at stake in Miss HerNia's film, where the association of decadence with decay and abjection is more apparent. The film depicts a body that seems to have been ravaged by a horrible skin disease. She invites those who gaze upon her body, as it lounges in the cosmos, to enjoy the meticulous crafting of distasteful costumes, and to call into question the prizing of beauty as a vague and spurious judgement of taste. The same is true of Bardsley and Marcel·lí Antúnez Roca's scenographies. A great deal of care and attention goes into the crafting of abject costumes and the wiring or stitching together of hybrid monstrosities. They render rot and decay through filigree and ornamentation. O'Brien's practice, too, brings sickness and decay into the orbit of desire and pleasure. His practice explores how intersections between illness and queerness might unsettle presumptions that consider maximal health and capability as viable bases for self-realization. This, too, appeals to decadent taste, just as it makes explicit how decadent taste is at one at the same time political.

Ron Athey's practice also involves the transgression of borders and conventional models of beauty. His performances make a decadent spectacle of porosity and rupture by recognizing the skin as the body's own border, and working with skin and the blood it holds as materials that traverse desire and abjection, attraction and repulsion, sensuality and sexuality. The political dimensions of his early practice take on added significance in the specific context of its staging, particularly given the 'polemic of blood' that governed how Athey and the performances that he made came to be viewed by conservative commentators at the height of the AIDS crisis in the early 1990s. However, while subject to and embroiled within a discourse of decadence at the time, Athey also resists a 'style' of evaluation based on perceptions of cultural breakdown. He crafts an uncommon sensibility based on the refusal of reproductive futurism and conventionally productive expenditures of energy.

An overarching concern underpinning this book has to do with the relationship of decadence to capitalism, and especially productivism. In the Introduction, I defined productivism as the introjection of productivity as a basis for self-realization, and the valorization of intensified productivity as a panacea for stagnant economies. I have been framing decadence as a process of falling and flowing away from the excesses of productivism, which invites consideration of more explicitly political issues. While O'Brien, Bardsley, jaamil olawale kosoko, The Uhuruverse, Athey, and Hasard Le Sin have all sought to elude, challenge, or reimagine these excesses, others over-identify or disidentify with them. This is especially true of Toshiki Okada, Toco Nikaido, and Wunderbaum. Okada's performers might move slowly, but they move as if in a catatonic stupor, haunted by compulsions serving a long-forgotten purpose. Nikaido creates super-saturated spectacles that pastiche the excesses of consumer capitalism, just as she augments the injunctions of productivism in the demands that she makes of her performers. Wunderbaum also references and exaggerates the supposedly corrosive influence that 'degenerate' and 'useless' art can have on a vulnerable populace, particularly when arts subsidy is made to compete with more 'useful' or 'productive' beneficiaries. These are performances that over-identify with productivism to points of absurdity, to breaking points, marking a striking contrast with notions of decadence that fixate on refinement and filigree, or the staging of an artificial paradise.

In exploring the politics of decadence, this book has been asking some fundamental questions about the shaping of decadence as a concept, and the entitlement of those empowered to define its parameters. Who is decadence for? Who is entitled to define decadence, and what happens to decadence as a practice to be embraced when it rubs shoulders with those intent on condemning it when they find it? My approach to decadence in this book has shared something of the literature scholar Matthew Potolsky's framing of decadence as 'a characteristic mode of reception, rather than a discernible quality of things or people'.[9] It has also been my intention to stretch Potolsky's insight beyond that which might unite a disparate group of decadent aficionados, opening out instead to practices, styles, and world views that bear little connection to decadence as it was conceived in fin de siècle Europe. Decadence in nineteenth-century art and literature circled around a number of key characteristics, including perversity, artificiality, egoism, and curiosity,[10] as well as exoticism, morbidity, and pessimism.[11] Decadence has also been widely regarded as a renunciation of the political, or as a stance reserved for an aristocratic and reactionary elite.[12] However, as I discussed in Chapter 3, kosoko and The Uhuruverse invite us to imagine decadence and especially the politics of decadence differently. The chapter explored some familiar themes, including entropy and pessimism, morbidity and the retrograde, and exoticism and alienation, but kosoko and The Uhuruverse put these regressive and oppressive characteristics into dialogue with Afrofuturism and political activism. In Alice Condé's terms, they make decadence 'affirmatory',[13] and invite those invested in the aesthetics as much as the politics of decadence to explore tensions between decadence as a practice of entropy, and what happens to this practice in a Black African-diasporic context, where it might serve ends that open out to social justice. On the face of it, this would seem very un-decadent given the close historical connections between decadence and philosophical pessimism, but the undoing of a world in such contexts also plays into the eschatological leanings of decadence. In the hands of kosoko and The Uhuruverse – as with O'Brien and Bardsley – the association of decadence with endings and the apocalyptic marks the beginning of *post*-apocalyptic thinking and doing, or that which comes after the end.

There is every reason to be thinking about the apocalypse today. As Jane Desmarais and David Weir write in their introduction to *The Oxford Handbook of Decadence*, the end of the world, which was 'once imagined as an event' in the twilight years of the nineteenth century, 'has since become a condition; and if decadence is a cultural response to a time of decline, that culture now seems more pertinent than ever as an expression of our contemporary predicament'.[14] The climate crisis is the most important factor underpinning this condition, which is an area that I hope will be explored in future studies.[15] Productivism, the cultish pursuit of novel innovations, and the myth of ever-expanding growth – once means to the end of wealth creation, now ends in themselves in productivist societies – must factor into how this apocalyptic condition is imagined. The uselessness, wastefulness, and outmodedness of theatre and performance may seem an odd place to start in thinking about the prospect of de-growth, for instance, but only so long as these terms are read in the light of productivism.[16] Each of these characteristics might just as well be steered along very different lines that are resistant to the apocalyptic ends of capitalism.

There are additional reasons why it is useful to consider the apocalypse as a condition: geopolitical crisis, for instance, or systemic racism, both of which put an all-too-literal spin on the ending of worlds. However, the demonstrable and measurable ways in which these examples play into the shaping of an apocalyptic condition are of a very different ilk to the kind of issue that tends to be decried in a recent spate of declinist literature. An example that I have been returning to at various points throughout this book is Ross Douthat's book *The Decadent Society: How We Became the Victims of Our Own Success* (2020). Douthat frames economic stagnation, secularization and declining birth rates, political and institutional sclerosis, and cultural exhaustion as symptoms of a 'decadent society'. These are familiar tropes that can be traced back through various periods of declinism, in this case following hot on the heels of conservative politicians and columnists who stoked the fires of a culture war at the turn of the twenty-first century in the United States.[17] As I explored in my discussion of kosoko and The Uhuruverse, there is a neocolonial dimension to much of this writing that traces back at least to the nineteenth century, and the racist condemnation of primitivism and an entropic slide into degeneracy if a nation risks contact with its 'bestial' others. Douthat's vaunting of the moon landing in 1969 as the last pinnacle of human achievement before a backward slide into societal decadence is part and parcel of this neocolonialism. It is also no accident that the moon landing offers fodder for The Uhuruverse to reimagine the race for space as a basis for staging an end to the ends of neocolonialism, and with it the economic structure – capitalism – that facilitates its perpetuation. As with kosoko, their concern with endings and the carefully crafted ruination of debilitating power – which appeals to a decadent sensibility – offers an alternative to the declinist diagnoses of societal decadence that have been a perennial concern of conservatives for nearly two centuries.

Our present century is no exception, as I explored in Chapter 5. Decadence is on the agenda again in the thick of an ascendant culture war, which was typified in February 2022 when a former culture secretary in the UK and the co-chairman of the Conservative Party at the time, Oliver Dowden, condemned left-wing activism and scholarship deriving from the arts, humanities, and social sciences, as 'a dangerous form of decadence'.[18] At the time of writing, the study of art and performance is being framed as useless relative to subjects that more explicitly serve the health and wealth of a nation. Those pursuing careers in the arts are being invited to 'Rethink. Reskill. Reboot' in ways that position art and artists as egregious extravagances relative to the utility of cyber and information security. In short, decadence is not a peripheral line of enquiry; it plays a role in the shaping of cultural and political discourse and policies, which are set to impact the lives and livelihoods of those whose interests and abilities depart from or are antithetical to the priorities of productivist enterprise.

There is substantive evidence documenting the economic impact of the arts in the years just prior to the pandemic, which adversely affected that impact.[19] There is also a substantive body of research to suggest that the arts can generate significant personal and social impact, whether through the 'ennoblement' of individuals and 'civilizing' qualities of art – which (thankfully) was more popular as a rationale for supporting the arts in the Victorian period than it is today – or through advancing various health and social benefits, including personal well-being, educational attainment, the regeneration of towns and cities, and community cohesion.[20] In other words, this body of evidence suggests that the arts can be instrumentalized in the service of personal and social transformation.

However, unlike more lucrative commercial productions with long run times playing in high-capacity spaces, it is also the case that the kinds of work I have been addressing in this book are unlikely to contribute all that much to a nation's GDP or productive capacity, although they may produce some of the personal and social impacts that advocates of the instrumental benefits of the arts have been plugging. It is also the case that arguments based on the instrumental benefits of the arts tend to ignore the fact that cultural production and reception is rife with inequality. This is what prompted Orian Brook, Dave O'Brien, and Mark Taylor, in their book *Culture is Bad for You: Inequality in the Cultural and Creative Industries* (2020), to suggest that we at least need to be cautious about *how* we come to value artistic practice. Those who 'make it' in the cultural arena often possess a degree of economic, social, and/or cultural capital, which is frequently the consequence of hereditary privilege. Consuming or participating in cultural production is also enjoyed by a minority of the population, and what is seen to 'count' as culture, and what not, has a habit of perpetuating inequalities. For whom is culture – theatre and performance included – 'essential'?

Decadence might form a starting point for engaging with some fundamental questions and issues regarding the borders that establish regimes of taste, the disciplining of behaviours in theatres and arts centres, and the attribution of value and significance. It is in the undoing of these borders, by those who are either marked as decadent or who perform decadence, that we might learn about entitlement and the establishment of meaningfulness or importance, or that which is deemed worthwhile and what not. If 'what is given value and worth can challenge and change inequality', as Brook, O'Brien and Taylor contend,[21] and what is accorded significance can challenge and change deep-seated prejudices and social and cultural blinkeredness, then decadence as a practice of transgression and of dethroning established hierarchies – not least what constitutes 'good' taste, and the 'goodness' of culture – offers welcome opportunities for intervening in the cultural-political arena.

Instead of advocating for the economic or social instrumentality of the arts, I have been making a case for the uselessness, wastefulness, outmodedness, and alternative productivities that can lend theatre and performance to decadence. Uselessness can be useful; wastefulness can be generative; outmodedness can give rise to emancipatory lines of flight; and productivity need not be put in the service of productivism, the myth of eternal growth, and techno-scientific and capitalistic codifications of progress, instead making a virtue of forms of creativity that are not so easily measured by or captured within productivist frameworks. If theatre and performance lend themselves to decadence, in these specific senses, then it would seem a decadence worthy of embrace, reclaiming it from the hands and mouths of those who undermine the possibility of practising and studying theatre, performance, and the arts and humanities more broadly. In other words, it is entirely possible that decadence might produce instrumental *effects* – particularly through acts of border crossing that are politically relevant and meaningful – without being instrumental*ized*.

This is not simply about advocating for the autonomous and intrinsic value of art and performance relative to instrumental rationales, although my argument certainly shares in aestheticism's pursuit of a different set of values to those inscribed by productivism in particular and capitalism in general. There are already plenty of accounts that make passionate and persuasive cases for the intrinsic value of making and engaging with art and literature, with advocates of *l'art pour l'art* and art for art's sake in fin de siècle France and Britain offering some of the most influential examples. Rather, in making a case for uselessness, wastefulness, outmodedness, and alternative productivities in performances that lend themselves to decadence, I have been forwarding arguments based neither on the autonomy of art – at least not in the sense of transcending the everyday – nor its instrumentality. Instead, decadent acts of border crossing of the kind explored in this book demand that the horizons that shape taste and decency, dispositions and orientations, and the legitimizing of productive uses of time, energy, and resource, be treated as that which might be negotiated through acts of refusal, breach, undoing, or more radical reimagining of the social field.

In her essay 'Poetry Is Not a Luxury', which was first published in 1977, Audre Lorde implores her readers to recognize how poetry can birth or illuminate emancipatory ideas, drawing inspiration from poetry 'as a revelatory distillation of experience, not the sterile word play that, too often, the white fathers distorted the word poetry to mean'.[22] Lorde is writing from the perspective of a queer Black feminist. From this standpoint, poetry has the capacity to foreshadow changes in society and culture that are yet to be realized or even accessible as ideas untethered from white European consciousness. This is why poetry is not a luxury for Lorde, but something more profound.

It is important to recognize the ways in which art and literature, theatre and performance, come to be understood and valued as platforms for anticipating alternative and more just futures for those who can ill-afford their relinquishment. I have no intention of suggesting otherwise. What I do want to encourage, though, is recognition of the desirability of art, literature, theatre, and performance *as* luxuries, provided these luxuries are not foreclosed to those who stand to gain most from their pleasures. I have hope for luxury yet: hope for the redistribution of bounty by means of its anticipation and manifestation in public spectacles; hope for the magic of unconventional glamour conjured by dissident bodies who refuse to conform with a culture that is not made for them; and hope for the radical potential of pleasure and its capacity to shift how we come to see particular things and activities as important or unimportant. There is a case to be made for the apparently frivolous, as frivolity can point towards things of great importance. There is a case to be made for inessentiality within structures that make a habit of categorizing useful services and occupations at the expense of counterparts deemed disposable in their inessentiality. There is also a case to be made for the simple enjoyment of useless things, or that which others deem to be a waste of time and energy, or that which is judged to be irrelevant by those with a vested interest in defining the relevant, or that which 'fails' to become more productive, or which 'fails' to continually grow and improve.

Theatre and performance are never going to achieve the same degree of social impact as welfare reform, for instance, or improvements in healthcare services, and they are never going to achieve the same degree of economic impact and potential for economic recovery and growth as a game-changing technology or resource. If we measure the value and benefits of theatre and performance against criteria that do not account for their unique qualities, then they are more easily condemned as useless, wasteful, outmoded, or unproductive in productivist terms – which is to say, as the decadent pursuits of those who think themselves above 'real' work and commitment to a productivist work ethic.

Instead, by acknowledging their lack of utility, where utility is understood in a strictly economic sense, we might come to recognize that lack as a valuable asset in societies that orient themselves around the instrumental uses of things and people, incessant growth, and intensified productivity. Also, by acknowledging that the act of gathering and attending to theatre in a shared space for an allotted time is an archaic use of time and resource, we might begin to value theatre and performance on their own terms, rather than as a competitor with more technologically innovative and economically lucrative areas of the Creative and Cultural Industries, such as on-demand and globally distributed media and streaming platforms. Further, the spending of time and expenditure of energy on the part of makers and performers is fundamentally entropic, both in terms of the resource intensity of most forms of theatre and performance that fall away from profitable commercial models, and in terms of the huge investments of time and energy that go into the making of theatre and performance, and the sharing of live performances night after night. This is not a 'productive' or 'sustainable' use of time and energy if we understand productivity and sustainability on an economic basis – but it can be a tremendously productive use of time and energy as a creative and explorative pursuit, and it can also sustain the interests and desires, passions and yearnings, of individuals and communities who derive pleasure from making and watching theatre and performance.

What we find across all of the performances considered in this book is not just an *idea* of decadence in the abstract; what we find are decadent spaces, materialities, desires, pleasures, times, and velocities that are grounded in and that emerge from the appearance and activities of bodies. Decadence in theatre and performance manifests as an embodied and enacted practice. Decadence is frequently derided in political rhetoric and commentary, but it also has the capacity to meet that derision with irresistible appearances and actions. For its conservative critics holding fast to a way of life that they regard as being eroded, the decadence of a society or its constituent parts – like art and performance – is there to be diagnosed and pathologized, together with all the practices and desires that they come to see as being in need of a cure. But for its advocates, the endings promised by decadence preempt the possibility of a future beyond the end that might be very different from the present in which we currently reside. A decadent theatre is a theatre of endings – the end of worlds, as much as a process of bringing things to an end, a praxis of decline – but decadent theatre and performance also promises new life, beginning again as a world dissolves each night, or starting afresh as the theatre's empty space becomes filled with artificial paradises that are yet to be realized.

Notes

Introduction

1. 'HERE RAW – Staging Decadence', HERE Arts Centre, New York City, 9 September 2021. http://here.org/shows/raw21-staging-decadence/?fbclid =IwAR1ceRaNhq_MnGBfLuPpShr0emQphuwkHJSdAKoUh_ewShc2wKJ _i2ESD9k, accessed 30 June 2022. This salon was one of several events associated with an Arts and Humanities Research Council Fellowship, titled 'Staging Decadence: Decadent Theatre in the Long Twentieth Century' (2020–2). For more on the Staging Decadence project, visit: www .stagingdecadence.com.
2. Normandy Sherwood qtd. in *Staging Decadence* [film], created by Adam Alston, Owen Parry, and Sophie Farrell, 12 May 2022, https://www .stagingdecadence.com/films, accessed 12 May 2022.
3. Normandy Sherwood, Interview with the author. HERE Arts Centre, New York, 9 September 2021.
4. Border crossing has been identified as a key facet of decadence. See Liz Constable, Dennis Denisoff, and Matthew Potolsky, 'Introduction', in Constable, Denisoff and Potolsky (eds), *Perennial Decay: On the Aesthetics & Politics of Decadence* (Philadelphia: University of Pennsylvania Press, 1999), pp. 1–32 (pp. 11 and 25); Matthew Potolsky, *The Decadent Republic of Letters: Taste, Politics, and Cosmopolitan Community from Baudelaire to Beardsley* (Philadelphia: University of Pennsylvania Press, 2013), p. 2.
5. *Decadēre*, meaning 'to fall' (*cadēre*) 'down' (*de-*). As Richard Gilman explains, the word 'decadence' was not used in Roman times; it first appears in Medieval Latin in the second millennium. Richard Gilman, *Decadence: The Strange Life of an Epithet* (New York: Farrar, Straus and Giroux, 1975), pp. 36–7.
6. Sherwood, Interview with the author.
7. adrienne maree brown, 'Introduction', in adrienne maree brown (ed.), *Pleasure Activism: The Politics of Feeling Good* (Chico and Edinburgh: AK Press, 2019), pp. 3–18 (p. 13).
8. Nia O. Witherspoon, Interview with the author. HERE Arts Centre, New York. 9 September 2021.
9. See Alice Condé, 'Decadence and Popular Culture', in Jane Desmarais and David Weir (eds), *Decadence and Literature* (Cambridge: Cambridge University Press, 2019), pp. 379–99 (p. 395).
10. Alice Rayner, *Ghosts: Death's Double and the Phenomena of Theatre* (Minneapolis and London: University of Minnesota Press, 2006), pp. 60–1. An article by Richard Schechner proved especially influential in fostering

this view of performance. See Richard Schechner, 'Theatre Criticism', *The Tulane Drama Review*, 9 (3) (Spring 1965), pp. 13–24 (p. 24).
11. Peggy Phelan, *Unmarked: The Politics of Performance* (New York: Routledge, 1993), p. 146.
12. Note that for Phelan, it is not just performance that 'becomes itself through disappearance'; subjectivity becomes itself through disappearance as well. Phelan's work on the ephemerality of performance has also been contested by numerous scholars, most famously in a well-rehearsed debate with Philip Auslander. See Philip Auslander, *Liveness: Performance in a Mediatized Culture* (London and New York: Routledge, 1999).
13. For an indicative example documenting the expanded breadth of Decadence Studies, see Jane Desmarais and David Weir (eds), *The Oxford Handbook of Decadence* (New York: Oxford University Press, 2022).
14. Ross Douthat, *The Decadent Society: How We Became the Victims of Our Own Success* (New York: Avid Reader Press, 2020), p. 11. There are echoes of Oswald Spengler in Douthat's writing, particularly with regard to cultural production. See Oswald Spengler, *The Decline of the West*, abridged by Helmut Werner (New York and Oxford: Oxford University Press, 1991), p. 158.
15. For North American examples of these diatribes in the puritanical vein, see Robert Bork, *Slouching Towards Gomorrah: Modern Liberalism and American Decline* (New York: Regan Books, 1997); Patrick J. Buchanan, *The Death of the West: How Dying Populations and Immigrant Invasions Imperil Our country and Civilization* (New York: Thomas Dunne Books, 2002). In France, some more recent writing derives from an Islamophobic fear of cultural contamination, and its impact on the perceived decline of a coherent national identity. See Alain Finkielkraut, *L'identité malheureuse* (Paris: Stock, 2013); Éric Zemmour, *Le Suicide Francais* (Paris: Albin Michel, 2014). David Fieni has also studied declinist literature stemming from the nexus between the Arab world and France. See David Fieni, *Decadent Orientalisms: The Decay of Colonial Modernity* (New York: Fordham University Press, 2020).
16. Giulia Palladini, 'Logic of Prelude: On Use Value, Pleasure, and the Struggle Against Agony', *Contemporary Theatre Review*, 'Interventions', 29 (4) (Winter/Spring 2019/20), https://www.contemporarytheatrereview.org/2020/logic-of-prelude-on-use-value-pleasure-and-the-struggle-against-agony/, accessed 2 February 2022.
17. Witherspoon, Interview with the author.
18. I am basing this definition on the work of Jean Baudrillard. See Jean Baudrillard, *The Mirror of Production*, trans. Mark Poster (St. Louis: Telos Press, 1975), pp. 17–19.
19. The term 'frenetic standstill' is drawn from Jonathan Trejo-Mathys translation of Hartmut Rosa's '*rasender Stillstand*', which is itself a translation of Virilio's term *l'intertie polaire*. Hartmut Rosa, *Social*

Acceleration: A New Theory of Modernity, trans. Jonathan Trejo-Mathys (New York: Columbia University Press, 2013), p. 15. This translation has also been used by others engaging with Rosa's work. See especially Bart Zantvoort, 'Political inertia and social acceleration', *Philosophy and Social Criticism*, 43 (4) (2017), pp. 707–23 (p. 717). Ivor Southwood describes a similar phenomenon as 'frenetic inactivity' and 'non-stop inertia'. See Ivor Southwood, *Non-stop Inertia* (Arlesford: Zer0 Books, 2011), p. 11. Studies of frenetic standstill were also anticipated in earlier studies of the postmodern condition. See especially Frederic Jameson, *The Cultural Turn: Selected Writings on the Postmodern, 1983–1998* (London and New York: Verso, 1998), p. 59.

20 Mark Fisher, *K-Punk: The Collected and Unpublished Writings of Mark Fisher (2004–2016)*, ed. Darren Ambrose (London: Repeater, 2018), p. 462, original emphasis. See also Mark Fisher, *Capitalist Realism: Is There No Alternative?* (Winchester and Washington: Zer0 Books, 2009). Fisher explains that 'capitalist realism' is not his coinage. He contextualizes it in light of a niche group of German pop artists in the 1960s, and parodic references to 'socialist realism' in work by Michael Schudson. See Fisher, *Capitalist Realism*, p. 16.

21 For an overview of these contributions in the UK context, see Creative Industries Council, 'The Economic Contribution of the Arts', 2 March 2021, https://www.thecreativeindustries.co.uk/facts-figures/industries-arts-culture-arts-culture-facts-and-figures-the-economic-contribution-of-the-arts, accessed 2 February 2022.

22 Richard Schechner, 'A New Paradigm for Theatre in the Academy', *TDR*, 36 (4) (Winter 1992), pp. 7–10 (p. 8). See also Johannes Birringer, *Media & Performance: Along the Border* (Baltimore and London: Johns Hopkins University Press, 1998), pp. 6–7.

23 José Esteban Muñoz, *Disidentifications: Queers of Color and the Performance of Politics* (Minneapolis and London: University of Minnesota Press, 1999), p. 19.

24 See Jane Desmarais, 'Decadence and the Critique of Modernity', in Desmarais and Weir, *Decadence and Literature*, pp. 98–114 (p. 98).

25 The prevalence of dandyism among aesthetes and decadents is illustrative. Rachilde and Jean Lorrain (another novelist and playwright associated with literary decadence) were famed for wearing gender-queer attire in public, and Rachilde even had an application to the police rejected for the right to continue to do so. See Frazer Lively, 'Introduction', in Kiki Gounaridou and Frazer Lively (ed. and trans.), *Madame La Mort and Other Plays* (Baltimore and London: Johns Hopkins UP, 1998), pp. 7–8.

26 Richard Vaughan, *Philip the Good: The Apogee of Burgandy* (London: Longmans, Green and Co. Ltd, 1970), pp. 56–7 and 143–5.

27 See Graham Pont, 'In Search of the *opera gastronomica*', in Anthony Corones, Graham Pont, and Barbara Santich (eds), *Food in Festivity:*

Proceedings of the Fourth Symposium of Australian Gastronomy (Sydney: Symposium of Australian Gastronomy, 1990), pp. 120–1.

28 Scot D. Ryersson and Michael Orlando Yaccarino, *Infinite Variety: The Life and Legend of the Marchesa Casati* (Minneapolis: University of Minnesota Press, 2004), p. 57; see also Catherine Spooner, 'Fashion: Decadent Stylings', in Jane Desmarais and David Weir (eds), *The Oxford Handbook of Decadence* (Oxford: Oxford University Press, 2022), pp. 417–41 (p. 431).

29 See, for instance, Adam Alston and Alexander Bickley Trott (eds), *Volupté: Interdisciplinary Journal of Decadence Studies*, 'Decadence and Performance', 4 (2) (Winter 2021). For an overview of West African and Caribbean playwrights associated with decadence, see Robert Stilling, *Beginning at the End: Decadence, Modernism, and Postcolonial Poetry* (Cambridge, MA and London: Harvard University Press, 2018). The Staging Decadence blog also features posts exploring theatre and decadence in China, Japan, Russia, the United States, and across western Europe, available at: www.stagingdecadence.com. For a selection of work by theatre historians who have explicitly addressed or touched on theatre, performance and decadence, see: Petra Dierkes-Thrun, *Salome's Modernity: Oscar Wilde and the Aesthetics of Transgression* (Ann Arbor: University of Michigan Press, 2011); Sos Eltis, 'Decadent Theater: New Women and "The Eye of the Beholder"', in Desmarais and Weir, *The Oxford Handbook of Decadence*, pp. 318–50; Sos Eltis, 'Theatre and Decadence', in Alex Murray (ed.), *Decadence: A Literary History* (Cambridge: Cambridge University Press, 2020), pp. 201–17.

30 *Femme fatales* and objectified women abound in decadent art and fiction, as do exotic figurations of 'the Orient'. Nonetheless, these tropes were often used to displace, mock or undermine jingoistic grandstanding, patriarchy, and normative codifications of gender and sexuality. There is also a rich history of women writing decadence. See, for instance, Katharina Herold and Leire Barrera-Medrano (eds), 'Women Writing Decadence', *Volupté: Interdisciplinary Journal of Decadence Studies*, 2 (1) (Spring 2019). For an instructive definition of 'decadent orientalism', see Fieni, *Decadent Orientalisms*, p. 3.

31 Matei Calinescu, *Five Faces of Modernity: Modernism, Avant-Garde, Decadence, Kitsch, Postmodernism* (Durham: Duke University Press, 1987), p. 155; Potolsky, *Decadent Republic of Letters*, p. 4.

32 Julia Skelly, *Radical Decadence: Excess in Contemporary Feminist Textiles and Craft* (London and New York: Bloomsbury, 2017); Jillian Hernandez, *Aesthetics of Excess: The Art and Politics of Black and Latina Embodiment* (Durham and London: Duke University Press, 2020).

33 Saidiya Hartman, *Wayward Lives, Beautiful Experiments: Intimate Histories of Riotous Black Girls, Troublesome Women and Queer Radicals* (London: Serpent's Tail, 2021), p. 23.

34 Richard Drake, 'Decadence, Decadentism and Decadent Romanticism in Italy: Toward a Theory of Decadence', *Journal of Contemporary History*, 17 (1) (January 1982), pp. 69–92 (p. 69).

35 Sianne Ngai, *Our Aesthetic Categories: Zany, Cute, Interesting* (Cambridge, MA: Harvard University Press, 2012), p. 7.
36 David Weir, 'Afterword: Decadent Taste', in Jane Desmarais and Alice Condé (eds), *Decadence and the Senses* (Cambridge: Legenda, 2017), pp. 219–28 (p. 221).
37 For discussions of this refusal, see Dave Beech's critique of Oscar Wilde's affirmation of idle leisure, and Kirsten MacLeod's writing on anti-capitalist decadent dilettantism and the refusal of productive use. Dave Beech, *Art and Postcapitalism: Aesthetic Labour, Automation and Value Production* (London: Pluto Press, 2019), pp. 86–8; Kirsten MacLeod, *Fictions of British Decadence: High Art, Popular Writing, and the Fin de Siècle* (Basingstoke and New York: Palgrave Macmillan, 2006), p. 29.
38 Rosa, *Social Acceleration*, pp. 13–14.
39 Alvin Toffler [and Heidi Toffler], 'The Future as a Way of Life', *Horizon*, 7 (3) (Summer 1965), pp. 108–15.
40 Jon McKenzie, *Perform or Else: From Discipline to Performance* (London and New York, 2001).
41 Critical Art Ensemble, 'Reinventing Precarity', *TDR*, 56 (4) (Winter 2012), pp. 49–61 (pp. 49–50).
42 See, for instance, Theron Schmidt, 'Troublesome Professionals: On the Speculative Reality of Theatrical Labour', *Performance Research*, 18 (2) (2013), pp. 15–26 (p. 15); Randy Martin, 'A Precarious Dance, a Derivative Sociality', *TDR*, 56 (4) (Winter 2012), pp. 62–77 (p. 66). See also Beech, *Art and Postcapitalism*, p. 8.
43 Graphs produced by the UK Office for National Statistics setting out national productivity levels between 1971 and the coronavirus outbreak in 2019 (both output per hour worked, and output per worker) show steady rises in the years running up to the 2008 financial crash, and a petering out and occasionally slight drops between 2008 and 2019. ONS, 'Labour Productivity', *Office for National Statistics*, 5 July 2019, https://www.ons.gov.uk/employmentandlabourmarket/peopleinwork/labourproductivity, accessed 2 February 2022. Labour productivity figures in the United States are more volatile over the same period, albeit with a general upward trend, but the gap between productivity and worker compensation has widened significantly since 2000. Benjamin Landy, 'Graph: Does Productivity Growth Still Benefit the American Worker?', *The Century Foundation*, 15 August 2012, https://tcf.org/content/commentary/graph-does-productivity-growth-still-benefit-the-american-worker/?agreed=1, accessed 2 February 2022. For critical analyses of declining growth and productivity, see Danny Dorling, *Slowdown: The End of the Great Acceleration – And Why it's Good for the Planet, the Economy, and Our Lives* (New Haven and London: Yale University Press, 2020); Robert J. Gordon, *The Rise and Fall of American Growth: The U. S. Standard of Living Since the Civil War* (Princeton and Oxford: Princeton University Press, 2016); Tim Jackson, *Post Growth: Life after Capitalism* (Cambridge and Medford,

MA: Polity Press, 2021); Sarah Sharma, *In the Meantime: Temporality and Cultural Politics* (Durham and London: Duke University Press, 2014).

44 Steven Pinker, *Enlightenment Now: The Case for Reason, Science, Humanism and Progress* (New York: Penguin, 2018), p. 329. The UK economy rebounded in 2021 with the fastest growth since the Second World War, but the 7.5 per cent growth it achieved was still less than the 9.4 per cent collapse it experienced in the previous year when parts of the economy were shut down. The end of the year also marked the beginnings of a significant cost of living crisis in the UK. See Russell Hotton, 'UK Economy Rebounds with Fastest Growth Since WW2', *BBC News*, 11 February 2022, https://www.bbc.co.uk/news/business-60344573, accessed 11 February 2022.

45 Francis Green et al., 'Is Job Quality Becoming More Unequal?', *Industrial & Labour Relations Review*, 66 (4) (2013), pp. 753–84 (p. 778).

46 A 2015 YouGov poll reports that 37 per cent of British workers believe that their job makes no meaningful contribution to the world, and a study by Schouten & Nelissen suggests that 40 per cent of workers in Holland believe that their job should not exist. See David Graeber, *Bullshit Jobs: A Theory* (London and New York: Penguin, 2018), p. xxii. According to another YouGov poll, 24 per cent of American workers say that their job does not make a meaningful contribution to the world. See Peter Moore, 'One Quarter of Americans Think Their Jobs are Meaningless', *YouGov*, 14 August 2015, https://today.yougov.com/topics/lifestyle/articles-reports/2015/08/14/one-quarter-americans-think-their-jobs-are-meaning, accessed 2 February 2022.

47 Judy Wajcman, *Pressed for Time: The Acceleration of Life in Digital Capitalism* (Chicago and London: University of Chicago Press, 2015), pp. 4–5 and 64–5.

48 Byung-Chul Han, *The Burnout Society*, trans. Erik Butler (Stanford: Stanford University Press, 2015), p. 10.

49 Paul Virilio, *Polar Inertia*, trans. Patrick Camiller (London: Sage, 2000), p. 21, original emphasis. The notion of 'intensive time' is a common trope in postmodern discourse and speed theory. See, for instance, David Harvey's writing on time-space compression, Manuel Castells's notion of 'timeless time', Frederic Jameson's remarks on a 'steady stream of momentum and variation that [. . .] seems stable and motionless', Helga Nowotny's writing on simultaneity in the 'extended present', and John Urry's concept of 'instantaneous time'. David Harvey, *The Condition of Postmodernity* (Oxford: Blackwell, 1990); Manuel Castells, *The Rise of the Network Society* (Oxford: Blackwell, 1996); Helga Nowotny, *Time: The Modern and Postmodern Experience*, trans. Neville Plaice (Cambridge: Polity Press, 1994), pp. 50–1; Jameson, *Cultural Turn*, p. 59; John Urry, *Sociology Beyond Societies: Mobilities for the Twenty-First Century* (London: Routledge, 2000). Modernist precedents also abound. Charles Baudelaire famously identified 'the ephemeral, the fugitive, the contingent' in modernity, and Walter Benjamin influentially explored how modernity antiquates the recent

past via the temporality and experience of 'shock'. Charles Baudelaire, *The Painter of Modern Life and Other Essays*, ed. and trans. Jonathan Mayne (New York: de Capo Press, n.d.), p. 12; Walter Benjamin, *Illuminations*, ed. Hannah Arendt, trans. Harry Zohn (London: Fontana, 1973), p. 90.

50 For examples, see Aaron Bastani, *Fully Automated Luxury Communism: A Manifesto* (London and New York: Verso, 2019); Robin Mackay and Armen Avanessian (eds), *#Accelerate: The Accelerationist Reader* (Falmouth: Urbanomic Media Ltd, 2017); Paul Mason, *Postcapitalism: A Guide to Our Future* (London: Penguin, 2015); Nick Srnicek and Alex Williams, *Inventing the Future: Postcapitalism and a World Without Work*, rev. ed. (London and New York: Verso, 2016). For instructive critiques of social acceleration and accelerationism (although Hassan anticipates acceleration*ism*), see Robert Hassan, *The Information Society* (Cambridge and Malden, MA: Polity Press, 2008); Benjamin Noys, *Malign Velocities: Accelerationism and Capitalism* (Winchester and Washington: Zero Books, 2014). For more controversial examples of radically libertarian accelerationism, see Nick Land, *Fanged Noumena: Collected Writings 1987–2007*, 6th edition, ed. Robin Mackay and Ray Brassier (Falmouth and New York: Urbanomic, 2018).

51 Kathi Weeks, *The Problem with Work: Feminism, Marxism, Antiwork Politics, and Postwork Imaginaries* (Durham and London: Duke University Press, 2011), p. 12.

52 Sara Ahmed, *Living a Feminist Life* (Durham and London: Duke University Press, 2017), p. 40.

53 See, for instance, Pirjo Lyytikäinen, 'Decadent Tropologies of Sickness', in Marja Härmänmaa and Christopher Nissen (eds), *Decadence, Degeneration, and the End: Studies in the European* Fin de Siècle (New York: Palgrave Macmillan, 2014), pp. 85–102. The Norwegian singer-songwriter's Jenny Hval's debut novel *Perlebryggeriet* (*Paradise Rot*, 2009) has also attracted the attention of scholars interested in contemporary decadence. See, for instance, Sally Blackburn-Daniels, '"His Red Flesh Their Forbidden Fruit": Permeable Bodies in Hval's *Paradise Rot*', paper presented at *Decadent Bodies*, Goldsmiths, University of London, London, 28–29 July 2022.

Chapter 1

1 BBC, 'The Artist Who Believes he's a Zombie', podcast, 4 April 2019, https://www.bbc.co.uk/news/av/disability-47813085, accessed 6 July 2022. See also Adam Alston, 'Martin O'Brien – Interview for Staging Decadence', *Staging Decadence Blog*, 26 July 2022, https://www.stagingdecadence.com/blog/martin-obrien, accessed 10 August 2022.

2 For more on these examples, see: Jenny Lawson, '*Eating Minds*: Fantasizing Undead, Becoming Zombie in Performance', *Studies in Theatre and Performance*, 34 (3) (2014), pp. 236–43; Claire Hind and Gary Winters,

Embodying the Dead: Writing, Playing, Performing (London: Red Globe Press, 2020); Teri Howson, 'Zombies, Time Machines and Brains: Science Fiction Made Real in Immersive Theatres', *Thesis Eleven*, 131 (1) (2015), pp. 114–26; Rebecca Schneider, 'It Seems As If... I Am Dead: Zombie Capitalism and Theatrical Labor', *TDR: The Drama Review*, 56 (4) (Winter 2012), pp. 150–62. Numerous scholars have also noted connections between performance and the living dead. See especially Herbert Blau, *Take Up the Bodies: Theatre at the Vanishing Point* (Urbana: University of Illinois Press, 1982), p. 83.

3 The extent of Rose's contributions to these collaborations have only recently gained focused attention. See Yetta Howard (ed.), *Rated RX: Sheree Rose with and After Bob Flanagan* (Columbus: Ohio State University Press, 2020). See also Adam Alston, 'Survival of the Sickest: On Decadence, Disease and the Performing Body', *Volupté: Interdisciplinary Journal of Decadence Studies*, 4 (2) (2021), pp. 130–56.

4 Amelia Jones, 'Rose/Flanagan/O'Brien: The Aesthetics of Resurrection', in Howard, *Rated RX*, pp. 98–109 (p. 101).

5 Martin O'Brien, 'Until the Last Breath is Breathed – Martin O'Brien Performance Lecture DaDaFest International 2018', *YouTube*, 14 January 2019, https://www.youtube.com/watch?v=dEvGjLgw-A0, accessed 27 March 2020.

6 Marina Warner, *Phantasmagoria: Spirit Visions, Metaphors, and Media into the Twenty-First Century* (Oxford and New York: Oxford University Press, 2006), p. 366.

7 Susan Sontag, *Illness as Metaphor and AIDS and Its Metaphors* (London: Penguin, 1991), p. 3.

8 Lúcio Reis Filho, 'No Safe Space: Zombie Film Tropes during the COVID-19 Pandemic', *Space and Culture*, 23 (3) (2020), pp. 253–8; Martin O'Brien, 'You Are My Death: The Shattered Temporalities of Zombie Time', *Welcome Open Research*, 5 (135) (2020), pp. 3–10 (p. 3).

9 O'Brien does not approach pathology as a subgenre of autobiography, although his work might be said to stage a resistant mode of embodied pathography based not on autobiography, but a falling away from biomedical discourses that shape and discipline sick bodies. For more on embodied pathography, see Emma Brodzinski, 'The Patient Performer: Embodied Pathography in Contemporary Productions', in Alex Mermikides and Gianna Bouchard (eds), *Performance and the Medical Body* (London: Bloomsbury, 2016), pp. 85–97.

10 See Martin O'Brien, 'Performing Chronic: Chronic Illness and Endurance Art', *Performance Research*, 19 (4) (2014), pp. 54–63 (p. 56).

11 O'Brien, 'Until the Last Breath is Breathed', from 01:11.

12 Priscilla Wald, *Contagious: Cultures, Carriers, and the Outbreak Narrative* (Durham and London: Duke University Press, 2008), pp. 52–3 and 67.

13 See Alan Kraut's notion of 'medicalized nativism' in Alan M. Kraut, *Silent Travelers: Germs, Genes, and the "Immigrant Menace"* (Baltimore: Johns

Hopkins University Press, 1994), p. 3. Numerous studies evidence a connection between the Covid-19 pandemic and increased xenophobia. For instance, see Zhuang She et al., 'Does COVID-19 Threat Increase Xenophobia? The Roles of Protection Efficacy and Support Seeking', *BMC Public Health*, 22 (485) (2022), https://doi.org/10.1186/s12889-022-12912-8, accessed 14 June 2022.

14 The World Health Organization formally identified the spread of coronavirus as a pandemic on 11 March 2020. The UK government did not implement its 'stay at home' message until 23 March 2020, although by this point many theatres, including the ICA, had already cancelled or postponed live performances.

15 Gianna Bouchard, 'Introduction: With (Dis-eased) Affection', in Martin O'Brien and David MacDiarmid (eds), *Survival of the Sickest: The Art of Martin O'Brien* (London: Live Art Development Agency, 2018), pp. 6–9 (p. 7).

16 Alphonso Lingis, 'Consecration', in O'Brien and MacDiarmid, *Survival of the Sickest*, pp. 22–4 (p. 23).

17 'Waiting Times' was a Welcome Trust Collaborative Awards in Humanities and Social Science project led by Laura Salisbury and Lisa Baraitser. For further information, see: https://waitingtimes.exeter.ac.uk/.

18 Lisa Baraitser, *Enduring Time* (London: Bloomsbury, 2017), p. 2, original emphasis. Baraitser positions her study of time's suspension in opposition to interminable time 'in the sense of Heidegger's account of boredom'; she is more concerned with the relationship between ethics and ontology, and in connecting suspended time to practices of care. Baraitser, *Enduring Time*, p. 4.

19 David Harvey, *The Condition of Postmodernity: An Enquiry into the Origins of Cultural Change* (Oxford: Blackwell, 1989), p. 147.

20 Elizabeth Freeman, *Time Binds: Queer Temporalities, Queer Histories* (Durham and London: Duke University Press, 2010), p. 3. See also Dana Luciano's writing on 'chronobiopolitics' in Dana Luciano, *Arranging Grief: Sacred Time and the Body in Nineteenth-Century America* (New York: New York University Press, 2007), p. 9. Note that Freeman forwards a critique of 'suspended time', but of a kind that focuses on nation-building events like the Olympics, and hence of a different ilk to the time-in-suspension explored by Baraitser. See Freeman, *Time Binds*, p. 6.

21 O'Brien, 'Performing Chronic', pp. 62–3.

22 Stephen Wright, 'The Fate of Public Time: Toward a Time Without Qualities', *North East West South*, 10 January 2008, https://northeastwestsouth.net/fate-public-time-toward-time-without-qualities-0/, accessed 16 February 2022. For more on the temporal commons, see Allen C. Bluedorn and Mary J. Waller, 'The Stewardship of the Temporal Commons', *Research in Organizational Behavior*, 27 (2006), pp. 355–96 (p. 357).

23 Baraitser conceives of the suspension of time 'as a viscous fluid'. Baraitser, *Enduring Time*, p. 1.
24 Alston, 'Martin O'Brien – Interview for Staging Decadence'.
25 O'Brien makes a similar point in the performance's programme notes. See Martin O'Brien, 'You Are My Death: The Shattered Temporalities of Zombie Time', in *The Last Breath Society (Coughing Coffin)*, programme notes (London: Institute for Contemporary Art, 2019), pp. 2–3 (p. 2).
26 Eirini Kartsaki, *Repetition in Performance: Returns and Invisible Forces* (London: Palgrave Macmillan, 2017), p. 124.
27 Chris Thorpe qtd. in Caridad Svich, 'Chris Thorpe', *Toward a Future Theatre: Conversations During a Pandemic* (London and New York: Methuen Drama 2022), para 8.185 [E-book viewer EPUB], https://www.bl.uk/.
28 Karmen MacKendrick, *Counterpleasures* (Albany: New York State University, 1999), pp. 65–6, original emphasis.
29 MacKendrick, *Counterpleasures*, pp. 3 and 12.
30 Lee Miller, 'Editorial Introduction', *Studies in Theatre and Performance*, 34 (3) (2014), pp. 191–200 (p. 194). For a discussion of the racial politics at stake in *Night of the Living Dead*, see Jack Halberstam, *Wild Things: The Disorder of Desire* (Durham and London: Duke University Press, 2020), pp. 164–6.
31 An interesting exception is the Halperin brothers' *Revolt of the Zombies* (1936), which depicts the 'horror' of a native Cambodian population refusing to work for their colonial masters. For contextualization of this and other zombie films exploring African-diasporic slavery, see Chera Kee, '"They Are Not Men . . . They Are Dead Bodies!": From Cannibal to Zombie and Back Again', in Deborah Christie and Sarah Juliet Lauro (eds), *Better off Dead: The Evolution of the Zombie as Post-Human* (New York: Fordham, 2011), pp. 9–23.
32 O'Brien, *Last(ing)*, SPILL Festival of Performance, Toynbee Studios, London, 11 April 2013. The crowning achievement of the protagonist of Joris-Karl Huysmans's decadent urtext *À rebours* (1884), Jean Floressas des Esseintes, is to devise a means whereby nourishment can be delivered by means of an enema. The decadent writer Jean Lorrain also died after an enema ruptured his colon.
33 O'Brien, 'Performing Chronic', p. 63. The term 'slow death' is drawn from Lauren Berlant, *Cruel Optimism* (Durham and London: Duke University Press, 2011), p. 95.
34 The category 'Zombie 2.0' is taken from Miller, 'Editorial Introduction', p. 196.
35 Martin O'Brien, 'The Unwell', *Martin O'Brien – Performance Artist*, https://www.martinobrienart.com/the-unwell.html, accessed 31 March 2020.
36 O'Brien, 'The Unwell'.
37 The cough as the 'creature voiced' is taken from Simon Bayly, *A Pathognomy of Performance* (Basingstoke: Palgrave Macmillan, 2011), pp. 166–7. See

also Martin O'Brien, 'Cough, Bitch, Cough: Reflections on Sickness and the Coughing Body in Performance', in Mermikides and Bouchard, *Performance and the Medical Body*, pp. 129–36 (p. 132).

38 Alison Kafer, *Feminist, Queer, Crip* (Bloomington: Indiana University Press, 2013), 2.
39 Kafer, *Feminist, Queer, Crip*, pp. 26–7.
40 Kafer, *Feminist, Queer, Crip*, p. 28.
41 Kafer is one of the most significant theorists of crip time, which she refers to in terms of a perennial lateness, additional time, and flexible standards of punctuality – in short, a 'reorientation to time'. See Kafer, *Feminist, Queer, Crip*, pp. 26–7. See also Irving Kenneth Zola, 'The Language of Disability: Problems of Politics and Practice', *Australian Disability Review*, 1 (3) (1988), pp. 13–21; Carol J. Gill, 'A Psychological View of Disability Culture', *DSQ: Disability Studies Quarterly*, 15 (4) (1995), pp. 16–19.
42 Kafer, *Feminist, Queer, Crip*, p. 39.
43 José Esteban Muñoz, *Cruising Utopia: The Then and There of Queer Futurity* (New York and London: New York University Press, 2009), p. 30.
44 Eric Cazdyn, *The Already Dead: The New Time of Politics, Culture, and Illness* (Durham and London: Duke University Press, 2012), p. 6.
45 For a meticulous consideration of Martin Heidegger's *Being and Time* (1927), see Peter Osborne, *The Politics of Time: Modernity and Avant-Garde* (London and New York: Verso, 1995), pp. 55–62, especially p. 57. For an overview of the distinction between a quantitatively-measured duration (*chronos*) and the exceptional time of 'a qualitative event that creates, arrests or changes time', see Kimberly Hutchings, *Time and World Politics: Thinking the Present* (Manchester and New York: Manchester University Press), p. 5. Note that *chronos* is often framed as being 'merely' endured, whereas O'Brien foregrounds endurance in his engagement with *kairos* as that which interrupts the standardization of *chronos*. See also Steven Shaviro's remarks on 'the slow meanders of zombie time' in Steven Shaviro, *The Cinematic Body* (Minneapolis: University of Minnesota Press, 2011), p. 98.
46 Cazdyn, *The Already Dead*, p. 9.
47 Cazdyn's management of leukaemia inspired certain aspects of *The Already Dead*. See Cazdyn, *The Already Dead*, pp. 9–10. Note that Cazdyn would also be sceptical of allegorical figurations of the zombie, which play an important role in O'Brien's practice. See pp. 201–4.
48 See Martin O'Brien, *Mucus Factory*, in *Access all Areas: Double DVD Set*, ed. and produced by Andrew Mitchell and Paula Gorini. Available in Lois Keidan and C.J. Mitchell, eds, *Access all Areas: Live Art and Disability* (London: Live Art Development Agency, 2012).
49 See David Weir, 'Afterword: Decadent Taste', in Jane Desmarais and Alice Condé (eds), *Decadence and the Senses* (Cambridge: Legenda, 2017), pp. 219–28 (p. 221).
50 Dodie Bellamy, *When the Sick Rule the World* (South Pasadena: Semiotext(e), 2015), p. 36.

51 Halberstam, *Wild Things*, p. 148.
52 Alston, 'Martin O'Brien – Interview for Staging Decadence'.
53 O'Brien, 'Until the Last Breath is Breathed'.
54 György Lukács, *Writer and Critic and Other Essays*, ed. and trans. Arthur Kahn (London: Merlin Press, 1978), p. 106.
55 Lukács, *Writer and Critic*, p. 106.
56 Lukács, *Writer and Critic*, pp. 107–8.
57 Jacques Derrida, 'The Deconstruction of Actuality: An Interview with Jacques Derrida', trans. Jonathan Rée, *Radical Philosophy*, 68 (Autumn 1994), pp. 28–41 (p. 32).
58 Sara Ahmed, *What's the Use? On the Uses of Use* (Durham and London: Duke University Press, 2019), p. 64.
59 O'Brien, 'Until the Last Breath is Breathed'.
60 O'Brien, 'Until the Last Breath is Breathed', my emphasis.
61 O'Brien, 'You Are My Death' (2020), p. 3.

Chapter 2

1 I explore these issues and relationships elsewhere. See Adam Alston, 'Decadence and the Antitheatrical Prejudice', in Dustin Friedman and Kristin Mahoney (eds), *Nineteenth-Century Literature in Transition: The 1890s* (Cambridge University Press, forthcoming). For an authoritative study of the relationships between decadence and symbolism, see Vincent Sherry, *Modernism and the Reinvention of Decadence* (New York: Cambridge University Press, 2015), pp. 6–7. For a discussion of decadence, embodiment and disembodiment, see John Stokes on the 'Paterian Paradox' in 'The Legend of Duse', in Ian Fletcher (ed.), *Decadence and the 1890s* (New York: Holmes and Meier Publishers, Inc.), pp. 151–71 (p. 151).
2 See James Bridle, *New Dark Age: Technology and the End of the Future* (London and Brooklyn: Verso, 2018), pp. 34–40 *passim*. See also Robert Hassan on 'digital magic' in *The Condition of Digitality: A Post-Modern Marxism for the Practice of Digital Life* (London: University of Westminster Press, 2020), pp. 51–2.
3 Mark Fisher, *Capitalist Realism: Is There No Alternative?* (Winchester and Washington: Zer0 Books, 2009), p. 2; Frederic Jameson, 'Future City', *New Left Review* 21 (May/June 2003), pp. 65–79 (p. 76). See also Fisher, *Ghosts of My Life: Writings on Depression, Hauntology and Lost Futures* (Winchester and Washington: Zer0 Books, 2014), pp. 8–9; Franco 'Bifo' Beradi, *After the Future*, ed. Gary Genosko and Nicholas Thoburn, trans. Arianna Bove et al. (Oakland and Edinburgh: AK Press, 2011), pp. 17–18; Paul Virilio, *The Futurism of the Instant: Stop-Eject*, trans. Julie Rose (Cambridge and Malden, MA: Polity Press, 2010), pp. 22–3 and 71.

4 Jon McKenzie, *Perform or Else: From Discipline to Performance* (London and New York: Routledge, 2001), pp. 12 and 97.
5 Sarah Hemming, 'Murdering the Text: Sarah Hemming on Julia Bardsley's Macbeth in Leicester, and Murder Is Easy in London', *The Independent*, 3 March 1993, https://www.independent.co.uk/arts-entertainment/theatre-murdering-the-text-sarah-hemming-on-julia-bardsleys-macbeth-in-leicester-and-murder-is-easy-1495320.html, accessed 24 February 2022. The UK slipped into a short recession in the early 1990s as a consequence of the US savings and loan crisis and an inflationary spiral associated with the Lawson Boom in the late 1980s.
6 For an instructive biographical overview, see Dominic Johnson, 'The Skin of the Theatre: An Interview with Julia Bardsley', *Contemporary Theatre Review*, 20 (3) (2010), pp. 340–52.
7 NRLA, 'Julia Bardsley: Aftermaths: A Tear in the Meat of Vision', *NRLA30*, 2020, https://nrla30.com/the-artists/julia-bardsley/, accessed 12 April 2022.
8 Bardsley has turned to Fisher's book in subsequent practice. In June 2017, she presented a collaborative performance, a 'Reading Room', with Dominic Johnson at Queen Mary, University of London, in which *Capitalist Realism* was read cover to cover. See http://www.airproject.qmul.ac.uk/whatson/.
9 Mark Fisher, *K-Punk: The Collected and Unpublished Writings of Mark Fisher (2004–2016)*, ed. Darren Ambrose (London: Repeater, 2018), p. 462, original emphasis.
10 Fisher, *Capitalist Realism*, p. 15.
11 The plague costumes in *Aftermaths* seem to reference the ten Plagues of Egypt more than the seven bowls (or plagues) depicted in Revelation 16.
12 'Je suis l'Empire à la fin de la decadence': translated variously as 'I am the Empire at the end of decadence', or 'I am the Empire in the last of its decline'. The latter translation can be found in Paul Verlaine, 'Languer', in Gertrude Hall (trans.), *Poems of Paul Verlaine* (New York: Duffield & Company, 1906), p. 79.
13 Jeffrey Jerome Cohen, 'Monster Culture (Seven Theses)', in Cohen (ed.), *Monster Theory: Reading Culture* (Minneapolis and London: University of Minnesota Press, 1996), pp. 3–25 (p. 6). Compare with Laura Bissell's writing on Bardsley's Plagues as 'both cyborgian and grotesque'. Laura Bissell, 'The Female Cyborg as Grotesque in Performance', *International Journal of Performance Arts and Digital Media*, 9 (2) (2013), pp. 261–74 (p. 261).
14 Cohen, 'Monster Culture', p. 7.
15 Cohen, 'Monster Culture', p. 12. See also Elaine L. Graham on the monster and the 'gates of difference' in Elaine Graham, *Representations of the Post/Human: Monsters, aliens and others in popular culture* (Manchester: Manchester University Press, 2002), p. 39 and 47–55 (*passim*).
16 Cohen, 'Monster Culture', p. 16.
17 Judith Halberstam, *Skin Shows: Gothic Horror and the Technology of Monsters* (Durham and London: Duke University Press, 1995), p. 12.

Mary Shelley describes Frankenstein's monster as 'hideous progeny', and bids them to 'go forth and prosper'. See Mary Shelley, *Frankenstein or The Modern Prometheus*, ed. M. K. Joseph (New York and Oxford: Oxford University Press, 1980), p. 10.

18 Frederic Jameson, *Archaeologies of the Future: The Desire Called Utopia and Other Science Fictions* (London and New York: Verso, 2007), pp. 231–2.

19 For more on utopia and the apocalypse, see Vita Fortunati, 'From Utopia to Science Fiction', in Krishan Kumar and Stephen Bann (eds) *Utopias and the Millenium* (London: Reaktion Books, 1993), pp. 81–9.

20 See, for instance, Roger Luckhurst, 'The Weird: A Dis/orientation', *Textual Practice*, 31 (6) (2017), pp. 1041–61 (p. 1046).

21 Eirini Kartsaki, 'Rehearsals of the Weird: Julia Bardsley's *Almost the Same (Feral Rehearsals for Violent Acts of Culture)*', *Contemporary Theatre Review*, 30 (1) (2020), pp. 67–90 (p. 68).

22 Mark Fisher, *The Weird and the Eerie* (London: Repeater, 2016), pp. 10–11 and 61. See also Jonathan Newell, *Weird Fiction 1832–1937: Disgust, Metaphysics and the Aesthetics of Cosmic Horror* (Cardiff: University of Wales Press, 2020). For an instructive literature review surveying key scholarship on British weird fiction, see James Machin, *Weird Fiction in Britain 1880–1939* (Cham: Palgrave Macmillan, 2018), pp. 5–11. Note that Lovecraft's interest in monstrous others was controversial even for its own time. For one of the more erudite accounts of Lovecraft's xenophobia, see Abel Alves, 'Humanity's Place in Nature, 1863–1928: Horror, Curiosity and the Expeditions of Huxley, Wallace, Blavatsky and Lovecraft', *Theology and Science*, 6 (1) (2008), pp. 73–88 (pp. 74–6 and pp. 82–3).

23 See Katharina Herold and Leire Barrera-Medrano (eds), 'Women Writing Decadence', *Volupté: Interdisciplinary Journal of Decadence Studies*, 2 (1) (Spring 2019). See also Nicole G. Albert, *Lesbian Decadence: Representations in Art and Literature of fin-de-siècle France*, trans. Nancy Erber and William Peniston (New York and York: Harrington Park Press, 2016); Elaine Showalter (ed.), *Daughters of Decadence: Stories by Women Writers of the Fin de Siècle* (London: Virago, 2016).

24 One might think here of the influence of Charles Baudelaire on French and English decadents in the nineteenth century. Although Baudelaire is often cited as a misogynist, feminist scholars have also revisited his work as evincing a more complex relationship to women and women's empowerment. See Michèle Roberts, 'Should Feminists Read Baudelaire?', *BBC Radio 4*, 28 March 2021, https://www.bbc.co.uk/programmes/m000tmhp, accessed 24 February 2022.

25 Julia Skelly, *Radical Decadence: Excess in Contemporary Feminist Textiles and Craft* (London: Bloomsbury, 2017), p. 4.

26 Skelly, *Radical Decadence*, p. 38.

27 Barbara Creed, *The Monstrous-Feminine: Film, Feminism, Psychoanalysis* (London and New York: Routledge, 1993), p. 151. See also Mary Russo,

The Female Grotesque: Risk, Excess and Modernity (New York and London: Routledge, 1995), p. 70.
28 Creed, *The Monstrous-Feminine*, p. 17.
29 Silvia Federici, *Caliban and the Witch: Women, the Body and Primitive Accumulation*, 2nd edition (New York: Autonomedia, 2014), p. 8. Federici is drawing on the work of Mariarosa Dalla Costa. See Mariarosa Dalla Costa, *Potere Femminile e Sovversione Sociale* (Venice: Marsilio Editori, 1972), p. 31.
30 Federici, *Caliban and the Witch*, pp. 11 and 40. As Federici explores, the sexual aspects of heresy that came to underpin many charges of witchcraft only become prominent after the spread of the plague in the mid-fourteenth century.
31 Charles Baudelaire, 'In Praise of Makeup', trans. Jane Desmarais, in Jane Desmarais and Chris Baldick (eds.), *Decadence: An Annotated Anthology* (Manchester and New York: Manchester University Press, 2012), pp. 22–4 (p. 23).
32 Marja Härmänmaa and Christopher Nissen, 'Introduction: The Empire at the End of Decadence', in Marja Härmänmaa and Christopher Nissen (eds), *Decadence, Degeneration, and the End: Studies in the European* Fin de Siècle' (New York and Basingstoke: Palgrave Macmillan, 2014), pp. 1–14 (p. 4).
33 Karmen MacKendrick, *Counterpleasures* (Albany: New York State University, 1999).
34 Härmänmaa and Nissen, 'Introduction', p. 4.
35 Sharon G. Feldman, 'An Aspiration to the Authentic: La Fura dels Baus', in *In the Eye of the Storm: Contemporary Theater in Barcelona* (Lewisburg: Bucknell University Press, 2009), pp. 75–102 (pp. 83–4). While referred to as 'The Madrilenian Scene', the movement quickly spread to other cities – including Barcelona.
36 Eva Bru-Domínguez, 'Becoming Undone: Colour, Matter and Line in the Artwork of Marcel·lí Antúnez', in Stuart Davis and Maite Usoz de la Fuente (eds), *The Modern Spanish Canon: Visibility, Cultural Capital and the Academy* (Abingdon and New York: Legenda, 2018), pp. 37–57 (pp. 38 and 54).
37 Steve Dixon, 'Cybernetic-Existentialism and Being-Towards-Death in Contemporary Art and Performance', *TDR*, 61 (3) (Fall 2017), pp. 36–55 (pp. 37–8).
38 Graham, *Representations of the Post/Human*, p. 183. Note that the original conceptualization of the cyborg was also focused on the achievement of homeostasis in space. See Manfred E. Clynes and Nathan S. Kline, 'Cyborgs in Space', in Chris Gray (ed.), *The Cyborg Handbook* (New York: Routledge, 1995), pp. 29–33. An early theorist of cybernetics, Norbert Weiner, also positioned cybernetics as an attempt to mitigate entropy, or 'nature's tendency to degrade the organized'. Norbert Weiner, *The Human Use of Human Beings: Cybernetics and Society* (n.c.: De Capo Press, 1954), p. 17.
39 Jennifer Parker-Starbuck, *Cyborg Theatre: Corporeal/Technological Intersections in Multimedia Performance* (Basingstoke and New York:

Palgrave Macmillan, 2011), pp. 44–5. Parker-Starbuck distinguishes 'abject bodies' from 'object bodies' and 'subject bodies' (as well as abject, object and subject technologies). In this example, it is more accurate to say that the robot is both abject and objectified, approximating without realizing cyborgian subjecthood. Parker-Starbuck also considers La Fura dels Baus in a chapter on Object Bodies, pp. 94–102.

40   I am paraphrasing a description of a cadaverous body 'becoming ornament' in a later work, *Epiphany* (1999). See Gabriella Giannachi, *Virtual Theatres: An Introduction* (London and New York: Routledge, 2006), p. 67.
41   Marcel·lí Antúnez Roca, *Systematurgy: Actions, Devices, Drawings* (Barcelona: Arts Santa Monica and Ediciones Polígrafa, 2015), p. 16.
42   Antúnez Roca, *Systematurgy*, p. 54.
43   Antúnez Roca, *Systematurgy*, pp. 49 and 68.
44   Hal Foster, *Compulsive Beauty* (London and Cambridge, MA: MIT Press, 1993), pp. 152 and 166; Walter Benjamin, 'Surrealism: The Last Snapshot of the European Intellingentsia', in Edmund Jephcott (trans.), Peter Demetz (ed.), *Reflections* (New York: Harcourt Brace Jovanovich, 1978), pp. 177–92 (p. 177 and pp. 181–2).
45   Matthew Causey, 'Postdigital Performance', *Theatre Journal*, 68 (3) (September 2016), pp. 427–41 (pp. 428 and 440).
46   See Liam Jarvis and Karen Savage, 'Introduction: Postdigitality: Isn't It All "Intermedial"?', in Jarvis and Savage (eds), *Avatars, Activism and Postdigital Performance: Precarious Intermedial Identities* (London: Bloomsbury, 2022), pp. 1–15 (p. 1).
47   Antúnez Roca, *Systematurgy*, p. 69. Antúnez Roca's posthumanism is in line with more balanced treatments of the topic that condemn the 'nightmare' of a culture that pitches bodies as 'fashion accessories', instead of recognizing that 'human being is first of all embodied being'. See N. Katherine Hayles, *How We Became Posthuman: Virtual Bodies in Cybernetics, Literature, and Informatics* (Chicago and London: University of Chicago Press, 1999), pp. 5 and 283.
48   Euripides, *The Bacchae and Other Plays*, trans. Philip Vellacott (London: Penguin Books, 1973), pp. 195–6.
49   Euripides, *The Bacchae*, p. 217.
50   Ovid, *Metamorphoses*, trans. A. D. Melville (Oxford and New York: Oxford University Press, 1998), p. 176.
51   Rachel Hann, *Beyond Scenography* (London and New York: Routledge, 2019), p. 28.

Chapter 3

1   David Fieni, *Decadent Orientalisms: The Decay of Colonial Modernity* (New York: Fordham University Press, 2020), p. 8, original emphasis.

2 See, for instance, Alain Finkielkraut, *L'identité malheureuse* (Paris: Stock, 2013); Éric Zemmour, *Le Suicide Francais* (Paris: Albin Michel, 2014). These are more extreme examples than Douthat's that forward xenophobic and misogynistic perspectives. Zemmour is also a far-right politician.
3 See, for instance, William S. Sadler, *Race Decadence: An Examination of the Causes of Racial Degeneracy in the United States* (Ann Arbor and London: University Microfilms International, 1981 [1922]). Sadler's thesis aligns with other texts of the period addressing 'degeneration'. See, for instance: E. Ray Lankester, *Degeneration: A Chapter in Darwinism* (London: Macmillan and Co., 1880); Cesare Lombroso, *Criminal Man*, trans. Mary Gibson and Nicole Hahn Rafter (Durham and London: Duke University Press, 2006); Max Nordau, *Degeneration*, trans. from the second German edition by George L. Mosse (Lincoln and London: University of Nebraska Press, 1993). See also Arthur de Gobineau's and Houston Stewart Chamberlain's writing on racial degeneration, which influenced Adolf Hitler's Aryanism. An instructive overview is available in Arthur Herman, *The Idea of Decline in Western History* (New York: The Free Press, 1997), pp. 54–63 *passim*. Hitler was influenced by Chamberlain, while Chamberlain worked in the shadow of Gobineau.
4 Alice Condé, 'Decadence and Popular Culture', in Jane Desmarais and David Weir (eds), *Decadence and Literature* (Cambridge: Cambridge University Press, 2019), pp. 379–99 (p. 395). See also David Weir and Jane Desmarais, 'Introduction: Decadence, Culture, and Society', in Jane Desmarais and David Weir (eds), *The Oxford Handbook of Decadence* (New York: Oxford University Press, 2022), pp. 1–17 (p. 13).
5 Matthew Potolsky, 'Decadence and Politics', in Alex Murray (ed.), *Decadence: A Literary History* (Cambridge: Cambridge University Press, 2020), pp. 152–66 (p. 152).
6 Potolsky, 'Decadence and Politics', pp. 152–3.
7 Oscar Wilde, 'The Soul of Man Under Socialism', in *Complete Works of Oscar Wilde, Vol. III: Poems, Essays and Letters* (London: Heron Books, 1966), pp. 371–96.
8 Alice Condé, 'Contemporary Contexts: Decadence Today and Tomorrow', in Desmarais and Weir, *The Oxford Handbook of Decadence*, pp. 96–114 (p. 98).
9 Cedric J. Robinson, *Black Marxism: The Making of the Black Radical Tradition*, 3rd edition (Dublin: Penguin, 2021), p. 66.
10 See Condé, 'Decadence and Popular Culture', p. 396.
11 See, for instance, jaamil olawale kosoko, *Syllabus for Black Love* (2021), https://static1.squarespace.com/static/5c74c0fb4d87115cde1dccfa/t/60edf06ac450ee4730810c0a/1626206331114/SFBL-zine-spreads.pdf, accessed 16 March 2022; kosoko, *Syllabus for Survival* (2020), https://static1.squarespace.com/static/5c74c0fb4d87115cde1dccfa/t/5e9f0d4a97b64409fdb9cdd6/1587481965196/Jaamil_ZINE_17.pdf, accessed 16 March 2022.
12 See Stacie Selmon McCormick, *Staging Black Fugitivity* (Columbus: Ohio State University Press, 2019), p. 11.

13 The content and language differ slightly from that documented in jaamil olawale kosoko, *Black Body Amnesia: Poems & Other Speech Acts*, ed. Dahlia (Dixon) Li and Rachel Valinsky (Brooklyn, NY: Wendy's Subway, 2022), pp. 73–81. All quotations are drawn from filmed documentation of the 2017 premiere, made available courtesy of the artist.
14 kosoko, Personal interview [video call], 20 May 2020.
15 See Brenda Dixon Gottschild, 'Where is the Theology?' (2018), p. 39 https://legacy.blackbox.no/wp-content/uploads/2020/01/BBTP-00_Gottschild.pdf, accessed 16 March 2022. The Gelede is another possible influence, which is a Yoruban masking tradition. Kimberley Miller has considered the gender non-conformity of the Gelede performer as 'a trickster figure, the Gelede dandy. He confounds our perceptions of what makes a male or a female, our perceptions of sex and gender'. Kimberley Miller, 'Cross-Dressing at the Crossroads: Mimic and Ambivalence in Yoruba Masked performance', in Susan Fillin-Yeh (ed.), *Dandies: Fashion and Finesse in Art and Culture* (New York and London: New York University Press, 2001), pp. 204–16 (p. 211).
16 Edgar Saltus, *The Philosophy of Disenchantment* and *The Anatomy of Negation* (N.C.: Underworld Amusements, 2014), p. 45.
17 See Nicolette Gable, '"Willful Sadness": American Decadence, Gender, and the Pleasures and Dangers of Pessimism', *Journal of Gender Studies*, 26 (1) (2017), pp. 102–11 (p. 103). Note that Gable's article draws on an 1897 essay titled 'Willful sadness in literature' by Louise Imogen Guiney.
18 kosoko, *Black Body Amnesia*, pp. 80 and 82.
19 Calvin L. Warren, 'ONTICIDE: Afro-pessimism, Gay Nigger #1, and Surplus Violence', *GLQ: A Journal of Lesbian and Gay Studies*, 23 (3) (2017), pp. 391–418 (pp. 394–6).
20 Calvin L. Warren, *Ontological Terror: Blackness, Nihilism, and Emancipation* (Durham and London: Duke University Press, 2018), p. 8.
21 The idea of Black non-being is historically determined. For instructive contextualization, see Stephanie E. Smallwood's writing on 'social annihilation', 'social death', and the purgatorial existence of commodified slaves in the eighteenth century. Stephanie E. Smallwood, *Saltwater Slavery: A Middle Passage from Africa to American Diaspora* (Cambridge, MA and London: Harvard University Press, 2007), pp. 60–1. See also Orlando Patterson's comparative study of 'social death', although it is less relevant to Warren's Afropessimism. Orlando Patterson, *Slavery and Social Death: A Comparative Study* (Cambridge, MA, and London: Harvard University Press, 2018), pp. 38–45 *passim*.
22 Nicole Serratore, 'Beyond Whiteness: A January Festival Wrap-Up', *American Theatre*, 2 February 2018, https://www.americantheatre.org/2018/02/02/beyond-whiteness-a-january-festival-wrap-up/, accessed 9 March 2022.
23 kosoko, 'personal interview'. For more on performance and trash, see João Florêncio and Owen Parry (eds), 'Trashing', *Dance Theatre Journal*, 24 (3) (2011).

24 Audre Lorde, 'Power', (1978), https://www.poetryfoundation.org/poems/53918/power-56d233adafeb3, accessed 9 March 2022.
25 James Baldwin, 'Stranger in the Village', in *Notes of a Native Son* (Beacon Press 1955), https://www.janvaneyck.nl/site/assets/files/2312/baldwin.pdf, accessed 16 March 2022.
26 Robinson, *Black Marxism*, p. 81.
27 Kodwo Eshun, *More Brilliant than the Sun: Adventures in Sonic Fiction* (London: Quartet Books, 1998), p. 140.
28 For more on spirit catching, see Brenda Dixon Gottschild, *The Black Dancing Body: A Geography from Coon to Cool* (New York and Basingstoke: Palgrave Macmillan, 2003), p. 260.
29 Andres Heisel, 'The Rise and Fall of an All-American Catchphrase: "Free, White, and 21"', *Jezebel*, 10 September 2015, https://theattic.jezebel.com/the-rise-and-fall-of-an-all-american-catchphrase-free-1729621311, accessed 9 March 2022.
30 See Marielle Pelissero, 'From the Figure to the Cipher: Figuration, Disfiguration and the Limits of Visibility', *Performance Research*, 23 (8) (2018), pp. 31–8 (p. 37).
31 kosoko, 'personal interview'.
32 See José Esteban Muñoz, *Disidentifications: Queers of Color and the Performance of Politics* (Minneapolis and London: University of Minnesota Press, 1999), pp. 12, 25, 31 and 97.
33 Warren, 'ONTICIDE', p. 397.
34 Warren, 'ONTICIDE', p. 397, original emphasis. See also Frank B. Wilderson III, *Red, White, and Black* (Durham: Duke University Press, 2010), p. 45; James Bliss, 'Hope Against Hope: Queer Negativity, Black Feminist Theorizing and Reproduction without a Future', *Mosaic*, 48 (2015), pp. 83–98.
35 Christina Sharpe, *In the Wake: On Blackness and Being* (Durham and London: Duke University Press, 2016), p. 14.
36 Saidiya V. Hartman, *Scenes of Subjection: Terror, Slavery, and Self-Making in Nineteenth-Century America* (New York and Oxford: Oxford University Press, 1997), pp. 19–20.
37 Ruby Sales, 'Ruby Sales: Where Does It Hurt?', *On Being with Krista Tippett*, 16 January 2020, https://onbeing.org/programs/ruby-sales-where-does-it-hurt/, accessed 9 March 2022.
38 Sharpe, *In the Wake*, pp. 17–18.
39 Warren, *Ontological Terror*, p. 13. See also David Marriott, 'Waiting to Fall', *CR: The New Centennial Review*, 13 (3) (Winter 2013), pp. 163–240 (p. 214).
40 Warren, *Ontological Terror*, p. 43.
41 The Uhuruverse has experienced multiple displacements which, at the time of writing, found them moving from Los Angeles to New Orleans. See The Uhuruverse, 'Uhuru Dream House', 13 July 2020, https://www.gofundme.com/f/UHURUDREAMHOUSE, accessed 25 February 2022.

42 The Uhuruverse says as much in a quasi-Wildean quip made backstage at a gig in 2015. Beatriz Moreno, 'Snatch Power Episode 1', *YouTube*, 25 October 2015, https://www.youtube.com/watch?v=Wy9seF6-j2Y, accessed 2 March 2022. The idea of a 'creatively strange' eccentricity is drawing on Madison Moore, *Fabulous: The Rise of the Beautiful Eccentric* (New Haven and London: Yale University Press, 2018), pp. 8 and 14.
43 For more on Vaginal Davis and the L.A. punk scene, see José Esteban Muñoz, '"The White to be Angry": Vaginal Creme Davis's Terrorist Drag', in Muñoz, *Disidentifications*, pp. 93–115.
44 Warren, *Ontological Terror*, p. 27.
45 See Simon Hattenstone, 'Star Trek's Nichelle Nichols: "Martin Luther King was a Trekker"', *The Guardian*, 18 October 2016, https://www.theguardian.com/tv-and-radio/2016/oct/18/star-trek-nichelle-nichols-martin-luther-king-trekker, accessed 25 May 2022.
46 See Reynaldo Anderson and Charles E. Jones, 'Introduction: The Rise of Astro-Blackness', in Anderson and Jones (eds), *Afrofuturism 2.0: The Rise of Astro-Blackness* (Lanham: Lexington Books, 2016), pp. vii–xviii (pp. ix–x).
47 Slavoj Žižek, *Living in the End Times* (London and New York: Verso, 2010), p. 84.
48 Žižek, *Living in the End Times*, p. 87, original emphasis. See also Franco 'Bifo' Beradi, *Futurability: The Age of Impotence and the Horizon of Possibility* (London and New York: Verso, 2017), p. 20.
49 Mark Fisher, 'acid communism (unfinished introduction)', in Mark Fisher, *K-Punk: The Collected and Unpublished Writings of Mark Fisher (2004–2016)*, ed. Darren Ambrose (London: Repeater, 2018), pp. 751–70. See also Fisher's writing on hauntology in *Ghosts of My Life: Writings on Depression, Hauntology and Lost Futures* (Winchester and Washington: Zer0 Books, 2014), p. 27. See also David Ayers's illuminating study of 'retroactive Utopias' in the work of William Burroughs. David Ayers, '"Politics Here is Death": William Burroughs's *Cities of the Red Night*', in Krishan Kumar and Stephen Bann (eds), *Utopias and the Millennium* (London: Reaktion Books, 1993), pp. 90–106.
50 August Brown, 'South L.A. Band Gives Voice to Trump-Era Fury', *Los Angeles Times*, 11 April 2017, https://www.latimes.com/entertainment/music/la-et-ms-f-u-pay-us-20170411-story.html?fbclid=IwAR0Xyy4VH9k52aR0aWphQ_rpNA-nOAsSNr5D0lr4wkW1to0skMK4FmAm7-s, accessed 26 February 2022.
51 William H. Grier and Price M. Cobbs, *Black Rage* (New York: Basic Books, 1968).
52 #SNATCHPOWER, 'S.W.P. (Snatches with Power) Live!', YouTube, 22 June 2016, https://www.youtube.com/watch?v=X8Li9qVWa_c, accessed 2 March 2022.
53 The Uhuruverse, 'DISOBEY!!', *Soundcloud*, July 2015, https://soundcloud.com/theuhuruverse/disobey, accessed 26 February 2022.
54 #SNATCHPOWER, 'BASIC ASS FAKE WHITE BITCH (BAFWB) The Uhuruverse X Niko Suki Produced by Onelle Woods', *YouTube*, 1 March

2017, https://www.youtube.com/watch?v=f2359FbpkIM, accessed 3 March 2022.

55 Nia O. Witherspoon qtd. in *Staging Decadence* [film], created by Adam Alston, Owen Parry, and Sophie Farrell, 12 May 2022, https://www.stagingdecadence.com/films, accessed 12 May 2022. Monica L. Miller makes a similar point, exploring how 'Africans dispersed across and around the Atlantic in the slave trade – once slaves to fashion – make fashion their slave'. Monica L. Miller, *Slaves to Fashion: Black Dandyism and the Styling of Black Diasporic Identity* (Durham and London: Duke University Press, 2009), p. 1.

56 See Helen Hester, *Xenofeminism* (Cambridge and Medford, MA: Polity Press, 2018), pp. 6–7.

57 See Simon Bayly, 'The End of the Project: Futurity in the Culture of Catastrophe', *Angelaki*, 18 (2) (2013), pp. 161–77 (pp. 162–5).

58 Seke Chimutengwende, 'Unfunky UFO: 2100AD', 15 January 2018, https://www.youtube.com/watch?v=IAvTRiegrPY, accessed 2 March 2022.

59 Žižek, *Living in the End Times*, p. 79.

60 Open Culture, 'Sun Ra Applies to NASA's Art Program: When the Inventor of Space Jazz Applied to Make Space Art', 10 September 2019, https://www.openculture.com/2019/09/sun-ra-applies-to-nasas-art-program.html, accessed 28 February 2022.

61 See Namwali Serpell, 'The Zambian "Afronaut" Who Wanted to Join the Space Race', *The New Yorker*, 11 March 2017, https://www.newyorker.com/culture/culture-desk/the-zambian-afronaut-who-wanted-to-join-the-space-race, accessed 2 March 2022. See also Namwali Serpell's historical and science fiction novel, *The Old Drift* (2019). A key section of the book explores the Zambian space programme.

62 Ytasha L. Womack, *Afrofuturism: The World of Black Sci-Fi and Fantasy Culture* (Chicago: Lawrence Hill Books, 2013), p. 16.

63 The phrase 'whitey on the moon' is the title of a spoken word poem by Gil Scott-Heron that features on the album *Small Talk at 125th and Lenox* (1970).

64 Serpell, 'The Zambian "Afronaut"'.

65 Ross Douthat, *The Decadent Society: How We Became the Victims of Our Own Success* (New York: Avid Reader Press, 2020), p. 1.

66 Douthat, *The Decadent Society*, p. 2.

67 Douthat, *The Decadent Society*, p. 6.

68 W. Ian Bourland, 'Afronauts', *Third Text*, 34 (2) (2020), pp. 209–29 (pp. 210 and 212). The quote from Cecil Rhodes is cited in Istvan Csicsery-Ronay, Jr, 'Science Fiction and Empire', *Science Fiction Studies*, 30 (2) (July 2003), pp. 231–45 (p. 234).

69 Aimé Césaire, *Discourse on Colonialism*, trans. Joan Pinkham (New York: Monthly Review Press, 2000), p. 31.

70 W. E. B. Du Bois, *The World and Africa* (New York: International Publishers, 1965), p. 1.

71 Derek Walcott, 'What the Twilight Says', *What the Twilight Says* (New York: Farrar, Strauss and Giroux, 1998), pp. 3–35 (p. 24).

72 Robert Stilling, *Beginning at the End: Decadence, Modernism, and Postcolonial Poetry* (Cambridge, MA and London: Harvard University Press, 2018), p. 141.
73 See, for instance, Eshun, *More Brilliant than the Sun*, p. 175. Mark Dery coined the term 'Afrofuturism' in 1993. See Mark Dery (ed.), *Flame Wars: The Discourse of Cyberculture* (Durham and London: Duke University Press, 1994).
74 Mark Sinker, 'Loving the Alien in Advance of Landing – Black Science Fiction', *The Wire*, 96 (February 1992), https://reader.exacteditions.com/issues/35378, accessed 9 March 2023.
75 tobias c. van Veen, 'The Armageddon Effect: Afrofuturism and the Chronopolitics of Alien Nation', in Anderson and Jones, *Afrofuturism 2.0*, pp. 63–90 (p. 65).
76 van Veen, 'The Armageddon Effect', p. 73. For an insightful historicization of alienation as a dissident practice in performance, see Daphne A. Brooks's writing on 'Afro-alienation acts'. Daphne A. Brooks, *Bodies in Dissent: Spectacular Performances of Race and Freedom, 1850–1910* (Durham and London: Duke University Press, 2006), pp. 4–6.
77 James Edward Ford, 'Introduction', *Black Camera*, 7 (1) (2015), pp. 110–14 (p. 110). See also McCormick, *Staging Black Fugitivity*, p. 12.
78 Paul Youngquist, *A Pure Solar World: Sun Ra and the Birth of Afrofuturism* (Austin: University of Texas Press, 2016), p. 33. Note that Sun Ra's interest in the 'slagheap' of the past sometimes ran counter to his professed rejection of the past in the new space age. For examples, see the sleeve notes on albums like *Atlantis* (1969) and *Continuation* (1970).
79 John S. Mbiti, *African Religions and Philosophy*, 2nd edition (Oxford: Heinemann, 1989), p. 23. Writing in the 1960s, Mbiti distinguished between consciousness of the future as a potentiality in traditional African ontologies, and the 'mathematical' concept of time, history and progress in the West. He regarded the importing of 'the future dimension of time' as being potentially beneficial for African nations, but he also warned that the displacement of traditional conceptions of time and history 'can get out of control and precipitate both tragedy and disillusionment'. Mbiti, *African Religions*, p. 27.
80 Alex Zamalin, *Black Utopia: The History of an Idea from Black Nationalism to Afrofuturism* (New York: Columbia University Press, 2019), p. 108.
81 Youngquist, *A Pure Solar World*, p. 44. See also pp. 135 and 196.
82 *Space Is the Place: Sun Ra and His Intergalactic Solar Arkestra*, written by Sun Ra and Joshua Smith, dir. John Coney (Plexifilm, 2003). The film was released in 1974, but shot in 1972.
83 See also Tavia Nyong'o's writing on 'tenseless time' and 'black polytemporality' in *Afro-Fabulations: The Queer Drama of Black Life* (New York: New York University Press, 2019), pp. 10 and 51.
84 Žižek, *Living in the End Times*, p. 84. See also José Esteban Muñoz's theorization of utopia in the years after the 1969 Stonewall Riots (i.e. the

same year as the Apollo moon landing). Muñoz, *Cruising Utopia: The Then and There of Queer Futurity* (New York and London: New York University Press, 2009), pp. 1–3.

Chapter 4

1 Given names follow surnames in Japan. However, I will be using a Western name order throughout because it is the order most commonly used when the Japanese artists and writers discussed in this chapter present or publish work outside of Japan. Diacritics have also been applied where appropriate, although there are exceptions. 'Nikaido' would usually include a macron (Nikaidō), but she presents her name as 'Nikaido'.
2 Frederick Jameson, 'Future City', *New Left Review*, 21 (May/June) (2003), pp. 65–79.
3 Marilyn Ivy, 'Critical Texts, Mass Artifacts: The Consumption of Knowledge in Postmodern Japan', in Masao Miyoshi and H. D. Harootunian (eds), *Postmodernism and Japan* (Durham and London: Duke University Press: 1989), pp. 21–46 (p. 21).
4 Tomiko Yoda, 'The Rise and Fall of Maternal Society: Gender, Labor, and Capital in Contemporary Japan', in Tomiko Yoda and Harry Harootunian (eds), *Japan After Japan: Social and Cultural Life from the Recessionary 1990s to the Present* (Durham and London: Duke University Press, 2006), pp. 239–74 (p. 240).
5 Makoto Itoh, *The World Economic Crisis and Japanese Capitalism* (Basingstoke: Macmillan Press, 1990), p. 181; Gavin McCormack, *The Emptiness of Japanese Affluence*, rev. ed. (New York and London: M. E. Sharpe, 2001), p. 80.
6 The LDP has been in power almost continuously since 1955, aside from two hiatuses: 1993–96 (coalition government led by Morihiro Hosokawa of the Japan New Party) and 2009–12 (Democratic Party of Japan).
7 IMF, 'General Government Gross Debt', World Economic Outlook, October 2019, https://www.imf.org/external/datamapper/GGXWDG_NGDP@WEO/OEMDC/ADVEC/WEOWORLD/JPN, accessed 31 January 2020.
8 See Sara Jansen, '"In What Time Do we Live?" Time and Distance in the Work of Toshiki Okada', *Etcetera*, 145 (2016), https://e-tcetera.be/in-what-time-do-we-live/, accessed 20 May 2022.
9 Byung-Chul Han, *The Burnout Society*, trans. Erik Butler (Stanford: Stanford University Press, 2015).
10 André Lepecki, *Exhausting Dance: Performance and the Politics of Movement* (New York and London: Routledge, 2006), p. 3.
11 Jonathan Crary, *24/7: Late Capitalism and the Ends of Sleep* (London and New York: Verso, 2014), pp. 8–9.
12 Peter Eckersall, 'Toshiki Okada's Ecological Theatre', *PAJ*, 43 (1) (January) (2021), pp. 107–15.

13 chelfitsch (2021) 'chelfitsch & Teppei Kaneuji "Eraser Mountain"', chelfitsch.net, https://chelfitsch.net/en/works/eraser-mountain/, accessed 20 March 2022.
14 Fisher finds Jacques Derrida, 'the inventor of that term, a frustrating thinker'. Fisher's own study of hauntology is more directly relevant to the lost futures of Japan's lost generation, and it also emphasizes aesthetics (particularly in music) above ontology and deconstruction. Mark Fisher, *Ghosts of My Life: Writings on Depression, Hauntology and Lost Futures* (Winchester and Washington: Zer0 Books, 2004), p. 16.
15 Jansen, 'In What Time Do we Live?'. Harry Harootunian makes a similar point, commenting on a 'future [that] could no longer be anticipated', and a past that 'had become a phantom'. Harry Harootunian, *Uneven Moments: Reflections on Japan's Modern History* (New York: Columbia University Press, 2019), p. 296.
16 Fisher, *Ghosts of My Life*, p. 18.
17 Fisher, *Ghosts of My Life*, p. 19.
18 Okada qtd. in M. Cody Poulton, 'Krapp's First Tape: Okada Toshiki's *Enjoy*', *TDR* 55 (2) (Summer) (2011), pp. 150–64 (p. 154).
19 Franco 'Bifo' Beradi, *Futurability: The Age of Impotence and the Horizon of Possibility* (London and New York: Verso, 2017), p. 94.
20 Tarō Okamoto qtd. in Takashi Murakami (ed.), *Little Boy: The Arts of Japan's Exploding Subculture* (New York: Japan Society; New Haven and London: Yale University Press, 2005), p. 2.
21 Johannes Birringer describes 'hyperdance' as a trait in late-twentieth-century European and North American dance practice that emphasizes the speed and intensity of movement, which he sees as a fitting reflection of the intensification and speed of transmission across information superhighways. See Johannes Birringer, *Media and Performance: Along the Border* (Baltimore and London: Johns Hopkins University Press, 1998), pp. 75–6 and pp. 86–7.
22 Kyoko Iwaki, 'Japanese Theatre after Fukushima: Okada Toshiki's *Current Location*', *New Theatre Quarterly*, 31 (1) (February) (2015), pp. 70–89 (pp. 70–1).
23 Iwaki, 'Japanese Theatre after Fukushima', pp. 70–1.
24 Nabuko Anan, 'Chapter 1: Girls' Time, Girls' Space', in *Contemporary Japanese Women's Theatre and Visual Arts: Performing Girls' Aesthetics* (Basingstoke: Palgrave Macmillan, 2016), para. 10.4 [E-book viewer EPUB], https://www.bl.uk/.
25 Anan, *Contemporary Japanese Women's Theatre and Visual Arts*, para. 11.26.
26 Adam Alston, 'Toco Nikaido – Interview for Staging Decadence', *Staging Decadence Blog*, 4 March 2021, https://www.stagingdecadence.com/blog/toco-nikaido-interview-for-staging-decadence, accessed 20 March 2022.
27 Lyn Gardner, 'Miss Revolutionary Idol Berserker Review – Merciless Japanese Pop-Culture Sendup', *The Guardian*, 23 June 2016, https://www

.theguardian.com/stage/2016/jun/23/miss-revolutionary-idol-berserker-review-merciless-japanese-pop-culture-sendup, accessed 20 March 2022.
28 Lepecki, *Exhausting Dance*, p. 7.
29 Yuji Sone, *Japanese Robot Culture: Performance, Imagination and Modernity* (New York: Palgrave Macmillan, 2017), p. 154.
30 Ian F. Martin, *Quit Your Band: Musical Notes from the Japanese Underground* (New York and Tokyo: Awai Books, 2016), p. 60.
31 Tsunku qtd. in Chris Campion, 'J-Pop's dream factory', *The Guardian*, 21 August 2005, https://www.theguardian.com/music/2005/aug/21/popandrock3, accessed 20 March 2022.
32 Gardner, 'Miss Revolutionary Idol Berserker Review'.
33 Sianne Ngai, *Our Aesthetic Categories: Zany, Cute, Interesting* (Cambridge, MA: Harvard University Press, 2012), p. 7.
34 Ngai, *Our Aesthetic Categories*, p. 202.
35 Ngai, *Our Aesthetic Categories*, pp. 14–15; see also pp. 192–7.
36 Ikuho Amano, *Decadent Literature in Twentieth-Century Japan: Spectacles of Idle Labor* (New York: Palgrave Macmillan, 2013), pp. 18–19.
37 Amano offers a fuller historicization of Japanese decadence than I can offer here. See Amano's commentary on the literary group *Pan no kai* (The Circle of Pan) the post-war *Buraiha* (the School of Decadence) associated with Ango Sakaguchi, and the short-lived journal *Blood and Roses* (1968–69) in Amano, *Decadent Literature*.
38 Jun'ichirō Tanizaki, *In Praise of Shadows*, trans. Thomas J. Harper and Edward G. Seidensticker (London: Vintage Books, 2001). Stefano Evangelista also explores how the writer Koizumi Yakumo (aka Lafcadio Hearn) 'used the myth of a democracy of the "beautiful" in Japan to criticize the degradation that, according to him, industrialization and capitalism had caused in Western societies'. Stefano Evangelista, 'Japan: Decadence and Japonisme', in Jane Desmarais and David Weir (eds), *The Oxford Handbook of Decadence* (Oxford University Press, 2021), p. 10. [E-book viewer EPUB], https://www.oxfordhandbooks.com/.
39 Ross Douthat, *The Decadent Society: How We Became the Victims of Our Own Success* (New York: Avid Reader Press, 2020), pp. 86–8; Mark Driscoll, 'Debt and Denunciation in Post-Bubble Japan: On the Two Freeters', *Cultural Critique*, 65 (Winter) (2007), pp. 164–87 (p. 164); McCormack, *Emptiness*, p. xi; Akira Moriki, *Nisen hatinen IMF senryô* (Tokyo: Kodansha, 2005); Tomiko Yoda, 'A Roadmap to Millennial Japan', in Yoda and Harootunian, *Japan After Japan*, pp. 16–53 (pp. 16–17).
40 Takashi Murakami, 'Earth in my Window', in Murakami, *Little Boy*, pp. 99–149 (p. 132).
41 Stephen Bertman, *Hyperculture: The Human Cost of Speed* (Westport and London: Praeger, 1998), p. 123; see also Douthat, *Decadent Society*. The idea of hyperculture extends Alvin and Heidi Toffler's concept of 'future shock', which has since been adapted in Douglas Rushkoff's theorization of 'present

shock'. See Alvin [and Heidi] Toffler, *Future Shock* (New York: Bantam, 1971); Douglas Rushkoff, *Present Shock: When Everything Happens Now*, New York: Penguin, 2013).

42 Yoda, 'A Roadmap to Millennial Japan', p. 21.
43 For a dramatization of the cultural politics surrounding *hikikomori*, see Yōji Sakate's play *The Attic* (*Yaneura*, 2002). See also Anne Allison, *Precarious Japan* (Durham and London: Duke University Press, 2013), pp. 1–3.
44 Marilyn Ivy, 'Revenge and Recapitulation in Recessionary Japan', in Yoda and Harootunian, *Japan After Japan*, pp. 195–215 (p. 196).
45 Thiam Huat Kam, 'The Common Sense that Make the "Otaku": Capital and the Common Sense of Consumption in Contemporary Japan', *Japan Forum*, 25 (2) (2013), pp. 151–73 (p. 160, my emphasis).
46 Akira Asada, 'Infantile Capitalism and Japan's Postmodernism: A Fairy Tale', trans. Kyoko Selden, in Masao Miyoshi and H. D. Harootunian (eds), *Postmodernism and Japan* (Durham and London: Duke University Press, 1989), pp. 273–8 (p. 275).
47 See Mardi Reason, 'Miss Revolutionary Idol Berserker: Inside the Out of this World', *Scenestr*, 2 September 2015, https://scenestr.com.au/arts/miss-revolutionary-idol-berserker-inside-the-out-of-this-world, accessed 20 May 2022. There are a number of *otaku* subcultures that celebrate intergenerational desires for eroticized two-dimensional images of young girls exhibiting some form of *kawaii ero* ('cute eroticism'). The extent to which this constitutes paedophilia is a matter of some debate. Some critics distinguish between adolescent girls and two-dimensional manga/anime characters (e.g. Patrick W. Galbraith), while others draw explicit parallels (e.g. Caroline Norma). See Patrick W. Galbraith, *The Moé Manifesto: An Insider's Look at the Worlds of Manga, Anime and Gaming* (North Clarendon: Tuttle Publishing, 2014); Patrick W. Galbraith, *Otaku and the Struggle for Imagination in Japan* (Durham and London: Duke University Press, 2019); Caroline Norma, 'Catharine MacKinnon in Japanese: Toward a Radical Feminist Theory of Translation', in Beverley Curran, Nana Sato-Rossberg, and Kikuko Tanabe (eds), *Multiple Translation Communities in Contemporary Japan* (London: Routledge, 2015), pp. 79–98 (pp. 85–6).
48 Tadashi Uchino, 'Globality's Children: The "Child's" Body As a Strategy of Flatness in Performance', *TDR*, 50 (1) (2006), pp. 57–66 (p. 58).
49 See Uchino, 'Globality's Children'. See also Anan's critique of Murakami's occlusion of women's perspectives in his theorization of superflatness. Anan, 'Chapter 4: "Little Girls" Go West?', para. 14.16. As she explores in this chapter, the dance troupe KATHY stage a very different kind of superflatness in a mode oriented around the perspectives of women.
50 Murakami, 'Earth in My Window', p. 100.
51 Takashi Murakami, 'Superflat Trilogy: Greetings, You Are Alive', in Takashi Murakami (ed.), *Little Boy: The Arts of Japan's Exploding Subculture* (New

52. Toco Nikaido, 'In Their Words: Miss Revolutionary Idol Berserker', *Barbican.org.uk*, 16 June 2016, https://www.barbican.org.uk/read-watch-listen/in-their-words-miss-revolutionary-idol-berserker, accessed 19 May 2022.
53. Allen C. Bluedorn and Mary J. Waller, 'The Stewardship of the Temporal Commons', *Research in Organizational Behavior*, 27 (2006), pp. 355–96 (p. 357).
54. Amano, *Decadent Literature*, p. 15.
55. Ayaka Someya, 'Miss Revolutionary Idol Berserker', press release, 2018, http://missrevodolbbbbbbbberserker.asia/wp-content/uploads/2018/09/EnglishPR.pdf, accessed 5 March 2020. Amanda Waddell, teleconference interview, 12 May 2020.
56. Amanda Waddell, email correspondence with the author, 16 May 2020.
57. Waddell, teleconference interview.
58. A prominent figure associated with this discourse is Shintarō Ishihara, who was governor of Tokyo from 1999 until 2012, and a member of the House of Representatives between 1975 and 1999 and again from 2012 until 2014. For paternalist commentators like Ishihara, principles centering around law, self-control, and commitment to public virtue have been threatened by 'the harmful excesses of motherhood and the maternal principle both inside and outside homes, encouraging uncontrolled egoism, narcissistic and hedonistic consumer culture, and the hysteria of entitlement and victimhood'. Yoda, 'The Rise and Fall of Maternal Society', p. 239.
59. Tom Wilson, personal interview, Shoreditch Town Hall, London, 11 March 2020.
60. Mark Fisher, *K-Punk: The Collected and Unpublished Writings of Mark Fisher (2004–2016)*, ed. Darren Ambrose (London: Repeater), p. 551.
61. Fisher, *K-Punk*, p. 552.

Chapter 5

1. Jim George, 'Introduction: Are the Culture Wars Over?', in Jim George and Kim Huynh (eds), *The Culture Wars: Australian and American Politics in the 21st Century* (South Yarra: Palgrave Macmillan, 2009), pp. 1–15 (p. 7).
2. Patrick J. Buchanan, *The Death of the West: How Dying Populations and Immigrant Invasions Imperil Our Country and Civilization* (New York: Thomas Dunne Books, 2002), pp. 6, 27 and 243–4.
3. Oliver Dowden, 'The Threat to Democracy: Defeating Cancel Culture by Defending the Values of the Free World', *Heritage Foundation*, 14 February 2022, https://www.heritage.org/europe/event/the-threat-democracy-defeating-cancel-culture-defending-the-values-the-free-world, accessed 22 April 2022.

4   For instance, see Joshua Chambers-Letson's commentary on the artist Félix González-Torres. Joshua Chambers-Letson, *After the Party: A Manifesto for Queer Color of Life* (New York: New York University Press, 2018), pp. 149–50.
5   Andrew Hartman suggests that the culture wars were not consigned to the period running from 1989 to 1996, as debate in this period was informed by attitudes towards the legacy of radical and progressive activism in the 1960s. However, this period 'should perhaps be known as the "Era of Culture Wars" proper'. Andrew Hartman, *A War for the Soul of America: A History of the Culture Wars*, 2nd edition (Chicago: University of Chicago Press, 2019), p. 294. For a discussion of relevant precedent in the nineteenth and early-twentieth centuries, see Alan Howard Levy, *Government and the Arts: Debates over Federal Support of the Arts in America from George Washington to Jesse Helms* (Lanham: University Press of America, Inc., 1997).
6   Alex Palmer, 'When Art Fought the Law and the Art Won', *Smithsonian Magazine*, 2 October 2015, https://www.smithsonianmag.com/history/when-art-fought-law-and-art-won-180956810/, accessed 11 June 2021. Note that Jesse McBride, one of the two children featured in the exhibition, would later pose for a photograph by Judy Linn – only this time he appeared as a smiling eighteen-year-old looking down at Mapplethorpe's earlier photo of him. McBride also suggested that it was 'sick to equate [Mapplethorpe's earlier photograph] with pornography'. See Richard Meyer, 'The Jesse Helms Theory of Art', *October*, 104 (Spring 2003), pp. 131–48 (pp. 143–4).
7   Qtd. in Richard Serra, 'Art and Censorship', *Critical Inquiry*, 17 (3) (Spring 1991), pp. 574–81 (p. 578).
8   Camille Paglia, 'The Beautiful Decadence of Robert Mapplethorpe: A Response to Rochelle Gurstein', in *Sex, Art and American Culture: Essays* (New York: Viking, 1992), pp. 40–4.
9   For an overview of arguments expounding the negative influence of the arts – specifically theatre – see Jonas Barish, *The Antitheatrical Prejudice* (Berkeley: University of California Press, 1981).
10 Qtd. in Cynthia Koch, 'The Contest for American Culture: A Leadership Case Study on The NEA and NEH Funding Crisis', 1998, http://www.upenn.edu/pnc/ptkoch.html, accessed 11 June 2021.
11 Fritz Kaiser, *Degenerate Art: The Exhibition Guide in German and English*, trans. anon (N.C.: Ostara Publications, 2012), p. 66.
12 Kaiser, *Degenerate Art*, p. 2.
13 Michael St. John, *Romancing Decay: Ideas of Decadence in European Culture* (Aldershot: Ashgate, 1999), p. xii.
14 St. John, *Romancing Decay*, p. xii.
15 Linda S. Kauffman, *Bad Girls and Sick Boys: Fantasies in Contemporary Art and Culture* (Berkeley: University of California Press, 1998), p. 19. The connection between Hitler's condemnation of 'degenerate' art and artistic censorship in North America during the culture wars was also made by Robert Brustein and Joshua Goldstein in 1989. See Brustein and Goldstein,

'Hitler, on Art', *New York Times*, 28 July 1989, https://www.nytimes.com/1989/07/28/opinion/op-ed-hitler-on-art.html, accessed 25 August 2021.
16 Qtd. in Kauffman, *Bad Girls and Sick Boys*, p. 19. The NEA was established in 1965 during Johnson's Presidency, and Alexander served as its chairwoman between 1993 and 1997.
17 Buchanan qtd. in Buchanan, *Death of the West*, p. 7.
18 Hartman, *A War for the Soul of America*, p. 2. See also Buchanan, *Death of the West*, pp. 6 and 8.
19 Libertarian writers have also described the 1960s as a period of social and cultural decadence. However, for the libertarian Jeff Riggenbach, such decadence was to be praised as 'the overall decay of the influence of traditional authority'. Jeff Riggenbach, *In Praise of Decadence* (New York: Prometheus Books, 1998), p. 108.
20 Robert Bork, *Slouching Towards Gomorrah: Modern Liberalism and American Decline* (New York: Regan Books, 1997), p. vii.
21 See Dominic Johnson, '"Does a Bloody Towel Represent the Ideals of the American People?": Ron Athey and the Culture Wars', in Dominic Johnson (ed.), *Pleading in the Blood: The Art and Performances of Ron Athey* (London: Live Art Development Agency; Bristol: Intellect, 2013), pp. 64–93 (p. 72).
22 Helms is a case in point. See Johnson, 'Bloody Towel', pp. 75–6.
23 Susan Sontag, *Illness as Metaphor* and *AIDS and Its Metaphors* (London: Penguin, 1991), pp. 146–7.
24 Lee Edelman, *No Future: Queer Theory and the Death Drive* (Durham and London: Duke University Press, 2004), pp. 2–3.
25 Recent curatorial work has clarified the importance of the controversy surrounding the performance at Patrick's Cabaret. Amelia Jones curated the first retrospective exhibition of Athey's work in 2021 – 'Queer Communion: Ron Athey' – which was presented at New York's Participant Inc. It featured a range of events, including a live-streamed recreation of *4 Scenes* on 16 February 2021. See also Johnson, 'Bloody Towel'.
26 'For the umpteenth time', writes Athey, 'I'm HIV-positive. Darryl Carlton – aka Divinity Fudge, the man whose blood was central in the work – isn't'. Ron Athey, 'Polemic of Blood: Ron Athey on the "Post-AIDS" Body', in Amelia Jones and Andy Campbell (eds), *Queer Communion: Ron Athey* (Bristol: Intellect, 2020), pp. 55–8 (p. 57). See also Dominic Johnson, 'Divine Fire: Ron Athey in Europe', in Jones and Campbell, *Queer Communion*, pp. 294–303 (p. 295).
27 See 'Congressional Record: July 25, 1994', p. 140 (p. 98), https://www.govinfo.gov/content/pkg/CREC-1994-07-25/html/CREC-1994-07-25-pt1-PgS17.htm, accessed 5 February 2020.
28 Ron Athey, *4 Scenes in a Harsh Life*, L.A. Center Theater, 15 October 1993. Filmed and directed by Louis Elovitz. Available at: https://vimeo.com/47239842, accessed 5 February 2021.
29 'Congressional Record'. Note that the same congressional record in which this letter is reproduced states that the Department of Health were

contacted 'after the fact', and that the paper towels in question 'could be troublesome'.
30 Jones and Campbell, *Queer Communion*, pp. 420–1.
31 'Congressional Record'.
32 Jesse Helms, 'It's the Job of Congress to Define What's Art', *USA Today*, September 8, 1989', in Richard Bolton (ed.), *Culture Wars: Documents from the Recent Controversies in the Arts* (New York: New Press, 1992), pp. 100–1 (p. 101).
33 'Roll Call Vote 101st Congress – 1st Session', *United States Senate*, 7 October 1989, https://www.senate.gov/legislative/LIS/roll_call_lists/roll_call_vote _cfm.cfm?congress=101&session=1&vote=00242, accessed 9 July 2021. Amendment No. 991 was defeated the following year in favour of a vague decency clause.
34 Karen Finley, Holly Hughes, John Fleck, and Tim Miller (the so-called 'NEA Four') made headlines after challenging a decision to rescind their NEA grants. NEA Chair John Frohnmayer enforced the recently approved decency clause as justification for rescinding their artist grants, despite successful peer review. The clause demanded that decisions about the allocation of NEA funds take into consideration 'general standards of decency and respect for the diverse beliefs and values of the American people'. The debate prompted by Frohnmayer's decision ended up in the Supreme Court. See Hartman, *A War for the Soul of America*, pp. 196–8. For more on NEA budget reductions, see Johnson, 'Bloody Towel', p. 73.
35 'Congressional Record'.
36 Meyer, 'Jesse Helms', p. 137.
37 'Congressional Record'.
38 Pat Robertson, 'Christian Coalition direct mail, October 25, 1989 (excerpt)', in Bolton, *Culture Wars*, pp. 123–5 (p. 124).
39 See Alyson Campbell and Dirk Gindt, 'Viral Dramaturgies: HIV and AIDS in Performance in the Twenty-First Century', in Alyson Campbell and Dirk Gindt (eds), *Viral Dramaturgies: HIV and AIDS in Performance in the Twenty-First Century* (Cham: Palgrave Macmillan, 2018), pp. 3–46 (pp. 8–9). See also Tim Dean, *Unlimited Intimacy: Reflections on the Subculture of Barebacking* (Chicago: University of Chicago Press, 2009), p. 91.
40 Athey, 'Polemic of Blood', p. 56.
41 Julia Yost, 'New York's Hottest Club Is the Catholic Church', *New York Times*, 9 August 2022. https://www.nytimes.com/2022/08/09/opinion/nyc -catholicism-dimes-square-religion.html, accessed 23 August 2022.
42 Rory Mulholland, 'Parisians Snap up "Butt Plugs" after "Tree" Fiasco', *The Local*, 2 December 2014, https://www.thelocal.fr/20141202/parisians-butt -plug-sex-toy-paul-mccarthy/, accessed 25 June 2021.
43 Tony Perucci, 'Irritational Aesthetics: Reality Friction and Indecidable Theatre', *Theatre Journal*, 70 (4) (December 2018), pp. 473–98 (p. 473).

44 Claudia Kammer, 'De kerstman die niet de straat op mocht', *NRC*, 12 October 2018, https://www.nrc.nl/nieuws/2018/10/12/de-kerstman-die-niet-de-straat-op-mocht-a2417443, accessed 25 June 2021.
45 Ross Douthat, *The Decadent Society: How We Became the Victims of Our Own Success* (New York: Avid Reader Press, 2020), p. 82.
46 Kristina Lee Podesva et al., 'Responses to the Recent Cuts to Arts Funding in the Netherlands', *Fillip*, Summer 2011, https://fillip.ca/content/responses-to-recent-dutch-arts-cuts, accessed 5 July 2021.
47 Arie Altena et al., 'A New Dark Age for Dutch Culture', Summer 2011, https://ariealt.home.xs4all.nl/dark_ages.html, accessed 5 July 2021.
48 Moosje Goosen, 'Going Dutch', *Frieze*, 1 January 2021, https://www.frieze.com/article/going-dutch-0, accessed 5 July 2021.
49 Adolf Loos, 'Ornament and Crime', *Ornament and Crime: Thoughts on Design and Materials*, trans. Shaun Whiteside (N.C.: Penguin Books, 2019), pp. 185–202 (pp. 188 and 195–6).
50 See, for instance, *Bossy Burger* (1991), *Painter* (1995) and the Caribbean Pirates project (2001–05).
51 The term 'infantile disorder' is taken from Patrick Buchanan, 'Where a Wall is Needed, *Washington Times*, November 22, 1989', in Bolton, *Culture Wars*, pp. 137–8 (p. 138).
52 Ralph Rugoff, 'Mr. McCarthy's Neighbourhood', in Ralph Rugoff, Kristine Stiles, and Giacinto Di Pietrantonio (eds), *Paul McCarthy* (London: Phaidon, 1996), pp. 32–87 (p. 14).
53 David Weir, 'Afterword: Decadent Taste', in Jane Desmarais and Alice Condé (eds), *Decadence and the Senses* (Cambridge: Legenda, 2017), pp. 219–28 (p. 221).
54 See Dominic Johnson's instructive discussion of kalliphobia in *Unlimited Action: The Performance of Extremity in the 1970s* (Manchester: Manchester University Press, 2019), p. 7; see also p. 177.
55 Georges Bataille, *The Accursed Share: An Essay on General Economy. Volume 1: Consumption*, trans. Robert Hurley (New York: Zone Books, 1991), p. 22.
56 Bataille, *Accursed Share*, p. 22.
57 For an instructive overview, see Eleonora Belfiore and Oliver Bennett, 'Autonomy of the Arts and Rejection of Instrumentality', in *The Social Impact of the Arts: An Intellectual History* (Basingstoke and New York: Palgrave Macmillan, 2008), pp. 176–90.
58 Dan Rebellato qtd. in *Staging Decadence* [film], created by Adam Alston, Owen Parry, and Sophie Farrell, 12 May 2022, https://www.stagingdecadence.com/films, accessed 12 May 2022.
59 Paul Bolton, 'Higher Education Funding in England' (House of Commons Library, 2021), p. 18, https://researchbriefings.files.parliament.uk/documents/CBP-7973/CBP-7973.pdf. See also Gavin Williamson, 'Guidance to the Office for Students – Allocation of the Higher Education

Teaching Grant funding in the 2021–22 Financial Year', Department for Education, 19 January 2021, https://www.officeforstudents.org.uk/media/a3814453-4c28-404a-bf76-490183867d9a/rt-hon-gavin-williamson-cbe-mp-t-grant-ofs-chair-smb.pdf, accessed 10 May 2022. Note that Williamson's letter does mention support for 'specialist providers' in the performing and creative arts that are 'world leading', although in time it became clear that this support was to be specifically geared around industry-facing graduate destinations and outcomes, rather than the range of careers and incomes that a university arts degree can provide.

60 Michelle Donelan and Nadhim Zahawi, 'Higher Education Policy Statement & Reform Consultation', Department for Education, 24 February 2022, pp. 9, 11, and 30, https://assets.publishing.service.gov.uk/government/uploads/system/uploads/attachment_data/file/1057091/HE_reform_command-paper-web_version.pdf, accessed 10 May 2022. Passing reference is made to the creative arts and humanities (pp. 11 and 36), but these are tokenistic gestures.

61 Donelan and Zahawi, 'Higher Education Policy Statement', p. 33.

62 Prime Minister's Office, 'PM: A New Deal for Britain', 30 June 2020, https://www.gov.uk/government/news/pm-a-new-deal-for-britain, accessed 30 June 2021.

63 BBC, 'Photographer "Devastated" by Government-Backed "Fatima" Dancer Advert', 15 October 2020, https://www.bbc.co.uk/news/entertainment-arts-54553828, accessed 30 August 2022.

64 CyberFirst, *This is a CyberFirst World: Annual Highlight Report 2019–20*, National Cyber Security Centre, https://www.ncsc.gov.uk/files/CF-421540-Annual-Report-2019-20-V6.pdf, accessed 27 April 2022.

65 ITV News, 'Covid: Rishi Sunak Says People in "All Walks of Life" are Having to Adapt for Employment', *ITV News*, 6 October 2020, https://www.itv.com/news/2020-10-06/rishi-sunak-suggests-musicians-and-others-in-arts-should-retrain-and-find-other-jobs, accessed 27 April 2022.

66 PA Media, 'Rishi Sunak Vows to End Low-Earning Degrees in Post-16 Education Shake-up', *The Guardian*, 7 August 2022, https://www.theguardian.com/politics/2022/aug/07/rishi-sunak-vows-to-end-low-earning-degrees-in-post-16-education-shake-up, accessed 17 August 2022. Sunak's initial campaign was unsuccessful, ceding victory to Liz Truss. However, Sunak replaced Truss as Prime Minister only fifty days after she took office, with Truss having lost the confidence of her party after a series of controversial policy U-turns.

67 Nadia Khomami, 'Theatre in UK Faces Exodus of Women After Pandemic, Study Finds', *The Guardian*, 9 October 2021, https://www.theguardian.com/stage/2021/oct/09/theatre-in-uk-faces-exodus-of-women-after-pandemic-study-finds, accessed 27 April 2022. The comment – which is alleged to have been said during a Downing Street teleconference meeting on the

future of the arts – was leaked by the actor Guy Masterson on Twitter on 2 August 2020.
68 See, for instance, Ayesha Hazarika, 'Nadine Dorries becoming Culture Secretary in the Reshuffle Shows Boris Johnson is Still the Master of Outrage', *iNews*, 16 September 2021, https://inews.co.uk/opinion/nadine-dorries-culture-secretary-cabinet-reshuffle-boris-johnson-master-outrage-1203302, accessed 27 April 2022.
69 Nadine Dorries, Tweet, 27 December 2017, https://twitter.com/NadineDorries/status/945973216778031110, accessed 27 April 2022.
70 Higher Education Policy Institute, 'Where and What did the New Cabinet Study?', 26 July 2019, https://www.hepi.ac.uk/2019/07/26/where-and-what-did-the-new-cabinet-study/, accessed 17 August 2022.
71 Dowden, 'The Threat to Democracy'.
72 Dowden, 'The Threat to Democracy'. See also Douthat, *The Decadent Society*. Note that Dowden's condemnation of universities as 'decadent' finds precedent during the culture wars in the United States in the 1990s. For a discussion of examples, see Mark Rawlinson, 'The Decadent University: Narratives of Decay and the Future of Higher Education', in Michael St John (ed.), *Romancing Decay: Ideas of Decadence in European Culture* (Aldershot: Ashgate, 1999), pp. 235–45 (p. 235).
73 Dowden, 'The Threat to Democracy'. The legislation that Dowden refers to was still being debated at the time of Dowden's speech, including proposals to sanction universities and students' unions for breaching existing legislation that protects freedom of speech in universities and colleges, and the appointment of a Free Speech and Academic Freedom Champion to the board of the Office for Students to investigate the no-platforming of speakers and the dismissal of academics because of their unpopular views. See Gavin Williamson, 'Higher Education: Free Speech and Academic Freedom', Department for Education, February 2021, p. 8, https://assets.publishing.service.gov.uk/government/uploads/system/uploads/attachment_data/file/961537/Higher_education_free_speech_and_academic_freedom__web_version_.pdf, accessed 11 May 2022. The report cites existing legislation that is meant to protect freedom of speech on campus. UK Public General Acts, 'Education (No. 2) Act 1986, Section 43', 1 August 2019, https://www.legislation.gov.uk/ukpga/1986/61/section/43, accessed 12 May 2022.
74 Joint Committee on Human Rights, 'Freedom of Speech in Universities', 27 March 2018, https://publications.parliament.uk/pa/jt201719/jtselect/jtrights/589/58909.htm#_idTextAnchor058, accessed 11 May 2022.
75 Adele Redmond, 'Arm's-Length Policy at Risk in "Contested Heritage" Debate', *Arts Professional*, 8 October 2020, https://www.artsprofessional.co.uk/news/arms-length-policy-risk-contested-heritage-debate, accessed 11 May 2022.
76 Andrew Anthony, '"She Often Speaks Without Thinking": Nadine Dorries, our New Minister for Culture Wars', *The Guardian*, 31 October 2021, https://

www.theguardian.com/politics/2021/oct/31/she-often-speaks-without-thinking-nadine-dorries-our-new-minister-for-culture-wars, accessed 27 April 2022.

77 Francis Fukuyama and Steven Pinker are noteworthy examples. See Fukuyama, *Liberalism and its Discontents* (London: Profile Books, 2022); Fukuyama, *Identity: Contemporary Identity Politics and the Struggle for Recognition* (London: Profile Books, 2019); Pinker, *Enlightenment Now: The Case for Reason, Science, Humanism and Progress* (New York: Penguin, 2018). See also Bradley Campbell and Jason Manning, *The Rise of Victimhood Culture: Microaggressions, Safe Spaces, and the New Culture Wars* (Cham: Palgrave Macmillan, 2018); Greg Lukianoff and Jonathan Haidt, *The Coddling of the American Mind: How Good Intentions and Bad Ideas are Setting up a Generation for Failure* (New York: Penguin, 2018); Douglas Murray, *The Madness of Crowds: Gender, Race and Identity* (London: Bloomsbury, 2019).

78 Pinker, *Enlightenment Now*, pp. 17 and 33.

79 Inspired by the Sokal affair, Helen Pluckrose, James A. Lindsay and Peter Boghossian published a number of hoax articles using various pseudonyms. See Helen Wilson (pseudonym), 'Human Reactions to Rape Culture and Queer Performativity at Urban Dog Parks in Portland, Oregon', *Gender, Place & Culture*, 27 (2) (2018), pp. 307–26; M. Smith (pseudonym), 'Going in Through the Back Door: Challenging Straight Male Homohysteria, Transhysteria, and Transphobia Through Receptive Penetrative Sex Toy Use', *Sexuality & Culture*, 22 (4) (2018), pp. 1542–60; Richard Baldwin (borrowed identity), 'Who are They to Judge? Overcoming Anthropometry Through Fat Bodybuilding', *Fat Studies* 7 (3) (2018), pp. i–xiii; Richard Baldwin (borrowed identity), 'An Ethnography of Breastaurant Masculinity: Themes of Objectification, Sexual Conquest, Male Control, and Masculine Toughness in a Sexually Objectifying Restaurant', *Sex Roles*, 79 (11–12) (2018), pp. 762–77.

80 Alexander Adams, 'On Identity Politics', in *Culture War: Art, Identity Politics and Cultural Entryism* (Exeter: Imprint Academic Ltd., 2019), pp. 84–105 (pp. 100–1). Adams draws on Émile Durkheim's writing on 'anomie'.

81 Pluckrose and Lindsay make this point most succinctly in *Cynical Theories: How Activist Scholarship Made Everything About Race, Gender, and Identity – and Why This Harms Everybody* (N.C.: Swift Press, 2020).

82 For more on the role of the internet in the unfolding of a culture war, see Angela Nagle, *Kill All Normies: Online Culture Wars from 4chan and Tumblr to Trump and the Alt-Right* (Winchester and Washington: Zer0 Books, 2017).

83 The British Academy has produced an evidence-based outline of the benefits of skills developed in the arts, humanities and social sciences to the wider economy and society in the UK context. British Academy, *Qualified for the Future: Quantifying Demand for Arts, Humanities and Social Science Skills* (London: The British Academy, 2020), https://www.thebritishacademy.ac.uk/publications/skills-qualified-future-quantifying-demand-arts-humanities-social-science/, accessed 17 August 2022.

84 Nuccio Ordine, *The Usefulness of the Useless*, trans. Alastair McEwen (Philadelphia: Paul Dry Books, 2017), p. 1.
85 Sara Ahmed, *What's the Use? On the Uses of Use* (Durham and London: Duke University Press, 2019), pp. 10 and 48.
86 Terry Eagleton makes a similar point. See Eagleton, 'Bodies, Artworks, and Use Values', *New Literary History*, 44 (4) (Autumn 2013), pp. 561–73 (p. 569).
87 James Graham qtd. in Caridad Svich, 'James Graham', *Toward a Future Theatre: Conversations During a Pandemic* (London and New York: Methuen Drama 2022), para 8.54 [E-book viewer EPUB]. Retrieved from https://www.bl.uk/. Note that Svich argues for the necessity of theatre in the collection's introduction. Svich, 'Introduction', *Toward a Future Theatre*, paras. 6.4 and 6.12.

Conclusion

1 'Decadence @ Iklectik', Iklectik Art Lab, London, 29 July 2022, https://iklectikartlab.com/decadence-iklectik/, accessed 2 August 2022.
2 Mieke Bal, *Endless Andness: The Politics of Abstraction According to Ann Veronica Janssens* (London: Bloomsbury, 2013), p. 3.
3 See Liz Constable, Dennis Denisoff, and Matthew Potolsky, 'Introduction', in Constable, Denisoff, and Potolsky (eds), *Perennial Decay: On the Aesthetics & Politics of Decadence* (Philadelphia: University of Pennsylvania Press, 1999), pp. 1–32 (pp. 11 and 25). Matthew Potolsky, *The Decadent Republic of Letters: Taste, Politics, and Cosmopolitan Community from Baudelaire to Beardsley* (Philadelphia: University of Pennsylvania Press, 2013), p. 2.
4 Matthew Potolsky has done much to challenge this limiting understanding of decadence. See Potolsky, *The Decadent Republic of Letters*, p. 6. For examples of texts propagating associations between decadence, individualism and atomization, see Paul Bourget, 'The Example of Baudelaire', trans. Nancy O'Connor, *New England Review*, 30 (2) (2009), http://cat.middlebury.edu/~nereview/30-2/Bourget.htm, accessed 9 August 2022; Havelock Ellis, 'A Note on Paul Bourget', in *Views and Reviews: A Selection of Uncollected Articles 1884-1932* (Boston: Houghton Mifflin, 1932), p. 52. For a detailed study of canonical texts that cemented links between decadence and individualism in the late-nineteenth and early twentieth centuries, see Regenia Gagnier, *Individualism, Decadence, and Globalization: On the Relationship of Part to Whole* (Basingstoke and New York: Palgrave Macmillan, 2010).
5 David Weir, 'Afterword: Decadent Taste', in Jane Desmarais and Alice Condé (eds), *Decadence and the Senses* (Cambridge: Legenda, 2017), pp. 219–28 (p. 221).
6 Oscar Wilde, 'The Preface', in *The Picture of Dorian Gray* (Croxley Green: Chiltern Publishing, 2020), pp. 5–6 (p. 6). Wilde is writing in the shadow of

Théophile Gautier, who famously wrote that '[t]he only things that are really beautiful are those which have no use'. Théophile Gautier, 'Preface', in Helen Constantine (trans.), *Mademoiselle de Maupin* (London: Penguin, 2005), pp. 3–37 (p. 23).
7 Holbrook Jackson identifies the first four of these characteristics as key decadent tropes in *The Eighteen-Nineties* (London: Cresset Library, 1988), p. 70.
8 Terry Eagleton, *The Ideology of the Aesthetic* (Oxford: Blackwell, 1990), p. 111.
9 Potolsky, *Decadent Republic*, p. 4.
10 These four characteristics are identified by Jackson as key decadent tropes in *The Eighteen-Nineties*, p. 76.
11 Potolsky adds these characteristics to Jackson's list in Potolsky, *Decadent Republic*, p. 2.
12 Liz Constable, Dennis Denisoff, and Matthew Potolsky succinctly outline these political associations, but they also offer an instructive challenge to the limiting ways in which the politics of decadent writing has tended to be considered. See Constable, Potolsky, and Denisoff, 'Introduction', pp. 25–6.
13 Alice Condé, 'Decadence and Popular Culture', in Jane Desmarais and David Weir (eds), *Decadence and Literature* (Cambridge: Cambridge University Press, 2019), pp. 379–99 (p. 395).
14 David Weir and Jane Desmarais, 'Introduction: Decadence, Culture, and Society', in Jane Desmarais and David Weir (eds), *The Oxford Handbook of Decadence* (New York: Oxford University Press, 2022), pp. 1–17 (p. 14).
15 At the time of writing, Dennis Denisoff is developing relevant projects exploring decadence and ecology, building on his book *Decadent Ecology in British Literature and Art, 1860–1910: Decay, Desire, and the Pagan Revival* (Cambridge: Cambridge University Press, 2022).
16 There is now a burgeoning literature on the desirability of de-growth. For an instructive overview, see Jason Hickel, *Less is More: How Degrowth Will Save the World* (London: Windmill, 2021). For early advocacy of de-growth, or 'low-entropy' values', see Jeremy Rifkin, with Ted Howard, *Entropy: A New World View* (Toronto: Bantam Books, 1981), p. 205.
17 Ross Douthat, *The Decadent Society: How We Became the Victims of Our Own Success* (New York: Avid Reader Press, 2020). See also remarks made by Senator Jesse Helms in 'Congressional Record: July 25, 1994', 140 (98), https://www.govinfo.gov/content/pkg/CREC-1994-07-25/html/CREC-1994-07-25-pt1-PgS17.htm, accessed 5 February 2020. See also Robert Bork, *Slouching Towards Gomorrah: Modern Liberalism and American Decline* (New York: Regan Books, 1997); Patrick J. Buchanan, *The Death of the West: How Dying Populations and Immigrant Invasions Imperil Our country and Civilization* (New York: Thomas Dunne Books, 2002). Declinist literature is also thriving in France, where it has taken on a much more xenophobic and racist character. See, for instance, Alain Finkielkraut, *L'identité malheureuse*

(Paris: Stock, 2013); Éric Zemmour, *Le Suicide Francais* (Paris: Albin Michel, 2014).

18 Oliver Dowden, 'The Threat to Democracy: Defeating Cancel Culture by Defending the Values of the Free World', Heritage Foundation, 14 February 2022, https://www.heritage.org/europe/event/the-threat-democracy-defeating-cancel-culture-defending-the-values-the-free-world, accessed 22 April 2022.

19 See, for instance, Cebr, *Contribution of the Arts and Culture Industry to the UK Economy*, report for Arts Council England, April 2019, https://www.artscouncil.org.uk/sites/default/files/download-file/Economic%20impact%20of%20arts%20and%20culture%20on%20the%20national%20economy%20FINAL_0_0.pdf, accessed 5 August 2022; National Endowment for the Arts, 'New Report Released on the Economic Impact of the Arts and Cultural Sector', 30 March 2021, https://www.arts.gov/news/press-releases/2021/new-report-released-economic-impact-arts-and-cultural-sector, accessed 5 August 2022.

20 For examples, see: All-Party Parliamentary Group on Arts, Health and Wellbeing, *Creative Health: The Arts for Health and Wellbeing*, 2nd edition, July 2017, https://www.culturehealthandwellbeing.org.uk/appg-inquiry/Publications/Creative_Health_Inquiry_Report_2017_-_Second_Edition.pdf, accessed 5 August 2022; Eleonora Belfiore and Oliver Bennett, *The Social Impact of the Arts: An Intellectual History* (Basingstoke and New York: Palgrave Macmillan, 2008); Geoffrey Crossick and Patrycja Kaszynska, 'Understanding the Value of Arts & Culture: The AHRC Cultural Value Project', *Cultural Trends*, 25 (4) (2016), pp. 273–6; House of Commons Digital, Culture, Media and Sport Select Committee, *Changing Lives: The Social Impact of Participation in Culture and Sport*, 11th report of session 2017–19, 14 May 2019 HC 734.

21 Orian Brook, Dave O'Brien, and Mark Taylor, *Culture is Bad for You: Inequality in the Cultural and Creative Industries* (Manchester: Manchester University Press, 2020), p. 10.

22 Audre Lorde, 'Poetry Is Not a Luxury', in *Sister Outsider* (London: Penguin Books, 2019), pp. 25–8 (pp. 25–6).

Works cited

Adams, Alexander, 'On Identity Politics', in *Culture War: Art, Identity Politics and Cultural Entryism* (Exeter: Imprint Academic Ltd., 2019), pp. 84–105.

Ahmed, Sara, *Living a Feminist Life* (Durham and London: Duke University Press, 2017).

Ahmed, Sara, *What's the Use? On the Uses of Use* (Durham and London: Duke University Press, 2019).

Albert, Nicole G., *Lesbian Decadence: Representations in Art and Literature of fin-de-siècle France*, trans. Nancy Erber and William Peniston (New York and York: Harrington Park Press, 2016).

Allison, Anne, *Precarious Japan* (Durham and London: Duke University Press, 2013).

All-Party Parliamentary Group on Arts, Health and Wellbeing, *Creative Health: The Arts for Health and Wellbeing*, 2nd edition, July 2017, https://www.culturehealthandwellbeing.org.uk/appg-inquiry/Publications/Creative_Health_Inquiry_Report_2017_-_Second_Edition.pdf, accessed 5 August 2022.

Alston, Adam, 'Decadence and the Antitheatrical Prejudice', in Dustin Friedman and Kristin Mahoney (eds), *Nineteenth-Century Literature in Transition: The 1890s* (Cambridge University Press, forthcoming).

Alston, Adam, 'Martin O'Brien – Interview for Staging Decadence', *Staging Decadence Blog*, 26 July 2022, https://www.stagingdecadence.com/blog/martin-obrien, accessed 10 August 2022.

Alston, Adam, 'Survival of the Sickest: On Decadence, Disease and the Performing Body', *Volupté: Interdisciplinary Journal of Decadence Studies*, 4 (2) (2021), pp. 130–56.

Alston, Adam, 'Toco Nikaido – Interview for Staging Decadence', *Staging Decadence Blog*, 4 March 2021, https://www.stagingdecadence.com/blog/toco-nikaido-interview-for-staging-decadence, accessed 20 March 2022.

Alston, Adam and Alexander Bickley Trott (eds), 'Decadence and Performance', *Volupté: Interdisciplinary Journal of Decadence Studies*, 4 (2) (Winter 2021).

Altena, Arie, et al., 'A New Dark Age for Dutch Culture', Summer 2011, https://ariealt.home.xs4all.nl/dark_ages.html, accessed 5 July 2021.

Alves, Abel, 'Humanity's Place in Nature, 1863–1928: Horror, Curiosity and the Expeditions of Huxley, Wallace, Blavatsky and Lovecraft', *Theology and Science*, 6 (1) (2008), pp. 73–88.

Amano, Ikuho, *Decadent Literature in Twentieth-Century Japan: Spectacles of Idle Labor* (New York: Palgrave Macmillan, 2013).

Anan, Nabuko, *Contemporary Japanese Women's Theatre and Visual Arts: Performing Girls' Aesthetics* (Basingstoke: Palgrave Macmillan, 2016).

Anderson, Reynaldo and Charles E. Jones, 'Introduction: The Rise of Astro-Blackness', in Anderson and Jones (eds), *Afrofuturism 2.0: The Rise of Astro-Blackness* (Lanham: Lexington Books, 2016), pp. vii–xviii.

Anthony, Andrew, '"She Often Speaks Without Thinking": Nadine Dorries, Our New Minister for Culture Wars', *The Guardian*, 31 October 2021, https://www.theguardian.com/politics/2021/oct/31/she-often-speaks-without-thinking-nadine-dorries-our-new-minister-for-culture-wars, accessed 27 April 2022.

Antúnez Roca, Marcel·lí, *Systematurgy: Actions, Devices, Drawings* (Barcelona: Arts Santa Monica and Ediciones Polígrafa, 2015).

Asada, Akira, 'Infantile Capitalism and Japan's Postmodernism: A Fairy Tale', trans. Kyoko Selden, in Masao Miyoshi and H.D, Harootunian (eds), *Postmodernism and Japan* (Durham and London: Duke University Press, 1989), pp. 273–8.

Athey, Ron, *4 Scenes in a Harsh Life*, L.A. Center Theater, 15 October 1993. Filmed and directed by Louis Elovitz, https://vimeo.com/47239842, accessed 5 February 2021.

Athey, Ron, 'Polemic of Blood: Ron Athey on the "Post-AIDS" Body', in Amelia Jones and Andy Campbell (eds), *Queer Communion: Ron Athey* (Bristol: Intellect, 2020), pp. 55–8.

Auslander, Philip, *Liveness: Performance in a Mediatized Culture* (London and New York: Routledge, 1999).

Ayers, David, '"Politics Here is Death": William Burroughs's *Cities of the Red Night*', in Krishan Kumar and Stephen Bann (eds), *Utopias and the Millennium* (London: Reaktion Books, 1993), pp. 90–106.

Bal, Mieke, *Endless Andness: The Politics of Abstraction According to Ann Veronica Janssens* (London: Bloomsbury, 2013).

Baldwin, James, 'Stranger in the Village', in *Notes of A Native Son* (Beacon Press, 1955), https://www.janvaneyck.nl/site/assets/files/2312/baldwin.pdf, accessed 16 March 2022.

Baldwin, Richard (borrowed identity), 'An Ethnography of Breastaurant Masculinity: Themes of Objectification, Sexual Conquest, Male Control, and Masculine Toughness in a Sexually Objectifying Restaurant', *Sex Roles*, 79 (11–12) (2018), pp. 762–77.

Baldwin, Richard (borrowed identity), 'Who are They to Judge? Overcoming Anthropometry Through Fat Bodybuilding', *Fat Studies*, 7 (3) (2018), pp. i–xiii.

Baraitser, Lisa, *Enduring Time* (London: Bloomsbury, 2017).

Barish, Jonas, *The Antitheatrical Prejudice* (Berkeley: University of California Press, 1981).

Bastani, Aaron, *Fully Automated Luxury Communism: A Manifesto* (London and New York: Verso, 2019).

Bataille, Georges, *The Accursed Share: An Essay on General Economy. Volume 1: Consumption*, trans. Robert Hurley (New York: Zone Books, 1991).

Baudelaire, Charles, 'In Praise of Makeup', trans. Jane Desmarais, in Jane Desmarais and Chris Baldick (eds), *Decadence: An Annotated Anthology* (Manchester and New York: Manchester University Press, 2012), pp. 22–4.

Baudelaire, Charles, *The Painter of Modern Life and Other Essays*, ed. and trans. Jonathan Mayne (New York: de Capo Press, n.d.).

Baudrillard, Jean, *The Mirror of Production*, trans. Mark Poster (St. Louis: Telos Press, 1975).

Bayly, Simon, *A Pathognomy of Performance* (Basingstoke: Palgrave Macmillan, 2011).

Bayly, Simon, 'The End of the Project: Futurity in the Culture of Catastrophe', *Angelaki*, 18 (2), pp. 161–77.

BBC, 'The Artist Who Believes he's a Zombie', podcast, 4 April 2019, https://www.bbc.co.uk/news/av/disability-47813085, accessed 6 July 2022.

BBC, 'Photographer "devastated" by Government-backed "Fatima" Dancer Advert', 15 October 2020, https://www.bbc.co.uk/news/entertainment-arts-54553828, accessed 30 August 2022.

Beech, Dave, *Art and Postcapitalism: Aesthetic Labour, Automation and Value Production* (London: Pluto Press, 2019).

Belfiore, Eleonora and Oliver Bennett, *The Social Impact of the Arts: An Intellectual History* (Basingstoke and New York: Palgrave Macmillan, 2008).

Bellamy, Dodie, *When the Sick Rule the World* (South Pasadena: Semiotext(e), 2015).

Benjamin, Walter, *Illuminations*, ed. Hannah Arendt, trans. Harry Zohn (London: Fontana, 1973).

Benjamin, Walter, *Reflections: Essays, Aphorisms, Autobiographical Writings*, trans. Edmund Jephcott, ed. Peter Demetz (New York and London: Harcourt Brace Jovanovich, 1978).

Beradi, Franco 'Bifo', *After the Future*, ed. Gary Genosko and Nicholas Thoburn, trans. Arianna Bove, et al. (Oakland and Edinburgh: AK Press, 2011).

Beradi, Franco 'Bifo', *Futurability: The Age of Impotence and the Horizon of Possibility* (London and New York: Verso, 2017).

Berlant, Lauren, *Cruel Optimism* (Durham and London: Duke University Press, 2011).

Bertman, Stephen, *Hyperculture: The Human Cost of Speed* (Westport and London: Praeger, 1998).

Birringer, Johannes, *Media & Performance: Along the Border* (Baltimore and London: Johns Hopkins University Press, 1998).

Bissell, Laura, 'The Female Cyborg as Grotesque in Performance', *International Journal of Performance Arts and Digital Media*, 9 (2) (2013), pp. 261–74.

Blackburn-Daniels, Sally, '"His Red Flesh Their Forbidden Fruit": Permeable Bodies in Hval's *Paradise Rot*', paper presented at *Decadent Bodies*, Goldsmiths, University of London, London, 28–29 July 2022.

Blau, Herbert, *Take Up the Bodies: Theatre at the Vanishing Point* (Urbana: University of Illinois Press, 1982).

Bliss, James, 'Hope Against Hope: Queer Negativity, Black Feminist Theorizing and Reproduction without a Future', *Mosaic*, 48 (2015), pp. 83–98.

Bluedorn, Allen C. and Mary J. Waller, 'The Stewardship of the Temporal Commons', *Research in Organizational Behavior*, 27 (2006), pp. 355–96.

Bolton, Paul, 'Higher Education Funding in England' (House of Commons Library, 2021), p. 18, https://researchbriefings.files.parliament.uk/documents/CBP-7973/CBP-7973.pdf.

Bolton, Richard (ed.), *Culture Wars: Documents from the Recent Controversies in the Arts* (New York: New Press, 1992).

Bork, Robert, *Slouching Towards Gomorrah: Modern Liberalism and American Decline* (New York: Regan Books, 1997).

Bouchard, Gianna, 'Introduction: With (Dis-eased) Affection', in Martin O'Brien and David MacDiarmid (eds), *Survival of the Sickest: The Art of Martin O'Brien* (London: Live Art Development Agency, 2018), pp. 6–9.

Bourget, Paul, 'The Example of Baudelaire', trans. Nancy O'Connor, *New England Review*, 30 (2) (2009), http://cat.middlebury.edu/~nereview/30-2/Bourget.htm, accessed 9 August 2022.

Bourland, W. Ian, 'Afronauts', *Third Text*, 34 (2) (2020), pp. 209–29.

Bridle, James, *New Dark Age: Technology and the End of the Future* (London and Brooklyn: Verso, 2018).

British Academy, *Qualified for the Future: Quantifying Demand for Arts, Humanities and Social Science Skills* (London: The British Academy, 2020), https://www.thebritishacademy.ac.uk/publications/skills-qualified-future-quantifying-demand-arts-humanities-social-science/, accessed 17 August 2022.

Brodzinski, Emma, 'The Patient Performer: Embodied Pathography in Contemporary Productions', in Alex Mermikides and Gianna Bouchard (eds), *Performance and the Medical Body* (London: Bloomsbury, 2016), pp. 85–97.

Brook, Orian, Dave O'Brien, and Mark Taylor, *Culture is Bad for You: Inequality in the Cultural and Creative Industries* (Manchester: Manchester University Press, 2020).

Brooks, Daphne A., *Bodies in Dissent: Spectacular Performances of Race and Freedom, 1850–1910* (Durham and London: Duke University Press, 2006).

brown, adrienne maree, *Pleasure Activism: The Politics of Feeling Good*, ed. adrienne maree brown (Chico and Edinburgh: AK Press, 2019).

Brown, August, 'South L.A. Band Gives Voice to Trump-era Fury', *Los Angeles Times*, 11 April 2017, https://www.latimes.com/entertainment/music/la-et-ms-f-u-pay-us-20170411-story.html?fbclid=IwAR0Xyy4VH9k52aR0aWphQ_rpNA-nOAsSNr5D0lr4wkW1to0skMK4FmAm7-s, accessed 26 February 2022.

Bru-Domínguez, Eva, 'Becoming Undone: Colour, Matter and Line in the Artwork of Marcel·lí Antúnez', in Stuart Davis and Maite Usoz de la Fuente (eds), *The Modern Spanish Canon: Visibility, Cultural Capital and the Academy* (Abingdon and New York: Legenda, 2018), pp. 37–57.

Brustein, Robert and Joshua Goldstein, 'Hitler, on Art', *New York Times*, 28 July 1989, https://www.nytimes.com/1989/07/28/opinion/op-ed-hitler-on-art.html, accessed 25 August 2021.

Buchanan, Patrick J., *The Death of the West: How Dying Populations and Immigrant Invasions Imperil Our Country and Civilization* (New York: Thomas Dunne Books, 2002).

Buchanan, Patrick J., 'Where a Wall is Needed, *Washington Times*, November 22, 1989', in Richard Bolton (ed.), *Culture Wars: Documents From the Recent Controversies in the Arts* (New York: New Press, 1992), pp. 137–8.

Calinescu, Matei, *Five Faces of Modernity: Modernism, Avant-Garde, Decadence, Kitsch, Postmodernism* (Durham: Duke University Press, 1987).

Campbell, Alyson and Dirk Gindt, 'Viral Dramaturgies: HIV and AIDS in Performance in the Twenty-First Century', in Alyson Campbell and Dirk Gindt (eds), *Viral Dramaturgies: HIV and AIDS in Performance in the Twenty-First Century* (Cham: Palgrave Macmillan, 2018), pp. 3–46.

Campbell, Bradley and Jason Manning, *The Rise of Victimhood Culture: Microaggressions, Safe Spaces, and the New Culture Wars* (Cham: Palgrave Macmillan, 2018).

Campion, Chris, 'J-Pop's Dream Factory', *The Guardian*, 21 August 2005, https://www.theguardian.com/music/2005/aug/21/popandrock3, accessed 20 March 2022.

Castells, Manuel, *The Rise of the Network Society* (Oxford: Blackwell, 1996).

Causey, Matthew, 'Postdigital Performance', *Theatre Journal*, 68 (3) (September 2016), pp. 427–41.

Cazdyn, Eric, *The Already Dead: The New Time of Politics, Culture, and Illness* (Durham and London: Duke University Press, 2012).

CEBR, *Contribution of the Arts and Culture Industry to the UK Economy*, report for Arts Council England, April 2019, https://www.artscouncil.org.uk/sites/default/files/download-file/Economic%20impact%20of%20arts%20and%20culture%20on%20the%20national%20economy%20FINAL_0_0.pdf, accessed 5 August 2022.

Césaire, Aimé, *Discourse on Colonialism*, trans. Joan Pinkham (New York: Monthly Review Press, 2000).

Chambers-Letson, Joshua, *After the Party: A Manifesto for Queer Color of Life* (New York: New York University Press, 2018).

chelfitsch (2021) 'chelfitsch & Teppei Kaneuji "Eraser Mountain"', *chelfitsch.net*, https://chelfitsch.net/en/works/eraser-mountain/, accessed 20 March 2022.

Chimutengwende, Seke, 'Unfunky UFO: 2100AD', 15 January 2018, https://www.youtube.com/watch?v=IAvTRiegrPY, accessed 2 March 2022.

Clynes, Manfred E. and Nathan S. Kline, 'Cyborgs in Space', in Chris Gray (ed.), *The Cyborg Handbook* (New York: Routledge, 1995), pp. 29–33.

Cohen, Jeffrey Jerome, *Monster Theory: Reading Culture* (Minneapolis and London: University of Minnesota Press, 1996).

Condé, Alice, 'Contemporary Contexts: Decadence Today and Tomorrow', in Jane Desmarais and David Weir (eds), *The Oxford Handbook of Decadence* (New York: Oxford University Press, 2022), pp. 96–114.

Condé, Alice, 'Decadence and Popular Culture', in Jane Desmarais and David Weir (eds), *Decadence and Literature* (Cambridge: Cambridge University Press, 2019), pp. 379–99.

'Congressional Record: July 25, 1994', 140 (98), https://www.govinfo.gov/content/pkg/CREC-1994-07-25/html/CREC-1994-07-25-pt1-PgS17.htm, accessed 5 February 2020.

Constable, Liz, Dennis Denisoff, and Matthew Potolsky (eds), *Perennial Decay: On the Aesthetics & Politics of Decadence* (Philadelphia: University of Pennsylvania Press, 1999).

Corones, Anthony, Graham Pont, and Barbara Santich (eds), *Food in Festivity: Proceedings of the Fourth Symposium of Australian Gastronomy* (Sydney: Symposium of Australian Gastronomy, 1990).

Costa, Mariarosa Dalla, *Potere Femminile e Sovversione Sociale* (Venice: Marsilio Editori, 1972).

Crary, Jonathan, *24/7: Late Capitalism and the Ends of Sleep* (London and New York: Verso, 2014).

Creative Industries Council, 'The Economic Contribution Of The Arts', 2 March 2021, https://www.thecreativeindustries.co.uk/facts-figures/industries-arts-culture-arts-culture-facts-and-figures-the-economic-contribution-of-the-arts, accessed 2 February 2022.

Creed, Barbara, *The Monstrous-Feminine: Film, Feminism, Psychoanalysis* (London and New York: Routledge, 1993).

Critical Art Ensemble, 'Reinventing Precarity', *TDR*, 56 (4) (Winter 2012), pp. 49–61.

Crossick, Geoffrey and Patrycja Kaszynska, 'Understanding the Value of Arts & Culture: The AHRC Cultural Value Project', *Cultural Trends*, 25 (4) (2016), pp. 273–6.

Csicsery-Ronay, Jr, Istvan, 'Science Fiction and Empire', *Science Fiction Studies*, 30 (2) (July 2003), pp. 231–45.

CyberFirst, *This is a CyberFirst World: Annual Highlight Report 2019–20*, National Cyber Security Centre, https://www.ncsc.gov.uk/files/CF-421540-Annual-Report-2019-20-V6.pdf, accessed 27 April 2022.

Dean, Tim, *Unlimited Intimacy: Reflections on the Subculture of Barebacking* (Chicago: University of Chicago Press, 2009).

'Decadence @ Iklectik', Iklectik Art Lab, London, 29 July 2022. https://iklectikartlab.com/decadence-iklektik/, accessed 2 August 2022.

Denisoff, Dennis, *Decadent Ecology in British Literature and Art, 1860–1910: Decay, Desire, and the Pagan Revival* (Cambridge: Cambridge University Press, 2022).

Derrida, Jacques, 'The Deconstruction of Actuality: An Interview With Jacques Derrida', trans. Jonathan Rée, *Radical Philosophy*, 68 (Autumn 1994), pp. 28–41.

Dery, Mark (ed.), *Flame Wars: The Discourse of Cyberculture* (Durham and London: Duke University Press, 1994).

Desmarais, Jane, 'Decadence and the Critique of Modernity', in Jane Desmarais and David Weir (eds), *Decadence and Literature* (Cambridge: Cambridge University Press, 2019), pp. 98–114.

Desmarais, Jane and David Weir (eds), *Decadence and Literature* (Cambridge: Cambridge University Press, 2019).

Desmarais, Jane and David Weir (eds), *The Oxford Handbook of Decadence* (New York: Oxford University Press, 2022).

Dierkes-Thrun, Petra, *Salome's Modernity: Oscar Wilde and the Aesthetics of Transgression* (Ann Arbor: University of Michigan Press, 2011).

Dixon, Steve, 'Cybernetic-Existentialism and Being-towards-death in Contemporary Art and Performance', *TDR*, 61 (3) (Fall 2017), pp. 36–55.

Donelan, Michelle and Nadhim Zahawi, 'Higher Education Policy Statement & Reform Consultation', *Department for Education*, 24 February 2022, https://assets.publishing.service.gov.uk/government/uploads/system/uploads/attachment_data/file/1057091/HE_reform_command-paper-web_version.pdf, accessed 10 May 2022.

Dorling, Danny, *Slowdown: The End of the Great Acceleration – And Why it's Good for the Planet, the Economy, and Our Lives* (New Haven and London: Yale University Press, 2020).

Dorries, Nadine, Tweet, 27 December 2017, https://twitter.com/NadineDorries/status/945973216778031110, accessed 27 April 2022.

Douthat, Ross, *The Decadent Society: How We Became the Victims of Our Own Success* (New York: Avid Reader Press, 2020).

Dowden, Oliver, 'The Threat to Democracy: Defeating Cancel Culture by Defending the Values of the Free World', Heritage Foundation, 14 February 2022, https://www.heritage.org/europe/event/the-threat-democracy-defeating-cancel-culture-defending-the-values-the-free-world, accessed 22 April 2022.

Drake, Richard, 'Decadence, Decadentism and Decadent Romanticism in Italy: Toward a Theory of Decadence', *Journal of Contemporary History*, 17 (1) (January 1982), pp. 69–92.

Driscoll, Mark, 'Debt and Denunciation in Post-Bubble Japan: On the Two Freeters', *Cultural Critique*, 65 (Winter) (2007), pp. 164–87.

Du Bois, W. E. B., *The World and Africa* (New York: International Publishers, 1965).

Eagleton, Terry, 'Bodies, Artworks, and Use Values', *New Literary History*, 44 (4) (Autumn 2013), pp. 561–73.

Eagleton, Terry, *The Ideology of the Aesthetic* (Oxford: Blackwell, 1990).

Eckersall, Peter, 'Toshiki Okada's Ecological Theatre', *PAJ*, 43 (1) (January) (2021), pp. 107–15.

Edelman, Lee, *No Future: Queer Theory and the Death Drive* (Durham and London: Duke University Press, 2004).

Ellis, Havelock, 'A Note on Paul Bourget', in *Views and Reviews: A Selection of Uncollected Articles 1884–1932* (Boston: Houghton Mifflin, 1932).

Eltis, Sos, 'Decadent Theater: New Women and "The Eye of the Beholder"', in Jane Desmarais and David Weir (eds), *The Oxford Handbook of Decadence* (New York: Oxford University Press, 2022), pp. 318–50.

Eltis, Sos, 'Theatre and Decadence', in Alex Murray (ed.), *Decadence: A Literary History* (Cambridge: Cambridge University Press, 2020), pp. 201–17.

Eshun, Kodwo, *More Brilliant Than the Sun: Adventures in Sonic Fiction* (London: Quartet Books, 1998).

Euripides, *The Bacchae and Other Plays*, trans. Philip Vellacott (London: Penguin Books, 1973).

Evangelista, Stefano, 'Japan: Decadence and *Japonisme*', in Jane Desmarais and David Weir (eds), *The Oxford Handbook of Decadence* (New York: Oxford University Press, 2021), [E-book viewer EPUB], https://www.oxfordhandbooks.com/.

Federici, Silvia, *Caliban and the Witch: Women, the Body and Primitive Accumulation*, 2nd edition (New York: Autonomedia, 2014).

Feldman, Sharon G., 'An Aspiration to the Authentic: La Fura Dels Baus', in *In the Eye of the Storm: Contemporary Theater in Barcelona* (Lewisburg: Bucknell University Press, 2009), pp. 75–102.

Fieni, David, *Decadent Orientalisms: The Decay of Colonial Modernity* (New York: Fordham University Press, 2020).

Filho, Lúcio Reis, 'No Safe Space: Zombie Film Tropes During the COVID-19 Pandemic', *Space and Culture*, 23 (3) (2020), pp. 253–8.

Fillin-Yeh, Susan (ed.), *Dandies: Fashion and Finesse in Art and Culture* (New York and London: New York University Press, 2001).

Finkielkraut, Alain, *L'identité Malheureuse* (Paris: Stock, 2013).

Fisher, Mark, *Capitalist Realism: Is There No Alternative?* (Winchester and Washington: Zer0 Books, 2009).

Fisher, Mark, *Ghosts of My Life: Writings on Depression, Hauntology and Lost Futures* (Winchester and Washington: Zer0 Books, 2014).

Fisher, Mark, *K-Punk: The Collected and Unpublished Writings of Mark Fisher (2004–2016)*, ed. Darren Ambrose (London: Repeater, 2018).

Fisher, Mark, *The Weird and the Eerie* (London: Repeater, 2016).

Florêncio, João and Owen Parry (eds), 'Trashing', *Dance Theatre Journal*, 24 (3) (2011).

Ford, James Edward, 'Introduction', *Black Camera*, 7 (1) (2015), pp. 110–14.

Fortunati, Vita, 'From Utopia to Science Fiction', in Krishan Kumar and Stephen Bann (eds), *Utopias and the Millenium* (London: Reaktion Books, 1993), pp. 81–9.

Foster, Hal, *Compulsive Beauty* (London and Cambridge, MA: MIT Press, 1993).

Freeman, Elizabeth, *Time Binds: Queer Temporalities, Queer Histories* (Durham and London: Duke University Press, 2010).

Fukuyama, Francis, *Identity: Contemporary Identity Politics and the Struggle for Recognition* (London: Profile Books, 2019).

Fukuyama, Francis, *Liberalism and its Discontents* (London: Profile Books, 2022).

Gable, Nicolette, '"Willful Sadness": American Decadence, Gender, and the Pleasures and Dangers of Pessimism', *Journal of Gender Studies*, 26 (1) (2017), pp. 102–11.

Gagnier, Regenia, *Individualism, Decadence, and Globalization: On the Relationship of Part to Whole* (Basingstoke and New York: Palgrave Macmillan, 2010).

Galbraith, Patrick W., *The Moé Manifesto: An Insider's Look at the Worlds of Manga, Anime and Gaming* (North Clarendon: Tuttle Publishing, 2014).

Galbraith, Patrick W., *Otaku and the Struggle for Imagination in Japan* (Durham and London: Duke University Press, 2019).

Gardner, Lyn, 'Miss Revolutionary Idol Berserker Review – Merciless Japanese Pop-Culture Sendup', *The Guardian*, 23 June 2016, https://www.theguardian.com/stage/2016/jun/23/miss-revolutionary-idol-berserker-review-merciless-japanese-pop-culture-sendup, accessed 20 March 2022.

Gautier, Théophile, 'Preface', in *Mademoiselle de Maupin*, trans. Helen Constantine (London: Penguin, 2005), pp. 3–37.

George, Jim, 'Introduction: Are the Culture Wars Over?', in Jim George and Kim Huynh (eds), *The Culture Wars: Australian and American Politics in the 21st Century* (South Yarra: Palgrave Macmillan, 2009), pp. 1–15.

Giannachi, Gabriella, *Virtual Theatres: An Introduction* (London and New York: Routledge, 2006).

Gill, Carol J., 'A Psychological View of Disability Culture', *DSQ: Disability Studies Quarterly*, 15 (4) (1995), pp. 16–19.

Gilman, Richard, *Decadence: The Strange Life of an Epithet* (New York: Farrar, Straus and Giroux, 1975)

Goosen, Moosje, 'Going Dutch', *Frieze*, 1 January 2021, https://www.frieze.com/article/going-dutch-0, accessed 5 July 2021.

Gordon, Robert J., *The Rise and Fall of American Growth: The U. S. Standard of Living Since the Civil War* (Princeton and Oxford: Princeton University Press, 2016).

Gottschild, Brenda Dixon, *The Black Dancing Body: A Geography From Coon to Cool* (New York and Basingstoke: Palgrave Macmillan, 2003).

Gottschild, Brenda Dixon, 'Where is the Theology?', (2018), p. 39, https://legacy.blackbox.no/wp-content/uploads/2020/01/BBTP-00_Gottschild.pdf, accessed 16 March 2022.

Graeber, David, *Bullshit Jobs: A Theory* (London & New York: Penguin, 2018).

Graham, Elaine L., *Representations of the Post/human: Monsters, Aliens and Others in Popular Culture* (Manchester: Manchester University Press, 2002).

Green, Francis, et al., 'Is Job Quality Becoming More Unequal?', *Industrial & Labour Relations Review*, 66 (4) (2013), pp. 753–84.

Grier, William H. and Price M. Cobbs, *Black Rage* (New York: Basic Books, 1968).

Halberstam, Jack, *Skin Shows: Gothic Horror and the Technology of Monsters* (Durham and London: Duke University Press, 1995).

Halberstam, Jack, *Wild Things: The Disorder of Desire* (Durham and London: Duke University Press, 2020).
Han, Byung-Chul, *The Burnout Society*, trans. Erik Butler (Stanford: Stanford University Press, 2015).
Hann, Rachel, *Beyond Scenography* (London and New York: Routledge, 2019).
Härmänmaa, Marja and Christopher Nissen, 'Introduction: The Empire at the End of Decadence', in Marja Härmänmaa and Christopher Nissen (eds), *Decadence, Degeneration, and the End: Studies in the European Fin de Siècle* (New York and Basingstoke: Palgrave Macmillan, 2014), pp. 1–14.
Harootunian, Harry, *Uneven Moments: Reflections on Japan's Modern History* (New York: Columbia University Press, 2019).
Hartman, Andrew, *A War for the Soul of America: A History of the Culture Wars*, 2nd edition (Chicago: University of Chicago Press, 2019).
Hartman, Saidiya, *Scenes of Subjection: Terror, Slavery, and Self-Making in Nineteenth-Century America* (New York and Oxford: Oxford University Press, 1997).
Hartman, Saidiya, *Wayward Lives, Beautiful Experiments: Intimate Histories of Riotous Black Girls, Troublesome Women and Queer Radicals* (London: Serpent's Tail, 2021).
Harvey, David, *The Condition of Postmodernity* (Oxford: Blackwell, 1990).
Hassan, Robert, *The Condition of Digitality: A Post-Modern Marxism for the Practice of Digital Life* (London: University of Westminster Press, 2020).
Hassan, Robert, *The Information Society* (Cambridge and Malden, MA: Polity Press, 2008).
Hattenstone, Simon, 'Star Trek's Nichelle Nichols: "Martin Luther King was a Trekker"', *The Guardian*, 18 October 2016, https://www.theguardian.com/tv-and-radio/2016/oct/18/star-trek-nichelle-nichols-martin-luther-king-trekker, accessed 25 May 2022.
Hayles, N. Katherine, *How We Became Posthuman: Virtual Bodies in Cybernetics, Literature, and Informatics* (Chicago and London: University of Chicago Press, 1999).
Hazarika, Ayesha, 'Nadine Dorries Becoming Culture Secretary in the Reshuffle Shows Boris Johnson is Still the Master of Outrage', *iNews*, 16 September 2021, https://inews.co.uk/opinion/nadine-dorries-culture-secretary-cabinet-reshuffle-boris-johnson-master-outrage-1203302, accessed 27 April 2022.
Heisel, Andres, 'The Rise and Fall of an All-American Catchphrase: "Free, White, and 21"', *Jezebel*, 10 September 2015, https://theattic.jezebel.com/the-rise-and-fall-of-an-all-american-catchphrase-free-1729621311, accessed 9 March 2022.
Helms, Jesse, 'It's the Job of Congress to Define What's Art', *USA Today*, September 8, 1989', in Richard Bolton (ed.), *Culture Wars: Documents From the Recent Controversies in the Arts* (New York: New Press, 1992), pp. 100–1.
Hemming, Sarah, 'Murdering the Text: Sarah Hemming on Julia Bardsley's Macbeth in Leicester, and Murder Is Easy in London', *The Independent*, 3 March 1993, https://www.independent.co.uk/arts-entertainment/theatre

-murdering-the-text-sarah-hemming-on-julia-bardsleys-macbeth-in
-leicester-and-murder-is-easy-1495320.html, accessed 24 February 2022.
'HERE RAW – Staging Decadence', HERE Arts Centre, New York City,
9 September 2021. http://here.org/shows/raw21-staging-decadence/?fbclid
=IwAR1ceRaNhq_MnGBfLuPpShr0emQphuwkHJSdAKoUh_ewShc2wKJ
_i2ESD9k, accessed 30 June 2022.
Herman, Arthur, *The Idea of Decline in Western History* (New York: The Free Press, 1997).
Hernandez, Jillian, *Aesthetics of Excess: The Art and Politics of Black and Latina Embodiment* (Durham and London: Duke University Press, 2020).
Herold, Katharina and Leire Barrera-Medrano (eds), 'Women Writing Decadence', *Volupté: Interdisciplinary Journal of Decadence Studies*, 2 (1) (Spring 2019).
Hester, Helen, *Xenofeminism* (Cambridge and Medford, MA: Polity Press, 2018).
Hickel, Jason, *Less is More: How Degrowth Will Save the World* (London: Windmill, 2021).
Higher Education Policy Institute, 'Where and What Did the New Cabinet Study?', 26 July 2019, https://www.hepi.ac.uk/2019/07/26/where-and-what-did-the-new-cabinet-study/, accessed 17 August 2022.
Hind, Claire and Gary Winters, *Embodying the Dead: Writing, Playing, Performing* (London: Red Globe Press, 2020).
Hotton, Russell, 'UK Economy Rebounds With Fastest Growth Since WW2', *BBC News*, 11 February 2022, https://www.bbc.co.uk/news/business-60344573, accessed 11 February 2022.
House of Commons Digital, Culture, Media and Sport Select Committee, *Changing Lives: The Social Impact of Participation in Culture and Sport*, 11th report of session 2017-19, 14 May 2019 HC 734.
Howard, Yetta, (ed.), *Rated RX: Sheree Rose With and After Bob Flanagan* (Columbus: Ohio State University Press, 2020).
Howson, Teri, 'Zombies, Time Machines and Brains: Science Fiction Made Real in Immersive Theatres', *Thesis Eleven*, 131 (1) (2015), pp. 114–26.
Hutchings, Kimberly, *Time and World Politics: Thinking the Present* (Manchester and New York: Manchester University Press).
IMF, 'General Government Gross Debt', *World Economic Outlook*, October 2019, https://www.imf.org/external/datamapper/GGXWDG_NGDP@WEO/OEMDC/ADVEC/WEOWORLD/JPN (accessed 31 January 2020).
Itoh, Makoto, *The World Economic Crisis and Japanese Capitalism* (Basingstoke: Macmillan Press, 1990).
ITV News, 'Covid: Rishi Sunak Says People in "all Walks of Life" are Having to Adapt for Employment', *ITV News*, 6 October 2020, https://www.itv.com/news/2020-10-06/rishi-sunak-suggests-musicians-and-others-in-arts-should-retrain-and-find-other-jobs, accessed 27 April 2022.
Ivy, Marilyn, 'Critical Texts, Mass Artifacts: The Consumption of Knowledge in Postmodern Japan', in Masao Miyoshi and H. D. Harootunian (eds),

Postmodernism and Japan (Durham and London: Duke University Press: 1989).

Ivy, Marilyn, 'Revenge and Recapitulation in Recessionary Japan', in Tomiko Yoda and Harry Harootunian (eds), *Japan After Japan: Social and Cultural Life From the Recessionary 1990s to the Present* (Durham and London: Duke University Press, 2006), pp. 195–215.

Iwaki, Kyoko, 'Japanese Theatre After Fukushima: Okada Toshiki's *Current Location*', *New Theatre Quarterly*, 31 (1) (February) (2015), pp. 70–89.

Jackson, Holbrook, *The Eighteen-Nineties* (London: Cresset Library, 1988).

Jackson, Tim, *Post Growth: Life After Capitalism* (Cambridge and Medford, MA: Polity, 2021).

Jameson, Frederic, *Archaeologies of the Future: The Desire Called Utopia and Other Science Fictions* (London and New York: Verso, 2007).

Jameson, Frederic, *The Cultural Turn: Selected Writings on the Postmodern, 1983–1998* (London and New York: Verso, 1998).

Jameson, Frederic, 'Future City', *New Left Review*, 21 (May/June 2003), pp. 65–79.

Jansen, Sara, '"In What Time do we Live?" Time and Distance in the Work of Toshiki Okada', *Etcetera*, 145 (2016), https://e-tcetera.be/in-what-time-do-we-live/, accessed 20 May 2022.

Jarvis, Liam and Karen Savage, 'Introduction: Postdigitality: "Isn't It All Intermedial"?', in Jarvis and Savage (eds), *Avatars, Activism and Postdigital Performance: Precarious Intermedial Identities* (London: Bloomsbury, 2022), pp. 1–15.

Johnson, Dominic, 'Divine Fire: Ron Athey in Europe', in Amelia Jones and Andy Campbell (eds), *Queer Communion: Ron Athey* (Bristol: Intellect, 2020), pp. 294–303.

Johnson, Dominic, (ed.), *Pleading in the Blood: The Art and Performances of Ron Athey* (London: Live Art Development Agency; Bristol: Intellect, 2013).

Johnson, Dominic, 'The Skin of the Theatre: An Interview With Julia Bardsley', *Contemporary Theatre Review*, 20 (3) (2010), pp. 340–52.

Johnson, Dominic, *Unlimited Action: The Performance of Extremity in the 1970s* (Manchester: Manchester University Press, 2019).

Joint Committee on Human Rights, 'Freedom of Speech in Universities', 27 March 2018, https://publications.parliament.uk/pa/jt201719/jtselect/jtrights/589/58909.htm#_idTextAnchor058, accessed 11 May 2022.

Jones, Amelia, 'Rose/Flanagan/O'Brien: The Aesthetics of Resurrection', in Yetta, (ed.), *Rated RX: Sheree Rose With and After Bob Flanagan* (Columbus: Ohio State University Press, 2020), pp. 98–109.

Jones, Amelia and Andy Campbell (eds), *Queer Communion: Ron Athey* (Bristol: Intellect, 2020).

Kaiser, Fritz, *Degenerate Art: The Exhibition Guide in German and English*, trans. anon. (N.C.: Ostara Publications, 2012).

Kafer, Alison, *Feminist, Queer, Crip* (Bloomington: Indiana University Press, 2013).

Kam, Thiam Huat, 'The Common Sense That Make the "Otaku": Capital and the Common Sense of Consumption in Contemporary Japan', *Japan Forum*, 25 (2) (2013), pp. 151–73.

Kammer, Claudia, 'De Kerstman Die Niet de Straat op Mocht', *NRC*, 12 October 2018, https://www.nrc.nl/nieuws/2018/10/12/de-kerstman-die-niet-de-straat-op-mocht-a2417443, accessed 25 June 2021.

Kartsaki, Eirini, 'Rehearsals of the Weird: Julia Bardsley's *Almost the Same (Feral Rehearsals for Violent Acts of Culture)*', *Contemporary Theatre Review*, 30 (1) (2020), pp. 67–90.

Kartsaki, Eirini, *Repetition in Performance: Returns and Invisible Forces* (London: Palgrave Macmillan, 2017).

Kauffman, Linda S., *Bad Girls and Sick Boys: Fantasies in Contemporary Art and Culture* (Berkeley: University of California Press, 1998).

Kee, Chera, '"They are Not Men . . . They are Dead Bodies!": From Cannibal to Zombie and Back Again', in Deborah Christie and Sarah Juliet Lauro (eds), *Better Off Dead: The Evolution of the Zombie as Post-Human* (New York: Fordham, 2011), pp. 9–23.

Khomami, Nadia, 'Theatre in UK Faces Exodus of Women After Pandemic, Study Finds', *The Guardian*, 9 October 2021, https://www.theguardian.com/stage/2021/oct/09/theatre-in-uk-faces-exodus-of-women-after-pandemic-study-finds, accessed 27 April 2022.

Koch, Cynthia, 'The Contest for American Culture: A Leadership Case Study on The NEA and NEH Funding Crisis', 1998, http://www.upenn.edu/pnc/ptkoch.html, accessed 11 June 2021.

kosoko, jaamil olawale, *Black Body Amnesia: Poems & Other Speech Acts*, ed. Dahlia (Dixon) Li and Rachel Valinsky (Brooklyn, NY: Wendy's Subway, 2022).

kosoko, jaamil olawale, Personal interview [video call], 20 May 2020.

kosoko, jaamil olawale, *Syllabus for Black Love* (2021), https://static1.squarespace.com/static/5c74c0fb4d87115cde1dccfa/t/60edf06ac450ee4730810c0a/1626206331114/SFBL-zine-spreads.pdf, accessed 16 March 2022.

kosoko, jaamil olawale, *Syllabus for Survival* (2020), https://static1.squarespace.com/static/5c74c0fb4d87115cde1dccfa/t/5e9f0d4a97b64409fdb9cdd6/1587481965196/Jaamil_ZINE_17.pdf, accessed 16 March 2022.

Kraut, Alan M., *Silent Travelers: Germs, Genes, and the "Immigrant Menace"* (Baltimore: Johns Hopkins University Press, 1994).

Land, Nick, *Fanged Noumena: Collected Writings 1987–2007*, 6th edition, ed. Robin Mackay and Ray Brassier (Falmouth and New York: Urbanomic, 2018).

Landy, Benjamin, 'Graph: Does Productivity Growth Still Benefit the American Worker?', *The Century Foundation*, 15 August 2012, https://tcf.org/content/commentary/graph-does-productivity-growth-still-benefit-the-american-worker/?agreed=1, accessed 2 February 2022.

Lankester, E. Ray, *Degeneration: A Chapter in Darwinism* (London: Macmillan and Co., 1880).

Lawson, Jenny, 'Eating Minds: Fantasizing Undead, Becoming Zombie in Performance', *Studies in Theatre and Performance*, 34 (3) (2014), pp. 236–43.

Lepecki, André, *Exhausting Dance: Performance and the Politics of Movement* (New York and London: Routledge, 2006).

Levy, Alan Howard, *Government and the Arts: Debates Over Federal Support of the Arts in America From George Washington to Jesse Helms* (Lanham: University Press of America, Inc., 1997).

Lingis, Alphonso, 'Consecration', in Martin O'Brien and David MacDiarmid (eds), *Survival of the Sickest: The Art of Martin O'Brien* (London: Live Art Development Agency, 2018), pp. 22–4.

Lively, Frazer, 'Introduction', in Kiki Gounaridou and Frazer Lively (ed. and trans.), *Madame La Mort and Other Plays* (Baltimore and London: Johns Hopkins UP, 1998), pp. 7–8.

Lombroso, Cesare, *Criminal Man*, trans. Mary Gibson and Nicole Hahn Rafter (Durham and London: Duke University Press, 2006).

Loos, Adolf, 'Ornament and Crime', in Shaun Whiteside (trans.), *Ornament and Crime: Thoughts on Design and Materials* (N.C.: Penguin Books, 2019), pp. 185–202.

Lorde, Audre, 'Poetry Is Not a Luxury', *Sister Outsider* (London: Penguin Books, 2019), pp. 25–8.

Lorde, Audre, 'Power' (1978), https://www.poetryfoundation.org/poems/53918/power-56d233adafeb3, accessed 9 March 2022.

Luciano, Dana, *Arranging Grief: Sacred Time and the Body in Nineteenth-Century America* (New York: New York University Press, 2007).

Luckhurst, Roger, 'The Weird: A Dis/orientation', *Textual Practice*, 31 (6) (2017), pp. 1041–61.

Lukács, György, *Writer and Critic and Other Essays*, ed. and trans. Arthur Kahn (London: Merlin Press, 1978).

Lukianoff, Greg and Jonathan Haidt, *The Coddling of the American Mind: How Good Intentions and Bad Ideas are Setting up a Generation for Failure* (New York: Penguin, 2018).

Lyytikäinen, Pirjo, 'Decadent Tropologies of Sickness', in Marja Härmänmaa and Christopher Nissen (eds), *Decadence, Degeneration, and the End: Studies in the European Fin de Siècle* (New York: Palgrave Macmillan, 2014), pp. 85–102.

Machin, James, *Weird Fiction in Britain 1880-1939* (Cham: Palgrave Macmillan, 2018).

Mackay, Robin and Armen Avanessian (eds), *#Accelerate: The Accelerationist Reader* (Falmouth: Urbanomic Media Ltd, 2017).

MacKendrick, Karmen, *Counterpleasures* (Albany: New York State University, 1999).

MacLeod, Kirsten, *Fictions of British Decadence: High Art, Popular Writing, and the Fin de Siècle* (Basingstoke and New York: Palgrave Macmillan, 2006).

Marriott, David, 'Waiting to Fall', *CR: The New Centennial Review*, 13 (3) (Winter 2013), pp. 163–240.

Martin, Ian F., *Quit Your Band: Musical Notes From the Japanese Underground* (New York and Tokyo: Awai Books, 2016).
Martin, Randy, 'A Precarious Dance, a Derivative Sociality', *TDR*, 56 (4) (Winter 2012), pp. 62–77.
Mason, Paul, *Postcapitalism: A Guide to Our Future* (London: Penguin, 2015).
Mbiti, John S., *African Religions and Philosophy*, 2nd edition (Oxford: Heinemann, 1989).
McCormack, Gavin, *The Emptiness of Japanese Affluence*, rev. edition (New York and London: M. E. Sharpe, 2001).
McCormick, Stacie Selmon, *Staging Black Fugitivity* (Columbus: Ohio State University Press, 2019).
McKenzie, Jon, *Perform or Else: From Discipline to Performance* (London and New York: Routledge, 2001).
Meyer, Richard, 'The Jesse Helms Theory of Art', *October*, 104 (Spring 2003), pp. 131–48.
Miller, Lee, 'Editorial Introduction', *Studies in Theatre and Performance*, 34 (3) (2014), pp. 191–200.
Miller, Monica L., *Slaves to Fashion: Black Dandyism and the Styling of Black Diasporic Identity* (Durham and London: Duke University Press, 2009).
Moore, Madison, *Fabulous: The Rise of the Beautiful Eccentric* (New Haven and London: Yale University Press, 2018).
Moore, Peter, 'One Quarter of Americans Think Their Jobs are Meaningless', *YouGov*, 14 August 2015, https://today.yougov.com/topics/lifestyle/articles-reports/2015/08/14/one-quarter-americans-think-their-jobs-are-meaning, accessed 2 February 2022.
Moreno, Beatriz, 'Snatch Power Episode 1', *YouTube*, 25 October 2015, https://www.youtube.com/watch?v=Wy9seF6-j2Y, accessed 2 March 2022.
Moriki, Akira, *Nisen Hatinen IMF Senryô* (Tokyo: Kodansha, 2005).
Mulholland, Rory, 'Parisians Snap up "butt Plugs" After "Tree" Fiasco', *The Local*, 2 December 2014, https://www.thelocal.fr/20141202/parisians-butt-plug-sex-toy-paul-mccarthy/, accessed 25 June 2021.
Muñoz, José Esteban, *Cruising Utopia: The Then and There of Queer Futurity* (New York and London: New York University Press, 2009).
Muñoz, José Esteban, *Disidentifications: Queers of Color and the Performance of Politics* (Minneapolis and London: University of Minnesota Press, 1999).
Murakami, Takashi (ed.), *Little Boy: The Arts of Japan's Exploding Subculture* (New York: Japan Society; New Haven and London: Yale University Press, 2005).
Murray, Douglas, *The Madness of Crowds: Gender, Race and Identity* (London: Bloomsbury, 2019).
Nagle, Angela, *Kill All Normies: Online Culture Wars From 4chan and Tumblr to Trump and the Alt-right* (Winchester and Washington: Zer0 Books, 2017).
National Endowment for the Arts, 'New Report Released on the Economic Impact of the Arts and Cultural Sector', 30 March 2021, https://www.arts.gov

/news/press-releases/2021/new-report-released-economic-impact-arts-and-cultural-sector, accessed 5 August 2022.

Newell, Jonathan, *Weird Fiction 1832–1937: Disgust, Metaphysics and the Aesthetics of Cosmic Horror* (Cardiff: University of Wales Press, 2020).

Ngai, Sianne, *Our Aesthetic Categories: Zany, Cute, Interesting* (Cambridge, MA: Harvard University Press, 2012).

Nikaido, Toco, 'In Their Words: Miss Revolutionary Idol Berserker', *Barbican.org.uk*, 16 June 2016, https://www.barbican.org.uk/read-watch-listen/in-their-words-miss-revolutionary-idol-berserker, accessed 19 May 2022.

Nordau, Max, *Degeneration*, trans. from the second German edition by George L. Mosse (Lincoln and London: University of Nebraska Press, 1993).

Norma, Caroline, 'Catharine MacKinnon in Japanese: Toward a Radical Feminist Theory of Translation', in Beverley Curran, Nana Sato-Rossberg, and Kikuko Tanabe (eds), *Multiple Translation Communities in Contemporary Japan* (London: Routledge, 2015), pp. 79–98.

Nowotny, Helga, *Time: The Modern and Postmodern Experience*, trans. Neville Plaice (Cambridge: Polity Press, 1994).

Noys, Benjamin, *Malign Velocities: Accelerationism and Capitalism* (Winchester and Washington: Zero Books, 2014).

NRLA (2020) 'Julia Bardsley: Aftermaths: A Tear in the Meat of Vision', *NRLA30*, https://nrla30.com/the-artists/julia-bardsley/, accessed 12 April 2022.

Nyong'o, Tavia, *Afro-Fabulations: The Queer Drama of Black Life* (New York: New York University Press, 2019).

O'Brien, Martin, 'Cough, Bitch, Cough: Reflections on Sickness and the Coughing Body in Performance', in Alex Mermikides and Gianna Bouchard (eds), *Performance and the Medical Body* (London: Bloomsbury, 2016), pp. 129–36.

O'Brien, Martin, *Last(ing)*, Spill Festival of Performance, Toynbee Studios, London, 11 April 2013.

O'Brien, Martin, *Mucus Factory, in Access all Areas: Double DVD Set*, ed. and produced by Andrew Mitchell and Paula Gorini. Available in Lois Keidan and CJ Mitchell (eds), *Access all Areas: Live Art and Disability* (London: Live Art Development Agency, 2012).

O'Brien, Martin, 'Performing Chronic: Chronic Illness and Endurance Art', *Performance Research*, 19 (4) (2014), pp. 54–63.

O'Brien, Martin, 'Until the Last Breath is Breathed - Martin O'Brien Performance Lecture DaDaFest International 2018', *YouTube*, 14 January 2019, https://www.youtube.com/watch?v=dEvGjLgw-A0, accessed 27 March 2020.

O'Brien, Martin, 'The Unwell', *Martin O'Brien – Performance Artist*, https://www.martinobrienart.com/the-unwell.html, accessed 31 March 2020.

O'Brien, Martin, 'You are My Death: The Shattered Temporalities of Zombie Time', in *The Last Breath Society (Coughing Coffin)*, programme notes (London: Institute for Contemporary Art, 2019), pp. 2–3.

O'Brien, Martin, 'You are My Death: The Shattered Temporalities of Zombie Time', *Welcome Open Research*, 5 (135) (2020), pp. 3–10.

ONS (2019) 'Labour Productivity', Office for National Statistics, 5 July 2019, https://www.ons.gov.uk/employmentandlabourmarket/peopleinwork/labourproductivity, accessed 2 February 2022.

Open Culture, 'Sun Ra Applies to NASA's Art Program: When the Inventor of Space Jazz Applied to Make Space Art', 10 September 2019, https://www.openculture.com/2019/09/sun-ra-applies-to-nasas-art-program.html, accessed 28 February 2022.

Ordine, Nuccio, *The Usefulness of the Useless*, trans. Alastair McEwen (Philadelphia: Paul Dry Books, 2017).

Osborne, Peter, *The Politics of Time: Modernity and Avant-Garde* (London and New York: Verso, 1995).

Ovid, *Metamorphoses*, trans. A. D. Melville (Oxford and New York: Oxford University Press, 1998).

Paglia, Camille, 'The Beautiful Decadence of Robert Mapplethorpe: A Response to Rochelle Gurstein', in *Sex, Art and American Culture: Essays* (New York: Viking, 1992), pp. 40–4.

Palladini, Giulia, 'Logic of Prelude: On Use Value, Pleasure, and the Struggle Against Agony', *Contemporary Theatre Review*, 'Interventions', 29 (4) (Winter/Spring 2019/20), https://www.contemporarytheatrereview.org/2020/logic-of-prelude-on-use-value-pleasure-and-the-struggle-against-agony/, accessed 2 February 2022.

Palmer, Alex, 'When Art Fought the Law and the Art Won', *Smithsonian Magazine*, 2 October 2015, https://www.smithsonianmag.com/history/when-art-fought-law-and-art-won-180956810/, accessed 11 June 2021.

PA Media, 'Rishi Sunak Vows to End Low-Earning Degrees in Post-16 Education Shake-up', *The Guardian*, 7 August 2022, https://www.theguardian.com/politics/2022/aug/07/rishi-sunak-vows-to-end-low-earning-degrees-in-post-16-education-shake-up, accessed 17 August 2022.

Parker-Starbuck, Jennifer, *Cyborg Theatre: Corporeal/Technological Intersections in Multimedia Performance* (Basingstoke and New York: Palgrave Macmillan, 2011).

Patterson, Orlando, *Slavery and Social Death: A Comparative Study* (Cambridge, MA and London: Harvard University Press, 2018).

Pelissero, Marielle, 'From the Figure to the Cipher: Figuration, Disfiguration and the Limits of Visibility', *Performance Research*, 23 (8) (2018), pp. 31–8.

Perucci, Tony, 'Irritational Aesthetics: Reality Friction and Indecidable Theatre', *Theatre Journal*, 70 (4) (December 2018), pp. 473–98.

Phelan, Peggy, *Unmarked: The Politics of Performance* (New York: Routledge, 1993).

Pinker, Steven, *Enlightenment Now: The Case for Reason, Science, Humanism and Progress* (New York: Penguin, 2018).

Pluckrose, Helen and James Lindsay, *Cynical Theories: How Activist Scholarship Made Everything About Race, Gender, and Identity – And Why This Harms Everybody* (N.C.: Swift Press, 2020).

Podesva, Kristina Lee, et al., 'Responses to the Recent Cuts to Arts Funding in the Netherlands', *Fillip*, Summer 2011, https://fillip.ca/content/responses-to-recent-dutch-arts-cuts, accessed 5 July 2021.

Potolsky, Matthew, 'Decadence and Politics', in Alex Murray (ed.), *Decadence: A Literary History* (Cambridge: Cambridge University Press, 2020), pp. 152–66.

Potolsky, Matthew, *The Decadent Republic of Letters: Taste, Politics, and Cosmopolitan Community From Baudelaire to Beardsley* (Philadelphia: University of Pennsylvania Press, 2013)

Poulton, M. Cody, 'Krapp's First Tape: Okada Toshiki's Enjoy', *TDR*, 55 (2) (Summer) (2011), pp. 150–64.

Prime Minister's Office, 'PM: A New Deal for Britain', 30 June 2020, https://www.gov.uk/government/news/pm-a-new-deal-for-britain, accessed 30 June 2021.

Rawlinson, Mark, 'The Decadent University: Narratives of Decay and the Future of Higher Education', in Michael St John (ed.), *Romancing Decay: Ideas of Decadence in European Culture* (Aldershot: Ashgate, 1999), pp. 235–45.

Rayner, Alice, *Ghosts: Death's Double and the Phenomena of Theatre* (Minneapolis and London: University of Minnesota Press, 2006).

Reason, Mardi, 'Miss Revolutionary Idol Berserker: Inside the Out of This World', *Scenestr*, 2 September 2015, https://scenestr.com.au/arts/miss-revolutionary-idol-berserker-inside-the-out-of-this-world, accessed 20 May 2022.

Redmond, Adele, 'Arm's-length Policy at Risk in "contested Heritage" Debate', *Arts Professional*, 8 October 2020, https://www.artsprofessional.co.uk/news/arms-length-policy-risk-contested-heritage-debate, accessed 11 May 2022.

Rifkin, Jeremy with Ted Howard, *Entropy: A New World View* (Toronto: Bantam Books, 1981).

Riggenbach, Jeff, *In Praise of Decadence* (New York: Prometheus Books, 1998).

Roberts, Michèle, 'Should Feminists Read Baudelaire?', *BBC Radio 4*, 28 March 2021, https://www.bbc.co.uk/programmes/m000tmhp, accessed 24 February 2022.

Robertson, Pat, 'Christian Coalition Direct Mail, October 25, 1989 (excerpt)', in Richard Bolton (ed.), *Culture Wars: Documents From the Recent Controversies in the Arts* (New York: New Press, 1992), pp. 123–5.

Robinson, Cedric J., *Black Marxism: The Making of the Black Radical Tradition*, 3rd edition (Dublin: Penguin, 2021).

'Roll Call Vote 101st Congress – 1st Session', *United States Senate*, 7 October 1989, https://www.senate.gov/legislative/LIS/roll_call_lists/roll_call_vote_cfm.cfm?congress=101&session=1&vote=00242, accessed 9 July 2021.

Rosa, Hartmut, *Social Acceleration: A New Theory of Modernity*, trans. Jonathan Trejo-Mathys (New York: Columbia University Press, 2013).

Rugoff, Ralph, 'Mr. McCarthy's Neighbourhood', in Ralph Rugoff, Kristine Stiles, and Giacinto Di Pietrantonio (eds), *Paul McCarthy* (London: Phaidon, 1996), pp. 32–87.

Rushkoff, Douglas, *Present Shock: When Everything Happens Now*, New York: Penguin, 2013).
Russo, Mary, *The Female Grotesque: Risk, Excess and Modernity* (New York and London: Routledge, 1995).
Ryersson, Scot D. and Michael Orlando Yaccarino, *Infinite Variety: The Life and Legend of the Marchesa Casati* (Minneapolis: University of Minnesota Press, 2004).
Sadler, William S., *Race Decadence: An Examination of the Causes of Racial Degeneracy in the United States* (Ann Arbor and London: University Microfilms International, 1981 [1922]).
Sales, Ruby, 'Ruby Sales: Where Does It Hurt?', *On Being With Krista Tippett*, 16 January 2020, https://onbeing.org/programs/ruby-sales-where-does-it-hurt/, accessed 9 March 2022.
Saltus, Edgar, *The Philosophy of Disenchantment and The Anatomy of Negation* (N.C.: Underworld Amusements, 2014).
Schechner, Richard, 'A New Paradigm for Theatre in the Academy', *TDR*, 36 (4) (Winter 1992), pp. 7–10.
Schechner, Richard, 'Theatre Criticism', *The Tulane Drama Review*, 9 (3) (Spring 1965), pp. 13–24.
Schmidt, Theron, 'Troublesome Professionals: On the Speculative Reality of Theatrical Labour', *Performance Research*, 18 (2) (2013), pp. 15–26.
Schneider, Rebecca, 'It Seems As If . . . I Am Dead: Zombie Capitalism and Theatrical Labor', *TDR: The Drama Review*, 56 (4) (Winter 2012), pp. 150–62.
Serpell, Namwali, 'The Zambian "Afronaut" Who Wanted to Join the Space Race', *The New Yorker*, 11 March 2017, https://www.newyorker.com/culture/culture-desk/the-zambian-afronaut-who-wanted-to-join-the-space-race, accessed 2 March 2022.
Serra, Richard, 'Art and Censorship', *Critical Inquiry*, 17 (3) (Spring 1991), pp. 574–81.
Serratore, Nicole, 'Beyond Whiteness: A January Festival Wrap-Up', *American Theatre*, 2 February 2018, https://www.americantheatre.org/2018/02/02/beyond-whiteness-a-january-festival-wrap-up/, accessed 9 March 2022.
Sharma, Sarah, *In the Meantime: Temporality and Cultural Politics* (Durham and London: Duke University Press, 2014).
Sharpe, Christina, *In the Wake: On Blackness and Being* (Durham and London: Duke University Press, 2016).
Shaviro, Steven, *The Cinematic Body* (Minneapolis: University of Minnesota Press, 2011).
Shelley, Mary, *Frankenstein or The Modern Prometheus*, ed. M. K. Joseph (New York and Oxford: Oxford University Press, 1980).
Sherry, Vincent, *Modernism and the Reinvention of Decadence* (New York: Cambridge University Press, 2015).
Sherwood, Normandy, Interview with the author. HERE Arts Centre, New York, 9 September 2021.

Showalter, Elaine (ed.), *Daughters of Decadence: Stories by Women Writers of the Fin de Siècle* (London: Virago, 2016).

Sinker, Mark, 'Loving the Alien in Advance of Landing – Black Science Fiction', *The Wire*, 96 (February 1992), https://reader.exacteditions.com/issues/35378, accessed 9 March 2023.

Skelly, Julia, *Radical Decadence: Excess in Contemporary Feminist Textiles and Craft* (London and New York: Bloomsbury, 2017).

Smallwood, Stephanie E., *Saltwater Slavery: A Middle Passage From Africa to American Diaspora* (Cambridge, MA and London: Harvard University Press, 2007).

Smith, M. (pseudonym), 'Going in Through the Back Door: Challenging Straight Male Homohysteria, Transhysteria, and Transphobia Through Receptive Penetrative Sex Toy Use', *Sexuality & Culture*, 22 (4) (2018), pp. 1542–60.

#Snatchpower, 'BASIC ASS FAKE WHITE BITCH (BAFWB) The Uhuruverse X Niko Suki Produced by Onelle Woods', *YouTube*, 1 March 2017, https://www.youtube.com/watch?v=f2359FbpkIM, accessed 3 March 2022.

#Snatchpower, 'S.W.P. (Snatches With Power) Live!', *YouTube*, 22 June 2016, https://www.youtube.com/watch?v=X8Li9qVWa_c, accessed 2 March 2022.

Someya, Ayaka, 'Miss Revolutionary Idol Berserker', press release, 2018, http://missrevodolbbbbbbbberserker.asia/wp-content/uploads/2018/09/EnglishPR.pdf, accessed 5 March 2020. Amanda Waddell, teleconference interview, 12 May 2020.

Sone, Yuji, *Japanese Robot Culture: Performance, Imagination and Modernity* (New York: Palgrave Macmillan, 2017).

Sontag, Susan, *Illness as Metaphor and AIDS and Its Metaphors* (London: Penguin, 1991).

Southwood, Ivor, *Non-stop Inertia* (Arlesford: Zer0 Books, 2011).

Space is the Place: Sun Ra and His Intergalactic Solar Arkestra, written by Sun Ra and Joshua Smith, dir. John Coney (Plexifilm, 2003).

Spengler, Oswald, *The Decline of the West*, abridged by Helmut Werner (New York and Oxford: Oxford University Press, 1991).

Srnicek, Nick and Alex Williams *Inventing the Future: Postcapitalism and a World Without Work*, rev. edition (London and New York: Verso, 2016).

Staging Decadence [film], created by Adam Alston, Owen Parry and Sophie Farrell, 12 May 2022, https://www.stagingdecadence.com/films, accessed 12 May 2022.

Stilling, Robert, *Beginning at the End: Decadence, Modernism, and Postcolonial Poetry* (Cambridge, MA and London: Harvard University Press, 2018).

St. John, Michael, *Romancing Decay: Ideas of Decadence in European Culture* (Aldershot: Ashgate, 1999).

Stokes, John, 'The Legend of Duse', in Ian Fletcher (ed.), *Decadence and the 1890s* (New York: Holmes and Meier Publishers, Inc.), pp. 151–71.

Svich, Caridad, *Toward a Future Theatre: Conversations During a Pandemic* (London and New York: Methuen Drama, 2022).

Tanizaki, Jun'ichirō, *In Praise of Shadows*, trans. Thomas J. Harper and Edward G. Seidensticker (London: Vintage Books, 2001).
Toffler, Alvin [and Heidi Toffler], *Future Shock* (New York: Bantam, 1971).
Toffler, Alvin [and Heidi Toffler], 'The Future as a Way of Life', *Horizon*, 7 (3) (Summer 1965), pp. 108–15.
Uchino, Tadashi, 'Globality's Children: The "Child's" Body As a Strategy of Flatness in Performance', *TDR*, 50 (1) (2006), pp. 57–66.
The Uhuruverse, 'DISOBEY!!', *Soundcloud*, July 2015, https://soundcloud.com/theuhuruverse/disobey, accessed 26 February 2022.
The Uhuruverse, 'Uhuru Dream House', 13 July 2020, https://www.gofundme.com/f/UHURUDREAMHOUSE, accessed 25 February 2022.
UK Public General Acts, 'Education (No. 2) Act 1986, Section 43', 1 August 2019, https://www.legislation.gov.uk/ukpga/1986/61/section/43, accessed 12 May 2022.
Urry, John, *Sociology Beyond Societies: Mobilities for the Twenty-First Century* (London: Routledge, 2000).
van Veen, tobias c., 'The Armageddon Effect: Afrofuturism and the Chronopolitics of Alien Nation', in Anderson and Jones (eds), *Afrofuturism 2.0: The Rise of Astro-Blackness* (Lanham: Lexington Books, 2016), pp. 63–90.
Vaughan, Richard, *Philip the Good: The Apogee of Burgandy* (London: Longmans, Green and Co. Ltd, 1970).
Verlaine, Paul, *Poems of Paul Verlaine*, trans. Gertrude Hall (New York: Duffield & Company, 1906).
Virilio, Paul, *The Futurism of the Instant: Stop-Eject*, trans. Julie Rose (Cambridge and Malden, MA: Polity Press, 2010).
Virilio, Paul, *Polar Inertia*, trans. Patrick Camiller (London: Sage, 2000).
Waddell, Amanda, email correspondence with the author, 16 May 2020.
Waddell, Amanda, Teleconference interview, 12 May 2020.
Wajcman, Judy, *Pressed for Time: The Acceleration of Life in Digital Capitalism* (Chicago and London: University of Chicago Press, 2015).
Walcott, Derek, 'What the Twilight Says', in *What the Twilight Says* (New York: Farrar, Strauss and Giroux, 1998), pp. 3–35.
Wald, Priscilla, *Contagious: Cultures, Carriers, and the Outbreak Narrative* (Durham and London: Duke University Press, 2008).
Warner, Marina, *Phantasmagoria: Spirit Visions, Metaphors, and Media Into the Twenty-First Century* (Oxford and New York: Oxford University Press, 2006).
Warren, Calvin L., 'ONTICIDE: Afro-pessimism, Gay Nigger #1, and Surplus Violence', *GLQ: A Journal of Lesbian and Gay Studies*, 23 (3) (2017), pp. 391–418.
Warren, Calvin L., *Ontological Terror: Blackness, Nihilism, and Emancipation* (Durham and London: Duke University Press, 2018).
Weeks, Kathi, *The Problem With Work: Feminism, Marxism, Antiwork Politics, and Postwork Imaginaries* (Durham and London: Duke University Press, 2011).

Weiner, Norbert, *The Human Use of Human Beings: Cybernetics and Society* (N.C.: De Capo Press, 1954).

Weir, David, 'Afterword: Decadent Taste', in Jane Desmarais and Alice Condé (eds), *Decadence and the Senses* (Cambridge: Legenda, 2017), pp. 219–28.

Weir, David and Jane Desmarais, 'Introduction: Decadence, Culture, and Society', in Jane Desmarais and David Weir (eds), *The Oxford Handbook of Decadence* (New York: Oxford University Press, 2022), pp. 1–17.

Wilde, Oscar, 'The Preface', in *The Picture of Dorian Gray* (Croxley Green: Chiltern Publishing, 2020), pp. 5–6.

Wilde, Oscar, 'The Soul of Man Under Socialism', in *Complete Works of Oscar Wilde, Vol. III: Poems, Essays and Letters* (London: Heron Books, 1966), pp. 371–96.

Wilderson III, Frank B., *Red, White, and Black* (Durham, NC: Duke University Press, 2010).

Williamson, Gavin, 'Guidance to the Office for Students – Allocation of the Higher Education Teaching Grant Funding in the 2021–22 Financial Year', Department for Education, 19 January 2021, https://www.officeforstudents.org.uk/media/a3814453-4c28-404a-bf76-490183867d9a/rt-hon-gavin-williamson-cbe-mp-t-grant-ofs-chair-smb.pdf, accessed 10 May 2022.

Williamson, Gavin, 'Higher Education: Free Speech and Academic Freedom', Department for Education, February 2021, https://assets.publishing.service.gov.uk/government/uploads/system/uploads/attachment_data/file/961537/Higher_education_free_speech_and_academic_freedom__web_version_.pdf, accessed 11 May 2022.

Wilson, Helen (pseudonym), 'Human Reactions to Rape Culture and Queer Performativity at Urban dog Parks in Portland, Oregon', *Gender, Place & Culture*, 27 (2) (2018), pp. 307–26.

Wilson, Tom, Personal interview, Shoreditch Town Hall, London, 11 March 2020.

Witherspoon, Nia O., Interview with the author. HERE Arts Centre, New York. 9 September 2021.

Womack, Ytasha L., *Afrofuturism: The World of Black Sci-Fi and Fantasy Culture* (Chicago: Lawrence Hill Books, 2013).

Wright, Stephen, 'The Fate of Public Time: Toward a Time Without Qualities', *North East West South*, 10 January 2008, https://northeastwestsouth.net/fate-public-time-toward-time-without-qualities-0/, accessed 16 February 2022.

Yoda, Tomiko, 'A Roadmap to Millennial Japan', in Tomiko Yoda and Harry Harootunian (eds), *Japan After Japan: Social and Cultural Life From the Recessionary 1990s to the Present* (Durham and London: Duke University Press, 2006), pp. 16–53.

Yoda, Tomiko, 'The Rise and Fall of Maternal Society: Gender, Labor, and Capital in Contemporary Japan', in Tomiko Yoda and Harry Harootunian (eds), *Japan After Japan: Social and Cultural Life From the Recessionary 1990s to the Present* (Durham and London: Duke University Press, 2006), pp. 239–74.

Yost, Julia, 'New York's Hottest Club Is the Catholic Church', *New York Times*, 9 August 2022. https://www.nytimes.com/2022/08/09/opinion/nyc-catholicism-dimes-square-religion.html, accessed 23 August 2022.

Youngquist, Paul, *A Pure Solar World: Sun Ra and the Birth of Afrofuturism* (Austin: University of Texas Press, 2016).

Zamalin, Alex, *Black Utopia: The History of an Idea From Black Nationalism to Afrofuturism* (New York: Columbia University Press, 2019).

Zantvoort, Bart, 'Political Inertia and Social Acceleration', *Philosophy and Social Criticism*, 43 (4) (2017), pp. 707–23.

Zemmour, Éric, *Le Suicide Francais* (Paris: Albin Michel, 2014).

Zhuang, She, et al., 'Does COVID-19 Threat Increase Xenophobia? The Roles of Protection Efficacy and Support Seeking', *BMC Public Health*, 22 (485) (2022), https://doi.org/10.1186/s12889-022-12912-8, accessed 14 June 2022.

Žižek, Slavoj, *Living in the End Times* (London and New York: Verso, 2010).

Zola, Irving Kenneth, 'The Language of Disability: Problems of Politics and Practice', *Australian Disability Review*, 1 (3) (1988), pp. 13–21.

Index

24/7 89–90, 93–4, 96, 105–6

Abe, Shinzō 92
abjection 3, 15, 20, 27, 34–6, 38–41 *passim*, 43, 50, 53–4, 57, 63, 124, 143, 145–6, 170 n.39
abundance 6–7, 56, 106, 110
acceleration 16–18 *passim*, 23, 58, 80, 89, 97, 99, 102, 109, 161 n.50
acid communism 78, 174 n.49
Adams, Alexander 188 n.80
aesthetic category 13–15 *passim*, 102
aestheticism 2–3, 14, 108, 137, 144–5, 150, *see also* art for art's sake
Afrofuturism 66–7, 69, 72–3, 76–8 *passim*, 82, 84–7 *passim*, 147
Afropessimism 66–7, 69–75 *passim*, 76, 79, 81, *see also* pessimism
Afropunk 69, 76–8 *passim*, 81
Ahmed, Sara 19, 40, 137
AIDS 22, 113, 116–17, 120, 139, 146
AKB48 101
Ali, Muhammed 79
alien 72–3, 78, 81, 85
Alien Nation 84–5, 88
alienation 52, 68, 73, 75, 84, 88, 147, 176 n.76
Amano, Ikuho 107, 179 n.37
American Family Association 118
anachronistic 32, 65, 73, 81–2
Anan, Nabuko 97, 180 n.49
Anderson, Laurie 82
antiquated 10–11, 160–1 n.49
Antoinette, Marie 76

Antúnez Roca, Marcel·lí 15, 21, 43, 45–6, 56–63 *passim*, 144–5, 170 n.47
Epizoo 58
Hipermembrana 43, 46, 58–62 *passim*
JoAn, l'home de carn 57
'La vida sin amor no tiene sentido' 57
Metamembrana 59
Protomembrana 59
apocalypse 25, 27, 29, 36, 43, 45–51 *passim*, 53, 62–3, 84–6, 110, 147–8
post-apocalyptic 37, 41, 77, 147
Arcade, Penny 13
art for art's sake 2, 137, 150
Artaud, Antonin 56
artificial paradise 45, 55, 147, 153
arts and humanities 22–3, 112, 131–40 *passim*, 149–50
Arts Council England 135
Asada, Akira 105
asceticism 34
Athey, Ron 1, 15, 22, 47, 113, 115–22 *passim*, 139, 146
4 Scenes in a Harsh Life 113, 119, 122
Deliverance 119
Excerpted Rites Transformation 119
Martyrs & Saints 119
Augar, Philip 131
augment 11, 15, 22, 53, 63, 101–2, 105–6, 108–10, 146
Aum Shinrikyō 103
Auslander, Philip 156 n.12
austerity 122, 123, 126–8, 139

Bal, Mieke 143

Baldwin, James 72
Banana Gakuen Junjo Otome-
 gumi 97–8, 105
Baraitser, Lisa 31, 163 nn.17–18,
 164 n.23
Bardsley, Julia 15, 21, 43,
 47–55 passim,
 62–3, 144–6
 *Aftermaths: A Tear in the Meat of
 Vision* 43, 46–55 passim,
 62–3
 *Almost the Same (feral rehearsals
 for violent acts of
 culture)* 47
 Trans-Acts 47
Barish, Jonas 182 n.9
baroque 14
Barrie, Dennis 116, 121
Bart, Walter 124–5
Bataille, Georges 34, 122, 129
Baudelaire, Charles 6, 54,
 67, 160–1 n.49,
 168 n.24
Baudrillard, Jean 108, 156 n.18
beauty 14, 101, 116, 129, 140,
 144–6
Beech, Dave 159 n.37
Belfiore, Eleonora 185 n.57
Benjamin, Walter 58–9, 78, 160–1
 n.49
Bennett, Oliver 185 n.57
Beradi, Franco 45, 96
Berber, Anita 12
Bertman, Stephen 104–5
Bezos, Jeff 86
biopolitics 45, 58, 96
Birringer, Johannes 178 n.21
Bissell, Laura 167 n.13
Black Power 78–9, 112
#BlackLivesMatter 6, 76–7
Bloch, Ernst 37
Bluedorn, Allen C. 163 n.22
bodies 1, 5, 11, 26, 28, 30, 32, 36,
 38, 40–1, 43–63 passim,
 65–6, 68, 72, 74–5,
 81–2, 84, 88, 90, 96–7, 100,
 104–6, 109–10, 118, 120,
 130, 143–4, 146, 151–2
Bodomo, Nuotama 83
border crossing 2–3, 19, 45,
 52, 137, 143–6 passim,
 150–1
Bork, Robert 118, 121
Bouchard, Gianna 30
Bourget, Paul 6
Bourland, Ian 83
Bourriaud, Nicolas 108
Bowery, Leigh 13
Boyle, Shary 52
Branson, Richard 86
Bridle, James 166 n.2
Brook, Orian 149–50
brown, adrienne maree 3
Browning, Barbara 5
Bru-Domínguez, Eva 56
Buchanan, Patrick 112, 116–18,
 121, 139
burlesque 76

cabaret 76, 142
cancel culture 135
capability 16–17, 20, 27–8, 32,
 38–40, 67–8, 146
capitalism 1, 3, 6–9, 11, 15–18
 passim, 21, 23, 26–7, 31–2,
 37–8, 40, 44–5, 48–9, 53–4,
 58, 61–3, 66, 68, 75, 81,
 84, 88, 90, 94, 96, 105,
 107–10, 137, 146, 148, 150,
 see also postindustrial;
 productivism
 ends of 7, 11, 17, 23, 25, 148
 excesses of 11–12, 22, 40, 45,
 48, 97, 101–2, 105,
 108–10, 146
 racial capitalism 21, 68, 72, 75,
 77, 79, 81, 84–6, 88
capitalist realism 8, 45, 49, 54, 61, 81
Carpenter, John 73
Casati, Luisa 12
Caton, Shaun 47
Causey, Matthew 59

Index

Cazdyn, Eric 37–8
censorship 121, 125, 134–5
Césaire, Aimé 84
Charcot, Jean-Martin 58
chelfitsch 89, 91–6 *passim*
Chimutengwende, Seke 66
choreography 3, 77, 80–1,
   89–90, 92, 94–6, 98,
   102, 106, 109
Christian Action Network 117–18
chronic
   illness 20, 25–7, 29, 37–8, 41
   time 25, 32, 37–8, 41
chrononormativity 32–3, 41
civil rights 66, 69, 77, 80, 112, 118
climate 108, 148
Clinton, George 69, 72–3, 77
Cohen, Jeffrey Jerome 50–1
colonial 7, 13, 26, 35, 66, 83–6
   neocolonial 21, 66–7, 83–8
   passim, 148
communism 17
compression 20, 31–2, 41
   time-space compression 31–2
Condé, Alice 67–8
conservative 6–7, 22, 44, 66,
   83, 103, 105, 110, 113,
   115–16, 118, 146, 148–9,
   152
Conservative Party 22, 112–14,
   131–6 *passim*, 149
consume 3, 11, 18, 26–7, 37–8, 79,
   80, 93–4, 100–1, 103–4,
   106, 110, 138, 146, 149
   conspicuous consumption 79,
   125
contagion 27, 51, 116, 118, 121–2
corrupt 9, 27, 41, 45, 101, 114, 116,
   143
costume 1–2, 12–13, 46, 50, 63,
   65, 73–4, 78–9, 141, 143,
   145–6, *see also* garment
countercultural 12–13, 21, 56, 68,
   78–9, 83, 87, 112
counterpleasure 20, 35, 40, 54–5,
   57, 63, *see also* pleasure

Covid-19 1, 10, 16, 27, 29, 32, 36,
   94–5, 131–2, 138, *see also*
   pandemic
Crary, Jonathan 94
Creed, Barbara 53
crip 37
culture war 22–3, 111–40 *passim*,
   148–9
Cummings, Dominic 132
CyberFirst 131, 133, 139
cybernetic 21, 46, 56–9 *passim*, 61–3
cyborg 43, 46, 57
cystic fibrosis 20, 25–6, 28, 30, 38

d'Amato, Alfonse 115
d'Annunzio, Gabriele 1, 67
dance 3, 12, 50, 54, 65, 81, 89–90,
   93–4, 97–100 *passim*, 103,
   105, 131–33, 143, *see also*
   choreography
dandy 141, 143, 157 n.25, 172 n.15
Danto, Arthur C. 129
Davis, Angela 80
Davis, Vaginal 76, 174 n.43
Dean, Tim 121–2
death 5, 25–6, 28–30, 33, 35, 37–8,
   41, 58, 72, 115, 117, 120
Debord, Guy 108
decadence
   cultural politics of 12, 21–3, 32,
   67, 69, 71, 75, 88, 90, 124,
   130, 139, 150–1
   Decadence Studies 21, 156 n.13
decadent, *see also* decay; decline;
   uncommon
   aesthetic 2, 13, 15–16, 52, 68,
   71–2, 75, 87, 126, 146
   bodies 1, 21, 44–6, 62, 130, 146,
   152
   design 2–3 (*see also* costume;
   garment; scenographic;
   scenography)
   discourse 22, 91, 103–4, 107,
   113, 115, 117–18, 128–9,
   131, 136–7, 139, 152 (*see
   also* pejorative)

etymology of 2–3
historicity 40, 87, 102–3
imagination 3, 44, 63, 68, 130, 145
materiality 21, 44, 52, 62–3
practice 5, 19, 103, 139, 145, 153
scenographic 20, 46, 52, 61, 96
scenography 21, 46, 55, 61–3
sensibility 5, 9, 15–16, 22, 44, 122, 129, 137, 144, 146, 148
society 6, 22, 39, 66, 68, 84–6, 88, 104, 118, 134, 139, 148
decay 2–3, 12, 19, 25, 27, 36, 39–41, 43, 46, 54, 135, 144–6
decline 1, 2, 6–7, 12, 15, 23, 50, 66, 83, 92, 104, 112, 115, 122, 135, 139, 148, 153, *see also* decadence
declinism 7, 39, 66, 118, 148
degenerate 22–3, 115–18 *passim*, 121, 124, 128, 136, 146, 148
de-growth 148
Denisoff, Dennis 190 n.15
Derrida, Jacques 40, 178 n.14
Dery, Mark 176 n.73
design 2–3, 13, 18, 51, 56, 71, 76, 78, *see also* costume; scenography
Desmarais, Jane 147, 156 n.13
detritus 3, 96, 110, *see also* trash; waste
Deville, Coco 142
Dierickx, Wine 124
Dierkes-Thrun, Petra 158 n.29
disability 36, 165 n.41, *see also* capability; chronic, illness; crip; cystic fibrosis; health; sick
disidentification 11, 15, 73, 146
distaste 15, 19, 38, 39, 129–30, 144–5
Dixon, Steve 56

DIY 69, 78, 80–1, 86
Dornan, Robert 117
Dorries, Nadine 132
Douthat, Ross 6–7, 66–7, 75–6, 83–8 *passim*, 104–5, 127, 134, 148
Dowden, Oliver 22, 112, 114, 132–5 *passim*, 139, 149
Droste, Sebastian 12
Du Bois, W. E. B. 84
duration 28, 30, 35, *see also* temporal; time

Eagleton, Terry 145, 189 n.86
Eckersall, Peter 95
economic
 crisis 10, 22, 90, 101, 103, 113
 growth 6–8, 11, 23, 75, 91, 114, 129, 137, 139, 152
 productivity 5, 7, 10–11, 23, 129, 137, 152
 progress 19, 32, 75, 83
 reform 115, 120–3 *passim*, 130–2, 136–7, 139
 stagnation 7, 22, 83, 92, 96, 110, 148
 utility 5, 9, 114, 131, 150, 152
economy, *see also* productivism
 ailing 15, 29, 114, 128
 information and/or service 44, 46
 primacy of 123, 131, 139
Edelman, Lee 118–19
efficiency 2–3, 8–10, 16–17, 19, 85, 106, 128
Elagabalus 99, 109, 143
elitist 10, 67
Eltis, Sos 158 n.29
embodiment 5, 20–1, 25, 27–8, 40–1, 43, 50–1, 54, 75, 94
empire 1, 7, 13, 50, 83
enactment 5, 27–8, 45, 69, 93, 103, 110, 142–3, 152
endings 7, 11, 21, 25, 28–9, 43, 45–51 *passim*, 54, 85–6, 88,

107, 141, 147–8, 153, *see also* capitalism
end-of-history 6, 111
enervation 21, 61, 65–6, 68, 74–5, 84, 88, 96
Entartete Kunst 116–17
entropy 5, 21, 25, 57, 62, 66, 129, 136, 143, 147–8, 152
ephemeral 4–5, 104, 156 n.12, 160–1 n.49
erotic 39, 48, 50, 56, 59–60
Eshun, Kodwo 72
Euripides 59–60
Evangelista, Stefano 179 n.38
excess 1, 3, 14, 22, 34, 38, 41, 43, 50, 52, 58, 60–1, 79, 89–90, 97, 100–1, 104–5, 107–10, 122, 124, 134, 143, 146, *see also* capitalism
exhaustion 15, 18, 40, 83, 94, 122, 148

failure 22–3, 66–7, 78, 96, 125, 129–30, 134, 136, 151
fashion 26, 52, 76, 103, 105
Federici, Silvia 54, 169 n.30
Feldman, Sharon G. 56
feminist 14, 36, 52–4, 63, 66, 79, 112, 151, 168 n.24, *see also* xenofeminist
fetishize 13, 22, 50, 57, 81, 101, 105, 127
Fieni, David 66, 156 n.15
film 5, 26, 35–8 *passim*, 59–60, 65–6, 71, 73, 77–83 *passim*, 85–6, 99, 105, 123, 143, 145
fin de siècle 12–14, 25, 52, 67, 88, 104, 147, 150
Finley, Karen 184 n.34
Fisher, Mark 8, 45, 49, 78, 95–6, 108 n.20, 167 n.8, 178 n.14
Fitch, Lizzie 105
Flanagan, Bob 26, 38
Fleck, John 184 n.34

Floyd, George 80
Fornieles, Ed 94
Foster, Hal 58–9
Foucault, Michel 34
Frankl, Daniel 125–7
Freeman, Elizabeth 32, 163 n.20
frenetic 15, 17, 22, 73, 89, 105–6, *see also* productivism
frenetic standstill 8, 15, 22–3, 89–91, 93–4, 96, 103, 109, 156–7 n.19
Frohnmayer, John 184 n.34
FUCK U PAY US 77, 79
Fudge, Divinity P. 119, 183 n.26
fugitivity 21, 66, 85–7
Fukuyama, Francis 188 n.77
Fukuzawa, Yukichi 102–3
funding 112–21 *passim*, 123–5, 127–8, 130–2, 138–9, *see also* National Endowment for the Arts
Funkadelic 77
future shock 179–80 n.41
Futurists 17
futurity 27, 36–7, 40–1, *see also* Afrofuturism; No Future; utopia
cancellation of a cancelled future 45, 51, 62, 69, 88, 110

Gagnier, Regenia 189 n.4
Galbraith, Patrick W. 180 n.47
Gardner, Lyn 99, 102
garment 2–3, 13, 43, 46, 50, 52–4, 141, *see also* costume
Gautier, Théophile 6, 189–90 n.6
gay 70, 118–22 *passim*, *see also* queer
Gelede 172 n.15
gender 2, 20, 52–4, 59–60, 80, 98, 101, 107, 109–10, 118, 134–5, 143, 157 n.25, 158 n.30, 172 n.15

George, Jim 111
Gilman, Richard 155 n.5
Gloop, Oozing 142–3
Gómez-Peña, Guillermo 47
Gottschild, Brenda Dixon 70
Graham, James 138
growth 6–9 *passim*, 11, 17–20, 23, 27–8, 39–41, 48, 62, 75, 92, 96, 114, 129, 137, 139, 148, 150, 152, 159–60 n.43, 160 n.44, 190 n.16

Halberstam, Jack 38
Han, Byung-Chul 93
Hann, Rachel 46, 61
Harootunian, Harry 178 n.15
Hartman, Andrew 182 n.5
Hartman, Saidiya 14, 74
Harvey, David 31, 160 n.49
Hassan, Robert 161 n.50
hauntology 30, 95–6, 174 n.49, 178 n.14
Hawksley, Rozanne 52
Hayles, N. Katherine 170 n.47
health 18–20, 23, 27, 32, 36–41 *passim*, 67, 75–6, 88, 112–13, 128, 131, 136–7, 139, 146, 149, 151–2
hedonistic 34, 104, 106
Helms, Jesse 112–13, 118, 120–1, 139
  Helms Amendment 120
Hemsley, Alexandrina 66
Herman, Arthur 171 n.3
Hernandez, Jillian 14
HerNia, Miss 143, 145
Herold, Katharina 158 n.30
heteronormativity 12, 51, 70, 79, 119
Higher Education 22, 112, 130–8 *passim*
hikikomori 104, 180 n.43
Hind, Claire 25
hip-hop 3, 79

Hirata, Oriza 92
homophobic 77, 81, 113
Howard, Yetta 162 n.3
Hughes, Holly 184 n.34
Hutchings, Kimberly 165 n.45
Huysmans, Joris-Karl 2, 6, 12, 48, 63, 67, 164 n.32
Hval, Jenny 161 n.53
hyper
  active 15, 99–100
  commodification 14, 103
  culture 104–5, 179–80 n.41
hyper dance 97, 178

Ilyas, Suhail 36
immaterial 5, 21, 43–7 *passim*, 49, 52, 54, 59, 61–3
imperialism 12, 29, 66, 84
industrialisation 12, 16–17, 44, 67, 85, 88, 179 n.38, *see also* postindustrial
inefficiency 2–3, 9–10, 19
inertia 15, 29, 33, 36, 46, 65, 96, 102, 156–7 n.19
instrumentalism 8, 19, 70, 75, 82, 103, 107, 113, 129–30, 137, 139, 149–52 *passim*
Ishihara, Shintarō 181 n.58
Ivy, Marilyn 104
Iwaki, Kyoko 95, 97

Jackson, Holbrook 190 n.7
Jameson, Frederic 45, 51, 89–90, 160 n.49
Jansen, Matijs 124–6
Jansen, Sara 95
Janssens, Ann Veronica 143
Jarvis, Liam 170 n.46
Johnson, Boris 131–2, 135
Johnson, Dominic 167 n.6, 167 n.8, 183 n.21, 183 n.26, 184 n.34, 185 n.54
Jones, Amelia 26, 183 n.25
Jordà, Sergi 57–8

Index

J-pop 21, 97, 99
junkspace 89–90, 95–6, 109

Kafer, Alison 36, 165 n.41
kalliphobia 129–30
Kaneuji, Teppei 94, 96
Kartsaki, Eirini 33, 51
Kasōtsūka Shōjo 101
KATHY 97–8, 180 n.49
Kato, Masami 98
Kauffman, Linda S. 117
kawaii 101–2, 106–7, 180 n.47
King, Martin Luther 77, 79
Kirshenblatt-Gimblett, Barbara 5
Koolhaas, Rem 90
kosoko, jaamil olawale 15, 21, 65–6, 68–76 *passim*, 86–8, 146–8
   American Chameleon 69, 70
   Black Male Revisited 69
   #negrophobia 69
   Séancers 65, 69–76 *passim*, 86–8
K-pop 97, 99

La Fura dels Baus 56–7, 170 n.39
Land, Nick 161 n.50
Lawson, Jenny 25
Lepecki, André 5, 94, 100
liberalism 6–7, 111, 118, 135–6
Lindsay, James A. 188 n.79
Lingis, Alphonso 30
literature 5–6, 12, 14, 20–1, 44–5, 51, 67, 103–4, 141, 144–5, 147, 151
live art 5–6, 11, 14, 18–19, 47
Live Art Development Agency 66, 76–7, 83
Locke, Hew 13
Lolita 105
Loos, Adolf 128
Lorde, Audre 68, 72, 151
Lorrain, Jean 157 n.25, 164 n.32
lost generation 16, 22, 90–2, 94–5, 103
Louis XIV 12

Lovecraft, H. P. 52, 168 n.22
Luciano, Dana 163 n.20
Ludlam, Charles 13
Lukács, György 39
luxury 14, 19, 26, 33, 40, 61, 129–30, 151

McCarthy, Paul 23, 114, 123–30 *passim*, 139
McDermott, Phelim 47
Mackay, Robin 161 n.50
MacKendrick, Karmen 34, 54
McKenzie, Jon 17, 46, 57
MacLeod, Kirsten 159 n.37
Mapplethorpe, Robert 22, 113, 115–16, 118, 121, 127, 182 n.6
Martinez, Daniel Joseph 49
Marx, Karl 16–17
Marxism 39, 45, 68
Mbiti, John S. 85, 176 n.79
#MeToo 6
Miku, Hatsune 99
Miller, Kimberley 172 n.15
Miller, Lee 35
Miller, Monica L. 175 n.55
Miller, Tim 184 n.34
Mishima, Yukio 13, 103
misogyny 13, 168 n.24, 171 n.2
Mitchell, Allyson 52
modernity 3, 12, 15–17, 19, 21, 44, 62, 66–8, 94, 103, 160 n.49, *see also* postmodernity
monster 2, 36, 40, 50–1, 107
Montez, Mario 13
Moonlight, Sigi 142
Moore, Madison 174 n.42
morality 39, 97, 104–6, 112–14, 116–18, 121–3, 130, 139, 144
morbid 41, 147
Morning Musume 101
mortality 4, 10, 29, 38
Moten, Fred 5

Muñoz, José Esteban   5, 11, 37, *see also* disidentification
Murakami, Takashi   103–4, 106
Musk, Elon   86

Nagle, Angela   188 n.82
Nakayashiki, Norihito   97
National Endowment for the Arts   112, 116–18, 120–1, 139, 184 n.34
National Review of Live Art   47–8
nationalism   7, 77, 104
Nero   1
Ngai, Sianne   14–15, 102–3
nihilism   21, 62
Nikaido, Toco   15, 22, 90, 96–110 *passim*, 146, 177 n.1
   Crazy Girls Save the World   99
   Miss Revolutionary Idol Berserker: Extreme Voices   98–110 *passim*
   Miss Revolutionary Idol Berserker: Noise and Darkness   98
   Ms. Berserker ATTTTTACKS!! Elektro Shock Luv Luv Luv Shout!!!!!   98
Nkoloso, Edward Mukuka   82–3, 86
No Future   21, 45, 77, 87
NOISE   97
Nordau, Max   121
Nowotny, Helga   160 n.49
Nyong'o, Tavia   176 n.83

O'Brien, Dave   149–50
O'Brien, Martin   15, 20, 25–41 *passim*, 144, 146, 162 n.9, 165 n.45
   The Ascension   28
   If it Were the Apocalypse I'd Eat You to Stay Alive   28
   The Last Breath Society (Coughing Coffin)   29–35 *passim*
   Until the Last Breath is Breathed   28–9, 35, 38
   The Unwell   28, 36–7, 40
obscenity   116, 120–1, 145
obsolete   8–10, 18, 23, 46, 58–9, 81, 85, 108
occult   1, 45, 47–50, 52–3, 62–3
Okada, Toshiki   15, 22, 89–96 *passim*, 103, 109–10, 146
   Air Conditioner   91
   Eraser Mountain   89–90, 94–6
   Five Days in March   91
   Super Premium Soft Double Vanilla Rich   89, 92–6 *passim*
Okamoto, Tarō   97
Okpokwasili, Okwui   70
onticide   70–1, 73
opulence   1, 3, 6–7
Ordine, Nuccio   137
Organisation for Economic Co-operation and Development   19, 91
orgy   1, 43, 46, 59, 62–3, 120
Orientalism   66, 158 n.30
ornament   2–3, 19, 57, 128, 146
Osborne, Peter   165 n.45
otagei   21–2, 89–90, 92, 98–100, 103
otaku   21, 103–6 *passim*, 108, 110, 180 n.47
outbreak narratives   27, 29
outmoded   5, 8–12 *passim*, 15, 19, 23, 46, 52, 57–8, 69, 77, 81–2, 85, 87, 113, 132, 137, 140, 148, 150, 152
over-identification   11, 22, 101, 103, 107, 109, 146–7
Ovid   61

Palladini, Giulia   7
pandemic   1, 6, 10, 16, 20, 27, 29, 32–3, 36, 41, 98, 131–2, 138, 149, *see also* Covid-19
para-site   49, 51, 62
Parker-Starbuck, Jennifer   57, 170 n.39

Index

Parliament (band)   77, 81
Pater, Walter   67
Patterson, Orlando   172 n.21
Peele, Jordan   73
pejorative   3, 12, 27, 128
Perucci, Tony   124
perversion   3, 9, 11–12, 15, 46, 51, 54, 59, 63, 102, 105, 116, 121, 123–4, 128, 131, 147
pessimism   6, 21, 55, 67, 70, 147, *see also* Afropessimism
Phelan, Phelan   5, 156 n.12
Philip the Good, Duke of Burgundy   12
Pigpen   119
Pinker, Steven   136, 188 n.77
pleasure   1, 3, 7, 9, 15, 18–19, 27, 34, 37, 43–6 *passim*, 54, 58, 67, 104–6, 121, 144–6, 151–2
  counterpleasure   20, 35, 40, 54–5, 57, 63
  pleasure activism   3
Pluckrose, Helen   188 n.79, 188 n.81
policy   10, 20, 22, 91–2, 110, 114, 116, 120, 122–3, 127, 130–40 *passim*, 149
pop idol   89, 101–4, 107, 110
Poppy, Andrew   48–50
postdigital   59
post-Fordist   90–1, 97, 102, *see also* postindustrial
posthuman   45, 170 n.47
postindustrial   8, 14, 16–17, 19, 21, 44–5, 52, 56, 61–2, 75, *see also* post-Fordist
postmodernity   18, 95, 136, 157 n.19, 160 n.49
Potolsky, Matthew   67, 147, 189 n.4, 190 n.12
precarity   15, 17–18, 33, 44, 62, 92, 128
prelude   3, 7
productivism   8–12 *passim*, 14, 16–23 *passim*, 27–8, 32–4, 36–41 *passim*, 44–6, 52, 54, 57, 61–3, 67, 81, 85–8 *passim*, 89–97 *passim*, 101, 103–10 *passim*, 113, 128, 130, 132, 138–40, 146, 148–52 *passim*, *see also* frenetic, frenetic standstill
  anti-   19, 46, 128
  techno-productivism   57–63 *passim*
productivity   5–12 *passim*, 15–23 *passim*, 27–8, 32–41 *passim*, 46, 52, 54, 57, 60–3, 67, 72, 75–6, 89–91, 96, 101–5 *passim*, 109–10, 112–14, 122, 125, 127–31 *passim*, 136–40 *passim*, 146, 149–52 *passim*, 159 n.43, *see also* productivism; unproductivity
  alternative   8–9, 11, 61, 89, 113, 130, 137, 140, 150–1
progress   9, 12, 19, 21, 27–8, 32, 35–6, 40–1, 51, 54, 58–9, 62–3, 66–8, 75–6, 82–8 *passim*, 102, 118, 127, 135–6, 150, 176 n.79
progressive   3, 7, 11, 36, 66–7, 78, 87, 112–13, 116, 118, 120, 182 n.5
punk   21, 45, 66, 76–7, 79, 81, 87, 98, 119, *see also* Afropunk
puritan   7, 116, 118

queer   1, 6, 26, 28–9, 32, 34–5, 37–8, 41, 65, 70, 78–9, 113–21 *passim*, 146, 151
queercore   76–7
queering   12, 29, 35, 38–9, 75–7, 84, 122

Ra, Sun   69, 72, 77, 82, 85–6, 88
  Space is the Place   85–6, 88

Rachilde 2, 12, 13, 63, 157 n.25
racial capitalism 21, 68, 72, 75, 77, 79, 81, 84–6, 88, *see also* capitalism
racism 66–8, 74, 77, 80–1, 138, 148, 190–1 n.17
Rauschenberg, Robert 82
Rebellato, Dan 130
Remmers, Maartje 124–5
repetition 28, 30, 33, 72, 96
retro 46, 58, 63, 69, 77, 82, 87, 147, 174 n.49
revolution 6–7, 39, 78, 86
Rhodes, Cecil 83
Riggenbach, Jeff 183 n.19
Robertson, Pat 120–1
Robinson, Cedric J. 68, 72
Romero, George A. 26–7, 35–6, 38
Rosa, Hartmut 16, 156–7 n.19
Rose, Sheree 26, 162 n.3
Ruga, Athi-Patra 13
Rugoff, Ralph 128
ruin 19, 26–7, 37, 41
ruination 19, 27, 29, 39, 41, 70, 129, 148
Rutte, Mark 127

S&M 26, 28, 115, 119, 122
Sadler, William S. 171 n.3
St. John, Michael 117
St. Sebastian 1, 119
Sakaguchi, Ango 179 n.37
Sakate, Yōji 180 n.43
Sakurai, Keisuke 105
Sales, Ruby 68, 74–5
Saltus, Edgar 2, 12, 70
saturation 11, 13–14, 22, 89–90, 96, 106, 121, 146
Savage, Karen 170 n.46
scenographic 20, 46, 52, 61, 96
scenography 21, 46, 52, 55, 61–3, 70, 77–8, 80, 86–7, 89–90, 94, 96, 109, 124, 145
Schechner, Richard 5, 11, 155–6 n.10

Schiller, Friedrich 145
Schneider, Rebecca 5
Scholten, Marleen 124–6
Schopenhauer, Arthur 70
Seale, Bobby 80
Serpell, Namwali 175 n.61
Serrano, Andres 22, 113, 115–16
Serratore, Nicole 71
sexuality 12, 20, 22, 35, 39, 53, 59, 79–80, 97, 117–21 *passim*, 143, 146, 158 n.30, *see also* gay; heteronormativity; queer
Sharpe, Christina 74
Shaviro, Steven 165 n.45
Shelley, Mary 167–8 n.17
Sherry, Vincent 166 n.1
Sherwood, Normandy 1–3, 7, 19, 20
  Psychic Self Defense 1–3, 7
Shōgekijō 107
Shonibare, Yinka 13, 83
sick 1, 20, 26–7, 29, 32, 35–41 *passim*, 68, 84, *see also* chronic; capability; disability; health; outbreak narratives
  kingdom of the 20, 27–8, 38, 40–1
Sin, Hasard Le 15, 20, 141–6 *passim*
Singer, Roman 94
Sinker, Mark 84
Skelly, Julia 14, 52
slavery 26, 35, 70, 72, 74, 84, 135, 172 n.21, 175 n.55
slow 7, 20, 31, 33, 35–7, 45, 89–93 *passim*, 96, 110, 146, 165 n.45
Smallwood, Stephanie E. 172 n.21
Smith, Jack 2, 13
#SNATCHPOWER 77, 79
social justice 68, 76–7, 112–13, 134–6, 147
Sokal affair 188 n.79
Sone, Yuji 100

Sontag, Susan   20, 27, 118
Southwood, Ivor   157 n.19
Soyinka, Wole   13
space age   69, 78, 82, 85–6, 176 n.78
space race   76, 82–4, 86–7, 148
Spengler, Oswald   156 n.14
Spielberg, Steven   78
SPILL Festival of Performance   47
Srnicek, Nick   161 n.50
stagnation   6–8, 17–18, 20, 22, 83, 92, 96, 109–10, 148
Stelarc   56, 59
STEM   131
Stenslie, Stahl   56
Stilling, Robert   84, 158 n.29
Stokes, John   166 n.1
subversion   3, 14, 21, 26, 53–4, 85, 109, 129, 139
Sunak, Rishi   132, 186 n.66
superflat   90, 106, 110, 180 n.49
Supple, Tim   47
survival   28, 33, 36–7, 114
Svich, Caridad   138
symbolism   13, 44, 166 n.1

Takamura, Eri   98
Takarazuka Revue   98–9
Tanizaki, Jun'ichirō   2, 12, 103, 108
taste   2–3, 15, 19–20, 23, 25–7, 34, 36, 38–9, 41, 54, 104, 112, 116, 122, 128–30 *passim*, 143–6 *passim*, 150–1, *see also* distaste
Taylor, Diana   5
Taylor, Mark   149–50
technological innovation   7, 11, 46, 152
technology   9, 17, 20, 44–6 *passim*, 49–50, 56–63 *passim*, 66, 73, 81–2, 85, 101, 131–2, 138, 152, *see also* productivism
   cybernetic   21, 46, 56–9 *passim*, 61–3

cyborg   43, 46, 57
   on-demand   10
   postdigital   59
   Techno-Performance   46, 57–63 *passim*
   techno-scientific   63, 66, 85–8 *passim*, 150
teleology   34, 39–41
temporal   20, 26, 28, 31–2, 37–8, 40–1, 73, 85, 90, 93, 96, 106, 160–1 n.49, *see also* chrononormativity; duration; time
   commons   32–3, 106–7, 163 n.22
Tezuka, Natsuko   91
Thatcher, Margaret   8, 49, 135
Thorpe, Chris   33
time   7–11 *passim*, 13, 16, 18–23 *passim*, 25–38 *passim*, 40–1, 43, 45–6, 58, 78, 81–2, 86, 94, 96, 105–6, 108, 110, 137, 151–2, *see also* 24/7; duration; temporal; time-space compression; superflat; waiting; zombie
   curative   36
   end   45–6, 48–9, 51, 54
   suspension of   27, 31–2, 163 n.18, 163 n.20, 164 n.23
Toffler, Alvin and Heidi   179–80 n.41
Tolentino, Julie   119
Toussaint-Baptiste, Jeremy   72–3
transgression   2, 9, 47, 104, 112–13, 116, 127, 130, 137, 139, 141, 143–6 *passim*, 150
trash   3, 71, 75, *see also* detritus; waste
   trashy   71, 75, 99
travelling practice   2, 13
Trecartin, Ryan   71, 105
Trump, Donald   69, 76–8
Tsunku   101

Uchino, Tadashi   180 n.49
Udé, Iké   13
Uhuruverse, The   15, 21, 65–6, 68, 69, 76–88 *passim*, 146–8
  'Basic a$$ Fake White Bytch'   79
  'Bomaye! (Suspense)'   79–81
  The Brightest Oddest Strangest Star U Ever Did Saw up Close and Afar from Planet Earth to Mars and Beyond!!   77
  '[Dis]Obey!'   79
  'She D'evil'   77–8
  Unfunky UFO: 2100AD (residency)   65–6, 76, 81–3 *passim*
uncommon
  desire   39, 62, 122
  pleasure   19, 44, 46, 54
  sense   15, 38, 122, 129, 130, 137, 139, 146
university   22, 132–5 *passim*, *see also* arts and humanities; Higher Education
unproductivity   9, 40, 46, 95–6, 109, 124, 129, 139, 152
usefulness   2, 9, 15–16, 32–3, 39, 107, 124, 131, 137–8, 146, 150–1
uselessness   2, 8–12 *passim*, 15, 19, 22–3, 32–3, 46, 52, 63, 82, 89–90, 95–6, 102, 109, 113–6 *passim*, 123, 128–32 *passim*, 135–40 *passim*, 144–6, 148–52 *passim*
utilitarian   103, 107, 110, 137, 139
utility   3, 5, 9–10, 23, 31, 46, 96, 102, 107, 109, 113–14, 128–30, 137, 139–40, 144, 149, 152
utopia   36, 51, 63, 67, 69, 77–8, 82–3, 85–7, 110

Vaccaro, John   13
van Otterdijk, Maarten   124
van Veen, tobias c.   84

Verlaine, Paul   50, 54, 167 n.12
Viennese Actionism   56
Virilio, Paul   8, 18, 45
von Reinhold, Shola   14

Waddell, Amanda   98
waiting
  interminable   20, 27, 30–3 *passim*, 41
  Waiting Times   30–1, 163 n.17
Walcott, Derek   13, 84
Wald, Priscilla   29
Walker Arts Center   119–20
Warburton, Alan   94
Warhol, Andy   82
Warren, Calvin L.   68, 70–1, 73–5
waste   9, 108, 129, *see also* detritus; trash
wastefulness   5, 8–11 *passim*, 12, 15, 19, 23, 34, 46, 52, 63, 89–90, 102, 110, 113, 128–9, 131, 137–8, 140, 148, 150, 152
Waters, John   71
Weeks, Kathi   19
Weimar Republic   12, 117
Weiner, Norbert   169 n.38
Weir, David   15, 38, 129, 144, 147
weird   46, 51–2, 62, 168 n.22
Wilde, Oscar   2, 12, 68, 144–5
Wilders, Geert   128
Wilderson III, Frank B.   70
Williams, Alex   161 n.50
Wilson, Tom   108
Winters, Gary   26
Witherspoon, Nia O.   1, 3, 6–7, 14–15, 19, 79
  Priestess of Twerk   1, 3, 15, 19
woke   22, 112–14, 132–6 *passim*
Womack, Ytasha L.   83
Wright, Stephen   32
Wunderbaum   15, 22–3, 114, 124–30 *passim*, 139, 146
  Looking for Paul   114, 124–30 *passim*

The New Forest 124

xenofeminist 80
xenophobia 29, 81, 163 n.13,
    190 n.17

Yoda, Tomiko 91
Youngquist, Paul 85
YUBIWA Hotel 97–8

Zamalin, Alex 85

Zambia National Academy of
    Science, Space Research
    and Philosophy 82–3
zany 14–15, 102–3, 106
Zemmour, Éric 171 n.2
Zijlstra, Halbe 127–8
Žižek, Slavoj 78, 80, 81
Zombie 25–9 *passim*, 35–41 *passim*,
    164 n.31
    time 20, 26–9 *passim*, 35–7
        passim, 40–1

www.ingramcontent.com/pod-product-compliance
Lightning Source LLC
Chambersburg PA
CBHW071830300426
44116CB00009B/1499